MAKE THAT GRADE

FUNDAMENTALS OF IRISH LAW

MAKE THAT GRADE

FUNDAMENTALS
OF
IRISH LAW

Ruth Davenport

Gill & Macmillan

Gill & Macmillan Ltd
Hume Avenue
Park West
Dublin 12
with associated companies throughout the world
www.gillmacmillan.ie

© Ruth Davenport 2008

978 07171 44587

Print origination in Ireland by O'K Graphic Design

*The paper used in this book is made from the wood pulp of managed
forests. For every tree felled, at least one tree is planted, thereby renewing
natural resources.*

A CIP catalogue record for this book is available from the British Library.

CONTENTS

1

INTRODUCTION TO FUNDAMENTALS OF IRISH LAW

Learning Goals

At the end of this chapter you should:
- Start considering the challenges of and the approaches to the study of law.
- Be thinking about your own study style and your approach to studying law.
- Be familiar with some important internet resources.
- Appreciate some different legal terminologies.
- Have an understanding of key distinctions between criminal and civil law.

1 The Relevance of Law in Life and as a Topic of Study

We are all affected by legal regulations. We make contracts, have employment relationships, drive cars, pay rent and take out mortgages, have relationships and live in family groups. All these activities are surrounded by legal regulation.

An aspect which makes law interesting (and challenging) is that law is a dynamic subject: it changes frequently. Changes to the law may occur following a change in government and in line with manifesto promises. There may be European Union initiatives which prompt new laws. There may be a major court case, such as the recent Mr G case in which the High Court and Supreme Court acknowledged the access rights of unmarried fathers to their children in certain circumstances.

Law is responsive to society and to shifts in social expectations. A smoking ban in Ireland would not have been considered acceptable a decade or more ago. Years ago, marriage was the only accepted way of constructing family groups. Women had limited property-owning rights and earning rights. Divorce in Ireland is not much more than a decade old.

An important aspect of legal study and practice is the need to keep up to date with changes in the law and legal obligations. Ignorance of the law is not a defence. This is an old saying, but one which is still relevant today. It is no defence for a business to say, 'we were unaware of current health and safety requirements,' or 'we did not realise that this type of contract is illegal under the Competition Act.'

Legal awareness is an accepted part of our life as consumers, students, employees and partners.

1.1 *The impact of legal changes on individuals and businesses*

The furore over the changes to the provisional driving licence situation in autumn 2007 illustrates the real impact changes in the law make to our daily lives.

European Union law impacts on us all. It affects us as employees, consumers, businesses, and farmers too. If we take a package holiday European Union law gives us certain rights. A citizen of the EU may exercise their right to work, retire or access medical services in another EU country. As heavy users of mobile phones we benefit from the reductions of roaming charges introduced in June 2007 as a result of EU legislation.

Accepted social norms are often translated into legal rules. There is a moral and religious rule not to kill and this forms the basis of ancient law on murder and manslaughter.

As society develops, the law also evolves. The law concerning marriage is an example. The concept of a marriage being the imperative for a co-habiting couple was a religious requirement of Christianity. The law on judicial separation and divorce was a response to changing demands of society. The Civil Partnership Bill, which is to be published in 2008, is a further development: it proposes legislation facilitating co-habiting couples of the same sex, or of different sexes, to register a civil partnership. It will also establish a scheme of redress for cohabitants who qualify that will deal with the situation when the relationship breaks down or one of the partners dies.

2 *How to Use this Book*

This text aims to introduce you to fundamental concepts of Irish and European law. The range of law is vast, however, and an introductory text must start somewhere.

It focuses on the following areas of Irish and European law:
- the sources of law
- institutional framework of Irish and European law

- fundamentals of tort
- fundamentals of contract law
- aspects of criminal law
- consumer law
- European Union law
- aspects of human rights law
- general study skills.

Once you have acquired a fundamental understanding of these areas you will be able to research specific areas in the areas of business studies, accountancy, building surveying or human resources.

The book aims to enable you to discover and interpret information. It offers some suggestions about methods of reading and studying in general and for law in particular. Use it as a work book as well as a basic reference text. It will help you feel equipped and confident to answer problems and short-essay type questions and to research topic areas further.

2.1 Electronic legal resources

The book shows you how to use the internet to develop your skills in locating, evaluating and applying relevant legal information. You will be aware from studying in general that the key to progressing with any subject area, whether maths, engineering, psychology or law, is to work with the materials and get involved in the subject area. This is essential for real understanding and enjoyment, and also make revision much easier if you are facing end of course exams and assessment.

2.2 Aspects of legal study

The study of law has its own particular characteristics. You need to be aware of:
- Where the relevant law comes from (the source of the law).
- The fact that a number of different laws may be relevant to a situation.
- What the law covers (the scope of the law) and how it is interpreted.
- How the law could be applied to a situation, and any alternative interpretations.
- The court or other body that applies the law if a dispute is unresolved.
- Possible outcomes if the law is broken.

3 The Format of this Book

Each chapter contains a list of Learning Goals and Overviews. Sections include Questions and Key Points; most also include a number of Tasks. It is a good idea to work through these tasks, because they aim to explain fundamental aspects of the Irish and European legal orders. Each chapter ends with a series of Questions and a Summary. At the end of the book is a Glossary of Legal Terms.

Annotate the book and highlight significant points as you go along. Work through and with the material. This will help the process of assimilating the material, and revision.

4 An Introduction to Law and Legal Concepts

OVERVIEW

- The nature of law and legal regulation.
- Legal consequences.
- Introduction to legal databases.
- Distinctions between civil and criminal law.

4.1 The nature of law and legal regulation

Societies have social rules and legal rules. We can identify social traditions and morals, religious rules and customs that regulate behaviour. An example is that of queuing. There is no legal requirement to 'form an orderly queue'. However, if a queue disintegrates and becomes a free-for-all there can be legal consequences. If people push and hit others the criminal law of assault may be relevant. There may be non-criminal consequences, too, in the tort of battery. There may be health and safety implications.

4.2 Legal awareness — the scope of legal consequences

The range of legal consequences which can arise from an everyday situation is a good starting point to consider a key distinction in law, the difference between criminal and civil law.

TASK

Consider the following scenario and the issues below.

Kitty's Trip to the Supermarket

Kitty completed her weekly shopping at the local supermarket. After paying the cashier she found her exit blocked by a large store security officer. He insisted that she accompany him to the manager's office.

Kitty refused. He grabbed her by the arm and pushed her into the office, shouting, 'the aul' girls are the easiest to catch thieving!' A number of her neighbours protested to the security officer but they were pushed aside.

The door was locked behind her.

Twenty minutes later the security officer returned and apologised. He said there had been a case of mistaken identity.

Kitty was too upset to confront the manager and hurried out of the fire exit. On her way out, she tripped over the flex of a polishing machine which was blocking the exit. Her ankle was broken.

The supermarket manager asks you whether there may be any legal consequences from this series of events.

Questions:
1. Do you think the supermarket staff may have committed any criminal offences for which they could be prosecuted by the State?
2. Do you think the supermarket could be sued by Kitty and be found liable to pay compensation?

Key Points:
1. There may criminal offences of assault under the Non-Fatal Offences Against the Person Act 1997. By pushing her the security officer may be guilty of criminal assault. By locking Kitty in a room he could be guilty of false imprisonment under the Act.

   The obstruction of an exit may be a criminal offence under the Safety, Heath and Welfare at Work Act 2005, which places a duty on employers to ensure that so far as reasonably practicable means of access and egress from buildings are safe and unobstructed.
2. There may be issues for which Kitty will want to sue for compensation. There may be civil liability for the tort of battery and also for false imprisonment. The comment about 'the aul' ones ...' damages Kitty's reputation and is defamatory. This spoken defamation is called slander.

The obstruction of the exit is likely to constitute negligence on the part of the supermarket. The liability for these actions, although committed by the store detective and the cleaning staff, will fall on the supermarket due to the principle of vicarious liability.

Do not be concerned if you did not identify many of these possibilities. This is the starting point. By the end of your studies you will be able to explain these key points.

4.3 Distinctions between civil and criminal law

Whether an event may be a civil wrong or a criminal offence (or gives rise to both types of legal consequences) is important because it determines:

1 Who or what takes proceedings against the person or organisation alleged to be in the wrong.
2 What type(s) of proceedings can be taken and which court could hear a case.
3 What outcomes or results there may be in the case.

Note that an act or an omission (a failure to do something) can have both civil and criminal consequences.

Example: Aeongus rides his motorcycle at speed in a busy urban area. He tries to overtake a car, crosses over onto the wrong side of the road and collides with an oncoming car driven by Brian. Aeongus suffers minor injuries. Brian sustains serious facial injuries. Aeongus may be prosecuted for dangerous driving (a criminal offence). He may be sued by Brian for negligence (a civil wrong).

4.3.1 The aim or purpose of criminal law

The main aim of criminal law is to regulate and to protect society. Some criminal offences are hundreds of years old.
Question: List three criminal offences that you would consider to have existed for a considerable time.
Key points: Murder, theft, assault, fraud, rape.
The number of criminal offences is growing as society becomes more complex and more regulated. There are now criminal offences covering a range of activities, health and safety matters, driving,

consumer protection, smoking in public places, unfair competition, as well as the more 'obvious' criminal offences relating to harming individuals or interfering with property rights.

4.3.2 Elements for criminal liability

The law generally requires two elements for a criminal offence to be committed. There must be a criminal act or an omission and a certain guilty state of mind.

You will see these referred to in the Latin phrases *actus reus* (meaning an action) and *mens rea* (criminal state of mind).

4.4 Civil law

Civil law covers all aspects that are not criminal. Contract, tort, property law and family law are all examples of civil law.

4.4.1 The law of tort

The word 'tort' means 'wrong' (originally a French word, derived from the Latin *tortum*, meaning 'to twist'). It is used to describe a variety of laws which can be used to claim damages from a person who has committed a civil wrong — a tort. An action can be started in the appropriate court.

Usually a claimant will be bringing an action for damages, though other forms of remedy can be requested. For example, if someone is illegally occupying land an injunction can be sought to compel the person to leave the land.

This area of law has largely been created by the rulings of the judges in the courts. It forms part of the common law of Ireland (see Chapter 2).

Many legal situations fall under the category of a tort.

Scenarios

Declan enters Aidan's house without permission (the tort of trespass).

Alex rolls into the car in front as he was busy answering his mobile (the tort of negligence).

You read an article in the local paper which alleges a local councillor is corrupt. The allegations are inaccurate (the tort of defamation).

A doctor performs an operation without your consent (the torts of battery and negligence).

A neighbour is regularly holding loud parties at the house, disrupting the life of the neighbourhood (the tort of nuisance).

During a football match Brendan threatens to hit Aidan if he tackles him again. Aidan knows Brendan's reputation and feels genuinely threatened (the tort of assault).

Niamh invites friends around to her house for a barbecue. She knows that her conservatory is in a dangerous state. While there her friend Orla leans on the conservatory frame and falls through it, sustaining cuts and bruises (tort of liability under the Occupiers' Liability Act 1995).

4.4.2 The modern law of negligence

The modern tort of negligence was created by the judges when ruling in the famous case of *Donoghue v. Stevenson [1932]*.

This is one of the most influential cases of modern times and it came about because a woman in a café bought two bottles of ginger beer, one for herself and one for her friend. One bottle was contaminated with a snail.

The consumption of the ginger beer with added snail, and the sight of snail remains, caused the woman's friend shock and a gastric complaint. The woman's friend sued the manufacturer of the ginger beer for damages and won.

The judges ruled that the manufacturer should have taken reasonable care to ensure that their products were not defective and did not injure a consumer.

We will be looking at this area in Chapter 4. For the moment it is important to note that this area of law is crucial in the regulation of our day-to-day activities (e.g. driving a car, surveying a house, running a business, etc.).

5 An Introduction to Legal Study Skills

OVERVIEW

- Types of questions or tasks that may be set.
- Using the internet as an information resource.
- Writing legal essays and problem solving.
- Referencing.

The study of law has characteristics which mark it out from other subjects. If you recognise these features it can help you plan your study style during the course. It can direct your approach when answering essay or problem-style questions and can also help in revising for an end of course assessment or exam.

Question: Consider what features you may associate with the study of law.
Key points:

- Law is not a static subject — it changes constantly. It is important to have up-to-date information.
- Law can be detailed and precise.
- Law relies on authorities (such as an Act, statutory instrument, case).
- There can be uncertainty about whether an Act and/or case is relevant in any given situation and the facts in a particular situation are important.
- There are debates about whether a law is applicable and interpretations of the scope of the law may differ.

5.1 Types of questions or tasks that may be set

You may be asked to give specific advice or to write a report on a situation or topic. You may be asked to 'solve' a problem situation. You will have to summarise complex legal provisions in a readable way and cite authorities to support your answers.

1　You need to identify the relevant source(s) of law.
2　Then apply the law to the particular issue or facts with which you are presented.
3　If there is more than one interpretation you should deal with both possibilities.
4　Give the legal authority (the statute, case name, etc.) that you refer to.
5　Come to some sort of conclusion.

We will practise this approach as we go through the course. As you read legal documents such as judgments you will see this is the basic approach that judges adopt.

You may be faced with short 'essay-type' questions such as:

'"The Irish Constitution is a source of developing human rights for Irish citizens." Explain this statement.'

In essay-type questions you need to organise your material to show the reader/assessor that you have understood the question and select relevant points to support your answer.

A short introduction sets out how the essay will address the question. In formal essays you should avoid the use of 'I' and use the third person instead. So instead of saying, 'I will examine Article 40 of the Constitution ...', write, 'Article 40 of the Constitution will be examined ...' This may seem formal, but it is more appropriate in an essay or problem-solving answer than saying 'I think ...', 'in my opinion ...', etc.

5.2 Using the internet as an information resource

The use of electronic legal databases is an essential tool in locating legal information. There are many paper-based sources such as law reports, journals, printed copies of legislation and hundreds of textbooks covering every possible area of Irish and European Union law. If you are studying law as part of specialist course you may need to refer to a specialist textbook on, for example, employment law, nursing law or building and engineering law.

5.2.1 Internet resources for law

Electronic databases for law, provided by commercial firms, which charge subscriptions for access to the sites and the information in them, are a feature of law libraries and legal practice. Your academic institution may subscribe to one or more legal databases, such as LexisNexis. For obvious reasons we will focus on the sites which are free to access and use.

Question: Can you identify three advantages of electronic sources of legal information over paper sources?
Key Points:
You may have identified ease of access (you do not need access to a specialist law library), the fact that information can be updated quickly, the information can be retrieved and copied and compiled from electronic sources quickly and conveniently. You may also have mentioned that it may be cheaper to access information electronically than purchase volumes of books and updates and that storage of electronic information is not a problem.

There can also be disadvantages in using some of the information on law that is available on the internet. The internet contains a mass of excellent, usable information. It also, as we are all aware, contains a mass of unverifiable information posted by people and organisations seeking to advertise themselves or their product.

The sites we mention in this book are reputable, excellently updated and easily navigated sites. We mainly rely on the British and Irish Legal Information Institute (BAILII), the Irish Legal Information Initiative run by UCC (IRLII), the Irish Statute Book site and the Europa portal to European Union law. There are many other excellent sites, which this book will refer to from time to time.

There is a list of website addresses (correct at the time of writing) at the end of the book. You will soon become familiar with certain sites and will have your own preferences about the ease of access, searches and navigation of other sites. In your own research you may find it useful to consider the following aspects and approaches. Internet searches can be highly informative and interesting; they can also be very time-consuming and distracting.

5.2.2 Internet searches

You probably already have your own favourite internet search engine. Fundamental to effective searching is:

- Identification of the issue(s) you need to research.
- Selection of key words and modification or refining the search.
- Accessing the information and assessing its reliability and currency.
- Selecting relevant information and discarding other information.
- Keeping a record of websites used and dates accessed.

Many of the legal databases have their own inbuilt search engine, and it may take some time to get used to the requirements of each.

You should chose an internet information source that is reliable, verifiable (i.e. you can check on the source of the information) and updated regularly. If a site says 'last updated August 2001', it may be of very limited use for up-to-date information on the current state of the law. If it is an authoritative site it may still be highly relevant for explaining the situation in 2001, including the facts and interpretation of case law that may still be relevant.

Researching a problem and choosing search terms

Example: You are asked to research the following problem.
Marion and Hayden own a dog called Lassie. She is a breed of collie.
Normally she is on a rope in a fenced garden and there are 'Beware

of the Dog' signs on each gate. One day Lassie chews through the rope and attacks a person walking another dog in a nearby park. Discuss issues of liability raised by the situation.

1. Choose your search engine or electronic database. (For the purposes of this exercise we will use the BAILII site.)
2. Identify the key words and select some of them to identify relevant information. This is often a process of trial and error. You can connect them by using connecting words like 'and' or 'or'. There is no right way to do this. What you aim to do is get the most specific sources quickly without having to scan through a huge list of documents. For example, type in *dogs and liability* and limit or refine your search in the database box by selecting *Ireland*.
3. You will call up a range of documents including reports (consultation papers), the Control of Dogs Act 1986 and cases.
4. The BAILII site has a facility that enables you to sort results. The default option is to be sorted by relevance, and a percentage figure is given to indicate the degree of relevance. This relevance figure relates to the words you typed into the search and not the issue you are researching. So although the Control of Dogs Act 1986 has a 71 per cent rating it may be far more relevant to the issue than a working paper produced in 1977 with a relevance rating of 100 per cent.
5. Try some other search terms of your own, for example 'dog attack', and compare the results.

5.3 Writing legal essays and problem solving

5.3.1 Answering questions on legal topics

You may face various types of question that aim to assess your knowledge and understanding of legal issues. Questions are set to test your knowledge and understanding, not just your memory.

Questions may fall into the following categories:

- general short questions on a legal topic
- 'problem' questions that ask you to advise a person or to discuss the legal rights and obligations of a party
- case studies for you to discuss
- project-type questions.

5.3.2 Writing an answer

Producing an accurate and readable summary of the topic is another skill that you will be encouraged to practise. This is a transferable skill, i.e. one that you can use for other subjects and in the workplace.

When answering questions on areas of the law you need to support your answer with reference to legal authorities. This means making references to appropriate case law and/or provisions of an Act, the Constitution, etc. After you have worked through some of the tasks this will become second nature.

An approach to problem questions:
- identify the law
- apply the law to the facts
- come to some sort of conclusion.

Note that often there may be two or more possible 'correct' answers. The legal system thrives on different interpretations and arguments. If the point is debatable, you can say that it is debatable, and explain why.

Question: Outline three of the main differences between the criminal and civil law in Ireland.
Key Points:
- The purposes and aims of criminal law and civil law.
- A prosecution by the State in criminal action; in a civil action a plaintiff sues the defendant.
- The different processes involved, e.g. the role of the jury trial in criminal law for more serious cases.
- The mental element generally required for criminal guilt (*mens rea* element).
- Differing burdens of proof. The prosecution must prove guilt beyond reasonable doubt in criminal law. In civil law the plaintiff must prove their case on the balance of probabilities, i.e. that it was more likely than not that the events occurred as the plaintiff alleged.

Question: Why do you consider there are different standards of proof for criminal and civil trials?
Key Points:
- In criminal trials the stakes are higher. Before the abolition of the death penalty a convicted person could lose their life. The sanctions of imprisonment and other restrictive punishments require that the case should be proved beyond reasonable doubt.

- In civil cases the normal outcome is either a finding of liability and an award of damages or a dismissal of the case. Legal costs may then be awarded by the court. In criminal cases the outcomes may be an acquittal or a finding of guilt and then sentencing.

5.4 Referencing

You need to know how to reference your resources and sources of information. If you write an essay for a course or a report for an employer you should show where you obtained the information. This gives your research extra strength and credibility as it can be verified. Academic institutions have their own policies about referencing and may use different systems. Whether you use paper-based resources, such as textbooks, or electronic sources, such as the internet, it is essential that you become familiar with the appropriate method of referencing works that you refer to for essays and dissertations etc.

5.4.1 Referencing in general

Question: Why is it necessary to refer to sources (such as authors or reports) in the body of your essay and references afterwards?
Key Points:
- To comply with academic rules.
- To ensure that you acknowledge others' words and thoughts and do not plagiarise (pass off another person's work as your own).
- In order that your work can be verified and the reader can follow up on sources you have used.

5.4.2 Types of referencing

The Harvard system of referencing is a recommended system of referencing. This deals with the citation of authors/reports within the body of the text, for example:

> 'Law plays an important part in the definition and regulation of all kinds of social relationships, between individuals and between groups.' (Harris, 2007)

Citing case law

If you are referring to a case in an answer or essay (not in an exam situation) you should if possible provide the full name of the case and the reference of the law report. Even if you are looking at cases on the internet the report will often give the traditional paper-based source of the case, e.g. *Kelly v. Hennessy [1995] 3 IR 253*. It is conventional to either underline or italicise case names. This citation means the case was reported in 1995 in the Irish Reports series (IR) at page 253. If you refer to the case more than once you do not need to repeat the reference in full but can simply refer to *Kelly v. Hennessy*.

Reminders about referencing
Just as copying from a colleague, or copying paragraphs from a book without acknowledging the source or author, constitute plagiarism, copying directly from a website can also contravene a number of rules (including the law on copyright).

Do not copy and paste chunks of material from a relevant and reputable website. If you use a selected quote from an internet source you should place it in quotation marks and acknowledge the source at the end of your answer, together with the date; e.g. http://www.bailii.org/ (accessed 5/9/08). It is useful to include the date because the content of websites and internet resources can change frequently, and this is a record of the information as it was presented on the day.

REFERENCES

Harris, P. (2007) *An Introduction to Law* (7th edn). Cambridge: Cambridge University Press.
University of Limerick, *Cite it Right: A Guide to Referencing in UL Using the Harvard Referencing Style*. http://www.ul.ie/~library/pdf/citeitright.pdf (accessed 3/12/2007).

2

THE SOURCES OF IRISH LAW

Learning Goals

After studying this chapter you should be able to:
- Explain the function of legislation and case law.
- Explain the enactment of Acts of the Oireachtas and be familiar with the format of statutes.
- Understand the function and significance of delegated legislation.
- Explain the role of the Irish Constitution and apply key Articles to factual scenarios.
- Describe and differentiate between types of European Union law.
- Explain the significance of case law in the development of the law and the basic court structure in Ireland.
- Explain the status of the sources of law.
- Understand some of the approaches to interpreting statutes used by the judiciary.
- Use research skills to identify statutes, cases and EU law.

OVERVIEW

This chapter will consider each of the sources of law in turn. It is important to note the status of each type of law. If one source contradicts another, we must ask which law takes precedence. We consider the special status of constitutional law in Ireland. The position of European Union and European human rights law in Ireland will be discussed briefly. (These topics are covered in more detail in Chapters 8 and 9.)

There are five main sources of law:
1. legislation (primary legislation and delegated legislation)
2. constitutional law
3. case law or precedent
4. European Union law
5. human rights law.

1 Legislation

OVERVIEW

- The Oireachtas (the Dáil and Senate) passes legislation.
- Legislation is of two types: **Acts** (also called statutes and known as primary legislation); and **Statutory Instruments** or **Regulations** (also called delegated or secondary legislation).

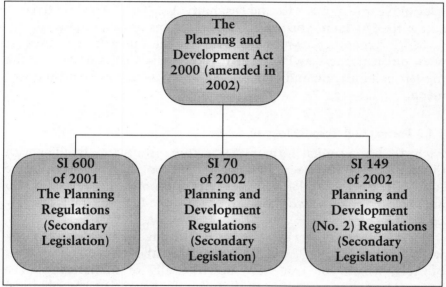

The relationship between primary and secondary legislation

1.1 Acts of the Oireachtas

The Government proposes legislation as part of its function. This may be to fulfil a manifesto statement, to respond to a situation in the state or to comply with European obligations. The proposed legislation is called a Bill. Bills are drafted by the relevant civil service department and the Office of the Parliamentary Counsel (OPC) to the Government. This office consists of lawyers who are specialists in drafting legislation.

1.1.1 Legislative procedure

The Bill goes through the legislative procedure set down in the Constitution. (Legislative procedure is discussed in more detail in Chapter 3.) An Act may come into force immediately in whole or in part, or at a later date. The process of debate and amendment can be protracted and for this reason only thirty to forty Acts are generally passed each year.

1.1.2 Locating Acts

The Irish Statute Book is the authoritative website. It provides access to Acts and Statutory Instruments from 1922 to 2006. Go to the website www.irishstatutebook.ie, click on 'Browse' and select the relevant year (e.g. 2005 for the Disability Act 2005). You will have to accept the Disclaimer before accessing statutes or other material.

More recent Acts can be accessed via the Oireachtas website at www.oireachtas.ie/ViewDoc.asp?fn=/home.asp. Click on 'Acts' in the top left-hand margin and then select 'New Acts' from the drop-down menu.

1.1.3 Format and Terminology of an Act

Each Act has a similar format or structure. To become familiar with this format and some terminology we will look at the Carer's Leave Act 2001. This is a relatively short Act. Do not be concerned if you are unclear about the wording and effect of the Act; our focus is solely on its structure.

First locate the Carer's Leave Act 2001 using the Irish Statute Book website. Look for the year 2001 as described above. You will see a list of Acts, which you can view alphabetically or numerically. (The Constitutional Amendments of that year are listed first.) Scroll down until you reach No. 19/2001 (the nineteenth Act of the Oireachtas of that year), which is the Carer's Leave Act, and click on that Act. Scroll down the Act and note how it is set out.

The number of the Act is given and then the **Long Title** gives a summary of its main purpose. It also gives the date it was passed by the Oireachtas (2 July 2001). Note that this does not necessarily mean that all or any part of an Act is in force, as the commencement of an Act can be delayed for a number of reasons. The Carer's Leave Act 2001 did, however, enter into force on this date.

You will see that the Act is arranged into **sections**.

The **Short Title** (section 1) is the usual way to refer to an Act (the citation of an Act). Once the full title of the Act has been given, if it is referred to frequently in a report or discussion, it may be abbreviated, for example the Carer's Leave Act 2001 may be referred to as the CLA 2001.

Section 2 is the **Interpretation** section. This defines relevant terms used by the Act such as 'Minister' and 'Employer'. It also refers the reader to other sections where definitions can be found.

Section 3 gives power to make **Regulations.** This is a typical form of section. It empowers the relevant minister (in this Act, the Minister for Enterprise, Trade and Employment) to pass regulations (secondary legislation) for any matter referred to in the Act, i.e. to make regulations generally for the purpose of giving effect to this Act.

The Act is then split into **Parts** setting out the various provisions.

Each **section** is split into **sub-sections** (ss). When referring to part of an Act in a report or answer is it not necessary to write out 'sub-section'. Write it as, for example, Section 4(5). Wherever possible you should refer to the relevant part of the Act specifically.

Question: Which provision in the Carer's Leave Act 2001 outlines the employee's obligation to give notice to the employer of an intention to take leave?
Answer: Section 9(1) Carer's Leave Act 2001.

TASK

This task involves using the website of the Houses of the Oireachtas to access recent legislation. Its purpose is to review the format of Acts, to identify situations in which an Act is passed but comes into force at a later date, and to introduce the topic of Statutory Instruments.

Go to www.oireachtas.ie. In the left hand margin click on 'Acts', then choose '1997–07'. Locate the Water Services Act 2007. This is an example of a complex Act, which was enacted by the Oireachtas on 14 May 2007. Due to the complexity of the provisions it was not possible to put the whole Act in force immediately; but we are concerned not with detailed content, but with the structure of the Act. Locate Section 3, the **Commencement** section. This is a typical section in an Act.

Question: When does the Act come into force?
Answer: When the minister (defined in Section 2 as the Minister for the Environment, Heritage and Local Government) makes an order fixing the dates. Parts of the Act can come into effect before others. The Order bringing provisions into effect is a statutory instrument.

1.2 Statutory instruments

Ministers have an important power to make **statutory instruments** (**SIs**) giving effect to or implementing legislation without the need to have every detail passed by the Oireachtas. They are cited using an S.I. number.

For example, the majority of the Safety, Health and Welfare at Work Act 2005 was brought into force on 1 September 2005 by S.I. No. 328 Safety, Health and Welfare at Work Act 2005 (Commencement) Order 2005.

Statutory instruments can also be used to add or change details or extra provisions in existing primary legislation (Acts), provided the Act allows for this.

1.2.1 The importance of statutory instruments

Statutory instruments are important in the legal system for a number of reasons.

- They save parliamentary time — there is a short, formal procedure allowing them to enter into force, compared with long debate and procedures before Bills become Acts.
- They allow for technical changes in the law.
- They are used as a way of implementing EU law into Irish law. An example of this is the S.I. No. 340/2005 Waste Management (Waste Electrical and Electronic Equipment) Regulations 2005 — the WEEE Regulations.
- They can be highly detailed and specific in a technical area.
- They often 'commence' part of the Act, i.e. make the Act come into full legal force.

However, they often attract less scrutiny and publicity than the progress of Bills, which raises questions about the transparency and level of public knowledge about provisions contained in statutory instruments.

Hundreds of statutory instruments are passed into law every year.

Question: How many Statutory Instruments were passed in 2005? Use the Irish Statute Book website to find the answer.

1.2.2 The validity and status of statutory instruments

The statutory instrument must comply with all the principles and requirements of the Act. The Act is often called the 'parent' Act because it gives birth to the statutory instrument. If there is any contradiction or conflict between the wording of the Act and the statutory instrument, the Act takes priority.

1.3 The status of legislation

All Acts and statutory instruments must comply with the provisions of the Constitution, otherwise the Act or part of an Act or statutory instrument can be struck down. Article 15.4 of the Constitution provides for this. This is the principle of constitutionality. Recently, in the publicised case of *CC v. Ireland* provisions of the Criminal Law (Amendment) Act 1935 were struck down as being unconstitutional. In the important case of *McGee v. AG and Anor [1974] IR 284*, a criminal statute of 1935 which made it illegal to sell, advertise, import or attempt to import contraceptives into the State was ruled as unconstitutional as it was contrary to the plaintiff's personal rights under Article 40 of the Constitution. (The Constitution has a higher status than legislation.)

2 The Constitution of Ireland — Bunreacht na hÉireann

The second source of law in Ireland is the Constitution or Bunreacht na hÉireann (the basic law of Ireland).

Constitutional law is an important and broad topic which could take up an entire textbook in itself. In this section we focus on certain key areas and we will be using the database of the Taoiseach's Office to access and consider these topics.

OVERVIEW

- Definition and purpose of a constitution.
- Elements of the Irish Constitution.
- Defining the functions of government: legislative; executive; judicial.
- Rights of the citizen.
- Status of the Constitution.
- Changes to the Constitution.

2.1 What is a constitution?

The written constitution of a state is usually the result of a major political event, after which the constitution is enacted as part of the process of resolution. It sets out the nature of the State and how it is to be organised. The first famous modern constitution was that of the United States in 1787, and the French constitution was largely modelled on principles in the US constitution. Both were the results of revolutions; and both were formal statements that declared that the power to organise and declare the institutions of state lay with the people (not with a monarch or a foreign power).

A constitution generally sets down:
1. The nature and the geographical borders of the state.
2. The institutions of the state and their functions and powers.
3. The rights of the citizens of the state.

A constitution generally has a special status in national law. It has a higher authority than other forms of domestic law. It may be **entrenched**, which means it requires a special legislative procedure and/or a referendum to change the Constitution. A Constitution is not a cast-iron guarantee of perpetual liberty, democracy and fraternity. Constitutional provisions are subject to interpretation and may be manipulated. Recent events in Zimbabwe and Pakistan show how constitutional provisions may be ineffective. We will be looking at case law in Ireland, which relies on constitutional rights to challenge certain actions of the State.

2.1.1 Introduction to terminology — the functions of government

Before looking at the structure and content of the Constitution we should be familiar with some important terms.

The law-making power of the state is known as the **legislative** power. The power to implement the law is the **executive** power. The enforcement of law is **judicial** power. In Ireland the Houses of the Oireachtas hold legislative power. The Taoiseach and the Government hold executive power. The courts and judges hold judicial power.

Generally the Constitution lays down a separation of powers so that only one institution holds certain powers and that personnel holding one type of power cannot exercise another type of power. An example of this is the fact that judges (the judicial function) cannot be TDs or senators and exercise legislative functions. However, we shall see that there are considerable overlaps between the institutions. An obvious overlap is the position of Government and of the Taoiseach. Ministers who exercise executive power also have legislative power as members of the Dáil. The judiciary, in the interpretation and application of law, can in certain cases be seen to be developing (or making) law, i.e. having a legislative function.

2.2 Introduction to the Irish Constitution

The present Constitution was written in 1937. It replaced the Constitution of the Irish Free State of 1922, which was written as a result of the War of Independence. The 1937 Constitution was largely the creation of Éamon de Valera. The language of the Constitution may seem outdated in places but in many respects it has moved with the times. The Preamble (or introduction), and Article 41 on the concept of the family, are examples of sections using the language of the 1930s. There have been significant formal changes (amendments) to the Constitution since 1937 and significant controversies about some of its contents. We will now consider the text of the Constitution and some of the key features and terminology.

Task: Locate the Irish Constitution on the internet

Go to the Department of the Taoiseach's website, www.taoiseach. gov.ie/. In the left-hand margin of the home page there are a number of options. Click on 'Department of the Taoiseach'. Use the search box and type 'Constitution'.

This will list a number of options: the first result gives access to the up-to-date Constitution. The most recent amendments to the Constitution were made in 2004, and this is the version you need to access.

Scan through the document briefly. Note that the Constitution was first enacted by the people (following a referendum) and became law on 29 December 1939. The Constitution has been amended a number of times, most recently following a referendum concerning the Irish citizenship of children born to foreign parents in Ireland.

The Constitution begins with the Preamble of 1937, which is religious in tone and refers to the struggle for independence.

2.3 The structure of the Irish Constitution

The Constitution consists of 50 Articles. It can be divided into topic areas for the purpose of our discussion. It is a relatively short document, considering that it deals with the apparatus of state and the rights of citizens. Its scope is subject to the interpretation of the relevant courts. Not all the key words within the Constitution are defined by the document. The scope of the rights of citizens has been developed by the Supreme Court, which has delivered a number of authoritative (and sometimes highly controversial judgments) on aspects of such areas of the Constitution as the right to life.

Task

Read through the Constitution and note its structure and main points. (This should take you about 30 minutes.)

2.4 *Summary of key Articles of the Constitution*

Article 3 contains the aspiration for a united Ireland to be brought about by peaceful means with the democratically expressed consent of a majority of the people in both jurisdictions (North and South).

Article 8 provides that Irish is the first national language and English is the second.

Article 9 deals with citizenship. This Article was changed by the most recent constitutional amendment. Prior to the amendment there had been a constitutional right to Irish citizenship to those born in Ireland, irrespective of whether either of the parents of the child was, or was entitled to be, an Irish citizen.

Article 12 deals with the role of the President. The nomination procedure is set out in Article 12.4.2 and the requirement that s/he be elected by direct vote of the people is contained in Article 12.2. The president holds office for a seven-year term and cannot be a member of either House of the Oireachtas. Under Article 13.3 every Bill passed by the Oireachtas requires the President's signature to become law.

Article 15 sets out provisions concerning the Oireachtas — the legislature. Under Article 15.2 'the sole and exclusive power of making laws for the State is ... vested in the Oireachtas'. It also provides that any law that is passed which is repugnant (contrary) to the Constitution will be invalid. The Constitution has a higher status than ordinary legislation.

Article 16 deals with the membership and constituency details of Dáil Éireann.

Article 18 deals with the Seanad, which has 60 members. Eleven are nominated, six are elected from universities and the remaining 43 are elected by members of the Dáil and others.

Articles 20–25 set out the legislative procedure and the steps that a Bill goes through before becoming an Act (refer to Chapter 3 for more detail on this). It divides Bills into Money Bills (defined in Article 22) and Non-Money Bills.

Article 26 allows the President (after consulting with the Council of State) to refer a Bill to the Supreme Court for a decision on whether the Bill is contrary to the Constitution.

Article 27 deals with amendment of the Constitution by referendum.

Article 28 outlines the functions of Government (the executive) and the Taoiseach.

Article 28A recognises the functions of local government.

Article 29 deals with international relations and gives authority to the

Government to conduct international relations. It contains detailed provisions relating to the European Union and the effect of EU law.

Article 30 outlines the appointment and functions of the Attorney General, the legal adviser to the Government.

Articles 31 and 32 establish the Council of State, which may be consulted by the President.

Article 33 establishes the office and powers of the Comptroller and Auditor General.

Articles 34–39: establishes the court structure, the judiciary and key principles such as the public administration of justice and the trial of criminal offences.

Article 40 lists the fundamental rights of citizens.

Article 41 describes the constitutional position and rights of the family.

Article 42 comprises rights relating to education.

Article 43 contains rights relating to private property.

Article 44 discusses rights relating to religion.

Article 45 describes the directing principles of social policy.

Articles 46 and 47 contain provisions governing the amendment of the Constitution and referendums.

Articles 48–50 contain provisions dealing with the validity of laws enacted prior to the Constitution.

A note on Article 50

Some of the older Acts which are still relevant today predate the independence of Ireland. Examples would be the Sale of Goods Act 1893 and the Partnership Act 1890. The Constitution provides that this 'old' law continues in force until repealed or amended. These were retained as part of the Irish legal system by virtue of the constitutional provision contained in Article 50.1 of the Constitution:

> Subject to this Constitution and to the extent to which they are not inconsistent therewith, the laws in force in Saorstát Eireann immediately prior to the date of coming into operation of this Constitution shall continue to be of full force and effect until the same or any of them shall have been repealed or amended by enactment of the Oireachtas.

However, many pre-independence Acts have now been repealed by the Statute Law Revision Act 2007 under a programme which aimed to 'tidy up' the long list of statutes in force. Under the 2007 Act over 3,200 statutes were repealed and other pre-independence Acts were expressly preserved.

The Constitution covers a wide range of matters. We shall focus on certain areas to highlight the importance of the Constitution in regulating the activities of the State:

- The institutions of the State.
- Legislative procedure (covered in Chapter 3).
- The status of international law and the incorporation of EU law.
- The extent of personal rights under the Constitution and the role of the Supreme Court in interpreting and defining the scope of these fundamental rights.

2.5 The institutions of the State

Under the Constitution the function of each institution is defined. Generally only the institution allocated a certain function may perform that specific task. If an institution 'oversteps' its power it may be said to be acting unconstitutionally.

The aim of giving each institution a certain function and limiting their function is to preserve democracy by ensuring that one institution never gets too much power. The powers of the legislature are separate and distinct from those of the judiciary. This aspect of 'separation of powers' is a recognised feature of many constitutions. The separation of powers theory states that there should be separate personnel in each institution and the institutions should have separate and distinct functions and powers. For example, under Article 35.3 no judge can be a member of the Oireachtas or hold any other office.

There are overlaps of institutions and personnel in the Irish constitutional structure, for example in the position of the Taoiseach, who is head of the executive branch of government and also sits and votes in the legislature. Another example is members of the executive (ministers), who make legislation in the form of statutory instruments.

2.5.1 The legislature — the Oireachtas (Article 15)

TASK

For an excellent overview of the function of the Oireachtas watch the short information video linked to the Houses of the Oireachtas website. This also introduces the topic of legislative procedure. You can visit the Oireachtas and watch proceedings: sittings are in public (Article 15.8.1). You can find details of how to arrange a tour on the Oireachtas website.

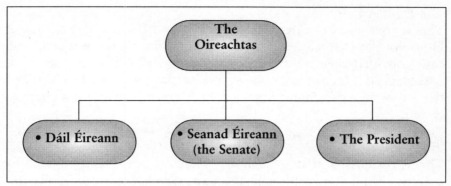

The Oireachtas comprises these three institutions

The Oireachtas sets its own rules of procedure and standing orders. Questions are decided on a majority of the votes of members present in the house.

Official documents and speeches have parliamentary privilege status (Article 15.12). This means that the makers of the statements cannot be sued for defamation or breach of confidentiality, or be prosecuted for criminal offences arising from statements made in either House. It is seen as essential for members of the Oireachtas to be able to speak freely without fear of litigation or prosecution. They may be subject to the rules of the Oireachtas in relation to words spoken. Under Article 15.3 members also have an immunity (except in certain situations) from arrest when in the House. Furthermore no TD or Senator can be forced to reveal the sources of information used in parliamentary debates.

The sole and exclusive power of making laws
Article 15.2.1 states that the 'sole and exclusive' power of making laws for the State is vested in the Oireachtas. The Constitution then goes on to provide for exceptions to this general rule. Laws may be created by subordinate bodies (local councils, which pass by-laws, are an example of this). Legislation can also be made by ministers in the form of statutory instruments.

Question: Can you think of any other body or institution that passes laws that will bind Ireland?
Key Point: The Institutions of the European Union can enact regulations, directives and decisions which become part of Irish law. (Article 29 of the Constitution regulates this area.)

The Dáil (Article 16)

This is comprised of directly elected TDs and is known as the lower House of the Oireachtas. It has more authority than the Seanad and can (provided there is the necessary majority) ensure legislation is passed even if the Seanad opposes the legislation. It has 166 TDs and the levels of representation within each constituency are subject to review.

The Seanad or Senate

This is comprised of sixty senators. They are not directly elected by citizens of the State, although the term *General Election* is used to describe their election, which is held within 90 days of the dissolution of the Dáil.

The Seanad is made up of:

• 11 senators nominated by the Taoiseach
• 43 senators elected by panels representing sectional interests in the State (e.g. administration; agriculture; culture and education; industry and commerce; labour)
• 6 senators elected by the graduates of NUI and the University of Dublin.

The panels are comprised of a number of types of politician (outgoing Seanad members, TDs, county councillors, etc.). As a result the political composition of the Seanad will generally mirror the strength of the parties in the Dáil.

TASK

Using the website of the Houses of the Oireachtas identify the current membership of the Seanad and whether they were elected (by panel or vote of university graduates) or nominated (by the Taoiseach). Use the 'Members' tab to locate the information.

The Seanad generally meets on two days a week (Wednesday and Thursday). Its main function is to scrutinise legislation sent to it by the Dáil. The Seanad can also commence (initiate) legislation, other than Money Bills or Bills, to alter the Constitution.

Members of the Seanad and of the Dáil sit together on Joint Committees to discuss and scrutinise legislative proposals.

Question:

What are your views on the method of selection of senators? Do you think that the method of selection makes the Seanad a democratically representative legislative institution?

Key Point:
This is a discussion point; there are no 'right' answers. However, reform of the Seanad has long been proposed by the Seanad itself. Proposals have included an expansion of membership of the Seanad to 65 and direct election of 32 members by citizens under the proportional representation (PR) system.

The President

The President is the Head of State. He or she is directly elected by citizens every seven years (Article 12) and can hold office for a maximum of two terms.

There is a formal procedure for nominating a candidate for a presidential election. A candidate needs the support of at least twenty members of the Oireachtas or at least four administrative counties. Presidential duties are mainly ceremonial.

Role of the President

The functions of the President are defined by the Constitution. The role has no executive power and the President acts on the advice (instructions) of the government (Article 13.9). All legislation must be signed into law by the President (Article 13.3.1).

Under Article 26 the President can refer Bills (other than a Money Bill or a Bill amending the Constitution) to the Supreme Court for a decision on a question as to whether all or part of the Bill is unconstitutional. If the Supreme Court decides that a provision is unconstitutional the President shall not sign the Bill into law.

2.5.2 The Government — the Executive

Under Article 28 the government consists of between seven and fifteen members. The government is responsible to the Dáil (Article 29). The government is collectively responsible for the departments of state, each of which is headed by a minister. The members of the government must be members of the Oireachtas.

Meetings of ministers are known as Cabinet meetings. Meetings of the Cabinet are confidential, unless a High Court order decides that disclosure should be made due to an overriding public interest or in the interests of the administration of justice.

The Cabinet operates under a principle of collective responsibility, which means that it speaks as one and each Minister must publicly support decisions taken in Cabinet meetings. Failure to toe the Cabinet line is likely to result in pressure to resign or dismissal by the President (on the advice of the Taoiseach).

The Taoiseach

The Head of the Government or Prime Minister is the Taoiseach. The Taoiseach appoints the Tánaiste (deputy prime minister).

The Taoiseach can ask a minister to resign at any time, 'for reasons which to him seem sufficient', and if the Minister does not resign the appointment may be terminated by the President on the Taoiseach's instruction.

If the Taoiseach resigns from office, all other government ministers are taken to have resigned, although the ministers continue to hold office pending the appointment of their successors (Article 28.11).

Matters such as the remuneration of government ministers, and the distribution and organisation of business among the departments of state, are all regulated in accordance with law.

Under Article 29.10 the Taoiseach must resign if s/he fails to retain the support of the majority in the Dáil (this is often referred to as a vote of no confidence).

Question:
Identify two aspects of the Taoiseach's power in the institutional order of the State, and a check or brake on the power of the Taoiseach.

Key Points:
The Taoiseach appoints the Tánaiste and other Ministers and has the constitutional power to dismiss Ministers. If the Taoiseach acts in a way which alienates his own Ministers and the Houses of the Oireachtas so that he can no longer retain a Dáil majority, he or she must resign from office.

2.5.3 The courts and judiciary: Articles 34 and 35

Although judges are formally appointed by the President, all the appointments are made on the instructions of the Government, which generally follow the advice of the Judicial Appointments Advisory Board (established under the Courts and Court Officers Act 1995).

Article 35 guarantees the independence of the judiciary.

Question: What do you consider 'independence of the judiciary' means and why is it necessary?

Key Points: Judges need to be secure in their position so that they can make fair and impartial judgments without fear of reprisal or dismissal if they make a decision contrary to the Government's viewpoint. A judge of the High Court or Supreme Court cannot be removed from office unless on grounds of incapacity or stated misbehaviour and both Houses of the Oireachtas must pass a resolution requiring removal of the judge.

Functions of the judiciary
Crotty v. An Taoiseach [1987] IR 713 at page 778:

> It is not within the competence of the Government, or indeed the Oireachtas to free themselves from the constraints of the Constitution ... They are both creatures of the Constitution and are not empowered to act free from the restraints of the Constitution. To the judicial organ of Government alone is given the power conclusively to decide if there has been a breach of constitutional restraints. (As per Walsh, cited in *McKenna*.)

TASK
The aim of this task is for you to exercise an important constitutional right — observing the process of justice in public — and to familiarise yourself with court procedures.

Visit your local court and watch a case or cases in progress. The public have a constitutional right (under Article 34) to access to most court hearings (subject to exceptions for family law and other cases). This is the best way to see the Irish court system in action. You can find details of the courts and their sitting times on the Courts Service website. The Supreme Court sits in the Four Courts in Dublin. There is also public access to this court but as the appeals are based on points of law and paper documentation the important work of the Supreme Court can be less engaging than the action in your District and Circuit Courts.

2.6 The fundamental rights of citizens under the Constitution

2.6.1 Balancing rights
The rights of the citizen are set out throughout the Constitution. It is important to note that rights of the citizen are often qualified and not absolute rights.

Question: Do you think the right to free speech is an absolute right? Should a person be constitutionally entitled to say or publish *anything* about any topic or any person?

Key Points: This right of freedom of expression is set out in Article 40.6.1. The right of citizens to express freely their convictions and opinions is subject to considerations of 'public order and morality'. In addition the publication of 'blasphemous, seditious or indecent matter' is an offence.

There are other limitations to the right to 'free speech'. You cannot threaten serious physical violence against somebody orally or in writing: this would constitute an offence of threatening to kill or cause serious harm (Section 5 of the Non-Fatal Offences Against the Person Act 1997). In addition, if a statement is untrue and defamatory this 'freedom of expression' may result in a civil action for defamation.

It is an offence to broadcast or publish or speak in public in a threatening, abusive or insulting manner in relation to race, religion, nationality or sexual orientation if the words are intended or are likely to stir up hatred on these grounds (Prohibition of Incitement to Hatred Act 1989).The right of free speech has to be *balanced* with the rights of others not to be threatened, defamed, verbally assaulted, etc.

The interpretation and application of many constitutional rights have to be balanced as the rights of one citizen may contradict or impinge on the rights of another citizen. The Supreme Court has had to balance the rights of the unborn child with the rights of a mother in difficult cases involving the issue of abortion.

The limitations or qualifications on rights which may be imposed by the State is a central theme of all human rights law and we shall return to this issue in Chapter 9.

2.6.2 Rights in relation to criminal trials (Article 38)

Trial of offences

Article 38.1 states that, 'No person shall be tried on any criminal charge save in due course of law.'

The Constitution does not defined 'due course of law' and it has been left to the judges to interpret this phrase. There is now the additional requirement under the European Convention on Human Rights Act 2003 to consider judgments of the European Court of Human Rights in defining concepts of fairness and 'due course of law'. (We shall consider this in more detail in Chapter 9.)

Question: What would you consider to be fundamental features of a fair criminal trial?
Key Points: You may have identified some or all of these:
• the right to be presumed innocent until proven guilty
• the prosecution must prove guilt beyond reasonable doubt

- the right to a trial by jury for serious offences (Article 38.5)
- the right to be present at your own trial (unless you have absconded)
- the right to present a defence and to have legal representation, irrespective of financial means
- evidence used against an accused person should have been lawfully obtained.

2.6.3 Personal rights under Article 40

Article 40.1 states the equality principle. This guarantees that all citizens, as human persons, will be treated as equal before the law. However, this does not mean that everyone has a right to be treated in the same way. The State is permitted to take note of the physical, moral and social differences between people. The laws can differentiate but must not do so on an unjust or unreasonable basis.

Question: Who decides what is ' unjust' or 'unreasonable' ?
Key Point: Ultimately it is left to the High Court and Supreme Court to make this judgment when deciding on the constitutionality of legislation.

De Burca v. Attorney General [1976] IR 38
The Juries Act 1927 allowed only men to serve on juries. Women had to formally apply to be a juror. This differential treatment meant that juries were largely comprised of male property owners. The Act was ruled unconstitutional by the court as it infringed the principle of equality. It also infringed the principle that a jury should be fairly representative of society.

McKenna v. An Taoiseach (No. 2) [1995] IESC 11
This case was a constitutional challenge against the actions of the Government, which helped fund a campaign promoting a 'yes' vote in the 1995 referendum on divorce. The Supreme Court ruled that the Government's action was unconstitutional as it preferred the 'yes' voters to the 'no' voters. The importance of the concept of using a referendum to change the constitution was emphasised and the fact that the people are the 'guardians' of the Constitution. Mrs Justice Denham stated that Article 40.1:

> ... requires the organs of government in the execution of their powers to have due regard to the right of equality. The citizen

has the right to be treated equally. This includes the concept that in the democratic process, including referenda, neither side of an issue will be favoured, treated unequally, by the government.

One of the results of this judgment was the establishment of an independent Referendum Commission, which operates each time a referendum is called (Referendum Act 1998 as amended by the 2001 Act). Its role is to explain the subject matter of proposals and to keep the public informed.

2.6.4 The right to life under Article 40

The Constitution states (Article 40.3.2): 'The State shall, in particular, by its laws protect as best it may from unjust attack and, in the case of injustice done, vindicate the life, person, good name and property rights of every citizen.'

These rights are not absolute. The State recognises that even the right to life is not absolute.

Question: Can you identify any situation in which a person may be lawfully killed?
Key Point: You may have identified situations of self-defence in which one person is killed by another protecting his or her own life. In Ireland, before the abolition of the death penalty it was lawful for the State to execute those guilty of capital murder (the killing of gardaí or prison officers).

The right to life has generated discussion and controversy concerning the issue of abortion. In a number of extremely difficult and contentious cases in the 1990s the Supreme Court was faced with circumstances in which the rights of an unborn child were in conflict with the rights of the mother.

As a result of a number of Supreme Court rulings interpreting the scope of Article 40.3.3, the position in Irish law is that the termination of a pregnancy can occur in Ireland if the continuation of the pregnancy would cause a 'real and substantial risk to the life of the mother'.

Attorney General v. X and Others [1992] 1 IR 1
The first defendant, X, was a 14-year-old schoolgirl. She became pregnant as a result of rape. She wished to travel to the UK for an abortion. The High Court had imposed an injunction preventing her from travelling outside the State. The Supreme Court lifted this

injunction and stated that the risk of X committing suicide as a result of her situation meant there was a 'real and substantial risk to her life'. She could travel to the UK. The Court also said, as an *obiter* comment, that if she had sought an abortion in Ireland it would have been legal in these circumstances.

One of the results of this important decision was that a constitutional amendment was proposed to incorporate the 'real and substantial risk' proviso and to permit the introduction of legislation to legalise abortion in the situation of 'real and substantial risk', but not where the threat of suicide was the risk to the mother's health. The referendum was held in 1992 and was narrowly defeated, which meant that the threat of suicide of the mother can constitute 'real and substantial risk' to the mother, justifying a termination.

2.6.5 Other rights under Article 40

Parts of Article 40 are drafted in very general terms. Article 40.3.1 reads: 'The State guarantees in its laws to respect, and, as far as practicable, by its laws to defend and vindicate the personal rights of the citizen.' The Supreme Court has interpreted this Article widely and has recognised *unenumerated* constitutional rights. Rights that are not specifically mentioned by the Constitution, but have been created by the Courts, are known as unenumerated rights.

Unenumerated rights under Article 40 include a right to bodily integrity and a right to privacy.

A *right to bodily integrity*

The scope of this right is limited. It does not give a right to medical treatment and health protection in all situations. The principle was implied into the Constitution in the case of *Ryan v. Attorney General [1965] IR 294*. A challenge to the fluoridation of water was brought. The Supreme Court noted that there was a right to protection of health and a right to bodily integrity. On the facts no breach of this was found as the court ruled no danger from the fluoridation process had been proved.

McGee v. Attorney General & Anor [1973] IESC

This case concerned the ban on the sale and importation of contraceptives into the Republic. The Supreme Court ruled that the ban infringed the personal rights of the plaintiff under Article 40. They referred to the right to bodily integrity as the ban could have serious health consequences for the plaintiff. It also infringed the unenumerated right of privacy in marital relations.

A right to privacy

An individual has a limited right to privacy and this principle was first stated in the *McGee* case above. The right to privacy is not absolute.

Question: Identify a situation in which a citizen's rights to privacy could be lawfully interfered with by the State.
Key Point: The State may investigate our affairs in order to prevent crime or to protect public security.

In the case of *Kennedy v. Ireland [1987] IR 533* the High Court ruled that tapping the telephones of Kennedy and Arnold (two journalists) without any justification constituted a breach of privacy rights.

We are all subject to surveillance of varying sorts, including CCTV recordings. The scope of privacy law is one that is evolving and is being developed by the European Court of Human Rights (see Chapter 9).

Other unenumerated rights that have been identified by the Court include:

• The right to criminal legal aid in order to have access to the courts (also supported by Article 38 above).
• The right to travel outside the State.
• The right to refuse medical treatment — provided the patient has full legal capacity.
• The right to earn a livelihood — unless there are legitimate and proportionate reasons for limiting the right.

2.7 Article 41 — the family

Under the Constitution the family has a special status. Article 41.1 states:

> The State recognises the Family as the natural primary and fundamental unit group of Society, and as a moral institution possessing inalienable and imprescriptible rights, antecedent and superior to all positive law.

The rights of the family have a special status in Ireland. The concept of family is a natural right, a basic right that is said to exist by virtue of our humanity and that cannot be given or taken away by human intervention.

Task: Access the Constitution and read all of Article 41. Is there any aspect which you think reads as outdated?

Key Point: There is no correct point to raise here: much will depend upon your outlook. However, the references in Article 41.2 to 'by her life within the home, woman gives to the State' and to 'the neglect of their duties in the home' (Art. 41.2.2) etc. may strike you as old-fashioned.

2.7.1 The definition of the family

Although Articles 41 and 42 of the Constitution refer to the family, the concept of 'family' is not defined in the Constitution. It has been left up to the Courts to define this concept.

Question: What do you understand by the term 'family'?

Key Points: You may have identified parents, children, grandparents, siblings and others such as aunts and uncles as members of a family. You may consider that an unmarried partner or stepchildren may be part of the family.

However, the concept of the constitutional 'family' in Ireland has been defined by the Irish courts to cover married relationships only. It does not cover the increasingly common situation of couples cohabiting without getting married. This has a significant impact on the rights of the fathers of children.

The State (Nicolaou) v. An Bord Úchtala [1966] IR 567

Facts: The father of a child born outside marriage challenged the constitutionality of the Adoption Act 1952. The Act allowed for the adoption of his child without his knowledge or consent.

The Supreme Court ruled that he had no constitutional rights to his child. The concept of 'family' under the Constitution was ruled to be limited to that of a **married** family.

N & Anor v. HSE & Others [2006] IESC 60

This was a much publicised case concerning 'Baby Ann'.

Facts: Baby Ann's parents offered her for adoption. The natural parents were unmarried at the time. The parents then withdrew their consent to adoption and got married a month before High Court proceedings. The High Court proceedings ordered the child to remain with the potential adoptive parents. The natural parents appealed to the Supreme Court.

The Supreme Court ruled that Baby Ann must be returned to her natural parents, initially on a phased basis until the baby adjusted.

The fact that her natural parents were now married was a vital factor in the Supreme Court's decision. Once the parents were married they became a family with rights under Article 41.

Mrs Justice McGuiness applied the decision of *In re JH [1985] IR 375* and quoted Chief Justice Finlay in that case, who interpreted the Guardianship of Infants Act 1964 as:

> ... involving a constitutional presumption that the welfare of the child, which is defined in s. 2 of the Act in terms identical to those contained in Art. 42, s. 1, is to be found within the family, unless the Court is satisfied on the evidence that there are compelling reasons why this cannot be achieved, or unless the Court is satisfied that the evidence establishes an exceptional case where the parents have failed to provide education for the child ...

Mrs Justice McGuiness found that there were no compelling reasons shown that Baby Ann's natural parents could not provide for her welfare in their care and custody. 'An additional and crucial factor ... is that, given her parents' marriage and the re-registration of her birth, there is now no realistic possibility that Ann can be adopted by the Doyles.'

The rights of the married family unit were emphasised in this judgment. The difficulty that this constitutional position can cause was noted.

2.7.2 The rights of children

At present under the Constitution there is no specific Article dealing with children's rights. Children of course have constitutional rights as part of a family, and a right to education under Article 41. In addition, if they become part of the criminal justice system they have rights in this situation.

The rights of children are protected by International Conventions such as the United Nations Convention on the Rights of the Child (this Convention is not incorporated into Irish law). There is also protection for children under EU law in relation to Council Regulation (EC) No. 2201/2003 of 27 November 2003 concerning jurisdiction and the recognition and enforcement of judgments in matrimonial matters and matters of parental responsibility. There is a proposed amendment to the Constitution to restate and extend constitutional protection of children, which is to be the subject of a referendum.

Task: Access the Constitution and read Articles 42 and 43. Now consider how the Constitution may impact on the following issues.

---

1. John is an autistic boy aged 18. The Health Board has just told his parents that there are no secondary school facilities available for him.
2. Martha has an argument with a school principal and removes her children from the school saying she will teach them at home instead. Is she entitled to do this?

Key Points:
1. Article 42 deals with the constitutional right to education. Article 42.4 provides that the State shall provide for free **primary** education. The scope of the phrase 'primary education' was discussed by the Supreme Court in *Sinnott v. Minister for Education [2001] IESC 63*. This was a complex and emotive case, and seven judges of the Supreme Court sat to decide the issue.

Facts: Jamie Sinnott was a young man aged 23 who had autism. Despite his mother's determination and pioneering work in highlighting the lack of service, he received little appropriate education from his region. He sued the Minister for Education through his mother (called a next friend) for failure to provide for free education, discrimination against him in the provision of free education facilities, failure to vindicate his right to education and, in particular, his right to receive a certain minimum education.

The High Court found the state was in breach of constitutional obligations under Article 42 and 42.4, imposed an obligation to provide and continue to provide for primary education and related ancillary services for this plaintiff, which would be open-ended and would continue as long as such education and services were reasonably required by him. The phrase 'primary education' was interpreted broadly and was not limited by age. The court awarded damages.

The Supreme Court overruled the judgment (although the damages were paid by the State). The issue, as summarised by Mrs Justice Denham, was the definition of 'the age to which a person is entitled to the provision of free primary education, whether the entitlement is for life or for childhood'. The court decided that primary education for the purposes of the constitutional right ends at the age of 18.

(Since the facts of the case arose the Education Act 1998 and Disability Act 2005 have made provision for special educational needs. You may have read of other contentious issues about the funding of and policy relating to provision and non-provision of facilities and education in this area.)

2. In Article 42.1 the State acknowledges that the 'primary and natural educator of the child is the Family'. There is a constitutional right to educate at home as set out in Article 42.2. The practical difficulties encountered by parents who sincerely believe that they are acting in their children's best interests in attempting to provide such education in the home are exemplified in the case decided by the court in *Director of Public Prosecutions v. Best [2000] 2 IR 17*. (Quoted in *Sinnott*.)

2.8 The Constitution and the EU

Article 29.4.10 provides:

> No provision of this Constitution invalidates laws enacted, acts done or measures adopted by the State which are necessitated by the obligations of membership of the European Union or of the Communities, or prevents laws enacted, acts done or measures adopted by the European Union or by the Communities or by institutions thereof, or by bodies competent under the Treaties establishing the Communities, from having the force of law in the State.

The effect of this provision and the European Communities Acts (as amended) is that the European Union can make laws that apply in Ireland without the sanction of the Oireachtas. It gives effect to directly applicable law and it provides that EU law is in theory exempt from having to comply with the Constitution, i.e. it provides that EU law has a higher status than the Constitution. It covers two types of law:

- law created by the EU institutions (Articles, Regulations, Directives, and the case law of the European Court of Justice)
- law created by the State to comply with the requirements of EU law (e.g. the implementation of a Directive).

2.8.1 EU law takes precedence over conflicting Irish Law

Where there is conflict between the laws of the EU and Ireland, EU law always takes priority.

This rule of the supremacy of EC law was a principle created by the European Court of Justice (ECJ) early in the EEC's history (*Case 6/64 Costa v. ENEL [1964] ECR 585*). The reason for the creation of the principle was to ensure that EC law was uniformly applied throughout the Community. It would undermine the whole Community legal order if member states could select which types of EC law they considered more important than national provisions. It would mean that Community law could be selectively applied. Although the principle of supremacy of EC law had not been included in the Treaty the ECJ developed the principle in a number of important cases.

Amministrazione delle Finanze dello Stato v. Simmenthal [1978] ECR 629:

> A national court which is called upon, within the limits of its jurisdiction, to apply provisions of Community law is under a duty to give full effect to those provisions, if necessary refusing of its own motion to apply any conflicting provision of national legislation, even if adopted subsequently, and it is not necessary for the court to request or await the prior setting aside of such provisions by legislative or other constitutional means.

The principle was firmly acknowledged in Ireland by the Supreme Court in the case of *Campus Oil v. Minister for Industry (No. 2) [1983] IR 82).*

Facts: The case arose out of a scheme which guaranteed the viability of the Whitegate Oil refinery. A number of challenges were brought against the scheme by traders. They relied on EC law on the free movement of goods to challenge domestic law. A preliminary ruling (then under Article 177 EC) was sought by the High Court from the ECJ. The preliminary ruling procedure was explained by the Supreme Court. Mr Justice Griffin also made it clear that rulings of the ECJ were to be followed by lower courts.

> In my opinion, it would be highly undesirable, to put it at its lowest, for this Court to interpret those articles in anticipation of the rulings of the Court of Justice. The plaintiffs should not be allowed to blow hot and cold in the course of the same proceedings between the same parties. It is for the Court of

Justice to interpret the provisions of the Treaty, and it is for our Courts to apply it. In my opinion ... the primary object of article 177 is to ensure the uniform interpretation of Community law within all member States, as otherwise the application of Community law by the national courts of the member States could lead to divergent application in different member States, or even to an application which would be contrary to the principles of Community law. It is for this reason that, although national courts, other than the court of last instance, have a discretion to seek preliminary rulings under article 177, the courts of last instance, whose cases set the important precedents, are obliged to refer to the Court of Justice any questions of Community law that have been raised.

In the *Attorney General v. X and Others* case above the Supreme Court also explicitly recognised that Irish courts must enforce European Community law and where community law conflicts with Irish law, including constitutional law, community law would take priority.

2.9 Amending the Constitution

The Irish Constitution is entrenched. That is, it requires a special procedure in order for it to be changed. The procedure is set out in Articles 46 and 47.

The Constitution has been amended many times, and each amendment requires a referendum. In 1972 the Constitution was amended to allow for Ireland's membership of the European Economic Community (EEC) and there have been other amendments to recognise major new European Treaties such as the Nice Treaty of 2002. The Belfast Agreement led to major amendments in 1998. Divorce was introduced by constitutional amendment in 1995.

3 The Common Law and Precedent

Ireland is a common law system. A common law system relies on the doctrine of precedent and the decisions of the judges to clarify legal principles. You will see it referred to as a case-based system. Other countries that have a common law system include the United States, Australia, and England and Wales. Due to historical reasons, other European countries have different types of legal system. Countries such as France and Italy have a system based on the ancient Roman law model, in which law was compiled into Themes or **Codes.** Their legal system is called a civil law legal system as it is based on framework codes.

A key feature of the common law system is the importance of case law decided by the judges in stating and developing the law. It is the judges who interpret the statutory provisions that come before them. Important principles that were created by common law include the laws of tort (Chapter 4) and contract (Chapter 5); and the criminal offences of murder and manslaughter were developed by the courts.

The common law system as it developed was flawed in many ways. It had a procedural rigidity. It relied on writs being issued, and if the basis of the claim did not 'fit the writ' the claim would fail. Remedies that could be granted were limited to monetary remedies. In particular the common law did not recognise or enforce the concept of a trust. A trust is created when a settler gives property (land or money) to a trustee to hold for the benefit of someone else.

The shortcomings in the common law system led to the creation of the law of equity by a separate set of English courts. The principles of equity or fairness became part of the mainstream court system from the 1870s and there are principles and precedents of equity which now form part of the common law system.

3.1 Precedent

The principle of precedent can be defined as requiring that legal principles decided by a higher court must be followed and applied by courts of a lower status unless there are reasons to depart from the earlier judgment.

3.1.1 Why have the rule of precedent?

The principle developed over centuries and is tied to the development of English law. Originally judges were not based in one area but went around the country hearing and deciding on cases 'on circuit'. Gradually it became judicial practice, in order to ensure uniformity and respect for the principle of justice, to interpret and apply the law uniformly, or in common, wherever the case was being decided. This is the origin of the term 'common law'. The practice developed of the more authoritative judgments from higher courts being followed by the lower courts, to ensure that a common law system was applied throughout the territory. In addition to ensuring a uniform, common system the system also has an 'efficiency aspect', because if a principle of law has been correctly decided it is more efficient to apply that principle to a similar situation than to try to 'reinvent the wheel' and decide the same issue again.

Law reports

This development was inextricably linked with the practice of **law reporting**. The principle of precedent relies on accurate records of cases and of the full judgments being made. There are different series and types of law report now. In this book we rely on those accessible online. There are many more sources, both paper-based and electronic databases, which are used by lawyers. These require payment to access.

3.1.2 Elements of the rule of precedent

Not all decisions are binding on courts of a lower status. A principle in a case is **binding** in a later case if all these elements are present:
- Part of the legal reasoning (the *ratio decidendi*) of the case.
- Decided by a higher court.
- No relevant differences between the two cases.

HIGHEST STATUS

The European Court of Justice
(Delivers binding judgments on matters of EU law which all national courts must follow)

The Supreme Court

The Court of Criminal Appeal

The High Court
Central Criminal Court
Special Griminal Court

The Circuit Court

The District Court

LOWEST STATUS

The hierarchy of the Irish courts

3.1.3 The hierarchy of the court structure

The principle of precedent relies on the courts being in ranking order. We shall look at the court structure in more detail in Chapter 3, but a brief explanation of the hierarchy of the Irish courts and the European Court of Justice is given in the diagram above.

3.1.4 What is a relevant principle (*ratio decidendi*) that creates a precedent?

This is a difficult question to answer and another aspect of the law where there are real differences in views of the essential reasoning and ratio of a case. These are complicated legal concepts and the identification of the exact principle established by a particular case generates much discussion, business (and money!) for lawyers. If a judge misinterprets the ratio of an earlier case or fails to apply it correctly this can provide grounds for an appeal.

For our purposes it is enough to note that it is the **legal principle** from the case, not the facts, which is the binding part of the judgment.

In *Donoghue v. Stevenson* the legal principle concerned negligence liability arising from a breach of reasonable care to a person who could be injured by actions or inactions. The fact that this case arose from a snail in a ginger beer bottle is irrelevant to the *ratio decidendi* of the case concerning the legal principle of duty of care. The **legal principle** would still be the same if a frozen and battered rat was found in a packet of frozen haddock or if a new car was sold with a manufacturing defect in its brakes that made it a dangerous vehicle.

3.1.5 Judgments

At the end of a case the judge(s) will give judgment. There may be a number of judgments depending on the number of judges. There will only be one judgment in the Circuit and High Court. There may be up to seven judges sitting in the Supreme Court on an important issue. Each judge may have a different viewpoint and may rely on different cases. If the judges are divided on the outcome, the majority view prevails over the **dissenting judgment** (which is why an odd number of judges sit to hear a case). A dissenting judgment can never form part of the *ratio*, as it has not decided the case, but has dissented from the majority verdict.

The judges do not indicate the key point of their judgment with words or headings such as, 'the fundamental point of my judgment is ...' It is a key legal skill to distil a judgment and get to the essence of the principle. The binding part of judgment is known as the *ratio decidendi* — the reasoning behind the case. There may be a number of slightly different *ratios* in a case as there may be a number of differing judgments.

Anything which is not a key legal principle (or proposition of law) decided in the case is termed an *obiter dicta* comment.

Task: *Identifying the ratio decidendi of a case*

Use the BAILII website. In the 'Search BAILII' box type '*Attorney General v. Whelan 1933*' and define your search by selecting 'Ireland' as the database.

A list of cases and reports will appear. Call up the Court of Criminal Appeal case of the *Attorney General v. Peter Whelan [1933] IR 518.*

Note: Due to the difficulty in identifying the essential principle of the case (the *ratio decidendi*) that binds a future court, a short one-judge judgment has been chosen. This case is also an excellent illustration of how old cases (this one from 1746) were relied upon as earlier precedents. Although decided in 1934 it is still a relevant principle. It concerns an appeal from a conviction for conspiracy to steal or larceny (now called theft) from the Circuit Court.

The conviction was appealed by the defendant. He claimed that he acted under duress and this should have been a defence entitling him to an acquittal.

Read the judgment through; do not worry about the archaic language. Try to identify some principles of Mr Justice Murnaghan's judgment that decide the case (the *ratio*).

Key Points: Look at Paragraph 8. The *ratio* of the case could be said to be:

Threats of immediate death or serious personal violence that overbear the ordinary power of human resistance can be a defence to a criminal action. This can be termed the defence of duress. If duress is applicable it must be shown that the overpowering of the person's will was operative at the actual time of the crime. (This is the defence of duress: note that the judge refers to the standard of 'ordinary power' or the power of a reasonable person.) The verdict was that the conviction should be quashed.

The judge also said that the defence of duress was limited and could never be pleaded in defence to a charge of murder. This principle was not strictly necessary to decide the case (as Whelan was charged with larceny, not murder). It is an important 'by the way' comment and is classed as *obiter dicta*.

3.1.6 Precedent and the position of the Supreme Court

The Supreme Court is the most authoritative domestic court and to ensure certainty in the interpretation and application of law the Supreme Court generally follows its own previous case law.

However, where the Supreme Court is convinced there is a strong reason to depart from its own previous decisions it can do so. For example in *McNamara v. ESB [1975]* the Supreme Court refused to follow its previous case law and ruled that an occupier owed a duty of care to a trespasser. (The law on occupiers' liability was uncertain as a result of differing standpoints and this prompted legislative action and the Occupiers' Liability Act 1995.)

Persuasive authorities

The judges will refer to binding precedents from the Irish jurisdiction. They may also refer to legal authorities from other jurisdictions. For example, in a recent constitutional case in the Irish Supreme Court cases from the Supreme Courts of Canada and California were relied upon.

3.2 The common law and law of equity

3.2.1 The law of equity

Historically the law of equity was a separate branch of law which developed as the common law form and procedures and writs were rigid and often operated to deprive a plaintiff of an appropriate remedy. A separate Court of Equity developed in parallel to the common law courts. It was more flexible in its procedure and looked to the overall fairness and equity of the proceedings. It created the concept of a **trust** and **trustees,** and new remedies such as the **injunction** (which compels a party to do something) and **specific performance** (an order which forces a party to complete a contract).

Judicial reforms led to the fusion of the courts of equity and the common law courts in the 1870s. Nowadays principles of equity can be argued in any civil court where the point is relevant.

Equitable principles are still very relevant today. Areas of law that are governed by equitable principles include: the law of trusts and the fiduciary duties of trustees under will and pension trusts; areas of family law; charities; and injunctions such as Mareva injunctions.

3.3 *The role of the judges in interpreting legislation (statutory interpretation)*

OVERVIEW

- The need for statutory interpretation.
- Guidelines used by the courts.
- The literal approach.
- The purposive approach.
- Presumptions.
- The Interpretation Act 2005.

The Irish legal system developed along the lines of the English legal system due to English rule over large parts of Ireland, and we have seen that Ireland is a **common law** system. The judges in the courts applied the legal principles that had been established by courts of higher status according to the rule of **precedent**. The rule of precedent is that a lower court is generally bound to follow the **legal principles** established in earlier decisions by higher courts. Much of the criminal law, the law of contract and tort was created by the judges in case law over hundreds of years.

A key role of judges is to **interpret** the law. This is referred to as statutory interpretation or statutory construction.

In Ireland the judges need to interpret the words in legislation and in the Constitution in order to make sense of their provisions. Language can be uncertain or ambiguous; and despite careful drafting and consideration, the meaning of words can be unclear or can change over time. An Act will often define its terms. The Occupiers' Liability Act 1995 (see Chapter 4) uses words such as 'premises', 'danger' and 'visitor'. These words have specific meanings in the Act. For example, in normal usage the word 'premises' means a building. Under the Occupiers' Liability Act the word 'premises' is defined to include land, water, vessels, vehicles and trains. Under the Interpretation Act 2005 certain common words used in all statutes are defined by the Act; so for example words and phrases such as 'weekday', 'full age', 'working day' and 'public holiday' are defined by the Act.

3.3.1 The meaning of words

The precise meaning of words is vital in the application of the law to a situation.

Assume that an offence states: 'It is a criminal offence to carry an offensive weapon in a public place.' Consider these examples:

Anna has a CS spray canister in her handbag in a shopping centre. Do you consider she could be guilty of this offence?

What are the important words in this offence that need definition?

Key Points: The concepts of offensive weapon (and whether it would cover the canister) would need to be defined and so would 'public place'.

Bernard lives in an area which has seen a spate of muggings. He is an electrician and makes sure he always carries one of his screwdrivers with him to 'defend' himself.

Key Points: Whether or not a screwdriver could be categorised as an offensive weapon would need to be considered. (You may consider the fact that the screwdriver can be a work tool may be relevant for the definition or may provide a defence to the charge.)

3.3.2 Judicial approaches to statutory interpretation

The courts have developed certain approaches or principles of statutory interpretation to assist in interpreting statutes that fail to adequately define a phrase or term.

The Interpretation Act 2005 provides that an ambiguous provision shall be given a construction that reflects the plain intention of the Oireachtas. The judges often use different methods to interpret words and may not refer specifically to the method of interpretation they are using. The primary methods of statutory interpretation are the literal rule and the purposive approach.

The literal rule

Words in a statutory provision should generally be given their ordinary meaning. This is the usual approach to statutory interpretation as it reflects the will of the Oireachtas, which passed the legislation.

Rahill v. Brady [1971] IR 69: 'in the absence of some special technical or acquired meaning the language of a statute should be construed according to its ordinary meaning'.

If the words have a special legal or technical meaning they will be given that meaning.

Burke v. Aer Lingus plc [1997] ILRM 148

Facts: A person was injured on the shuttle bus from plane to terminal building.

The claim centred on the words in the Warsaw Convention concerning international carriage by air (which are incorporated into airline tickets). The issue was whether the words 'embarking' and 'disembarking' included the shuttle bus trip.

The court ruled that as there was technical language attached to air travel the words should be interpreted in this context and the shuttle bus trip should constitute disembarkation for these purposes.

The purposive approach

This aims to fulfil the purpose of the legislation and it may involve interpreting an Act to cure a defect which has become apparent in the Act.

A statutory provision might be badly drafted and leave gaps in the law. In certain circumstances the literal meaning may not be appropriate. Where this is the situation the courts have interpreted the provision to prevent an absurd or inconsistent result which goes against the purpose of the Act.

The purposive approach is also referred to as the **teleological** approach to interpretation.

This approach is especially relevant when the provision derives from obligations of EU law. For example, a national provision which implements a Directive will be interpreted in line with the spirit and **purpose** of the EU legislation.

Nestor v. Murphy [1979] IR 326

The Family Home Protection Act 1976 provided that one spouse could not transfer the family home to another without the written consent of the other spouse. It was legislation that was aimed at protecting women living in the family home, to prevent the home being sold or mortgaged without their consent.

A husband and wife both entered and signed a contract of sale of their home to the plaintiffs. They then refused to go through with the sale, arguing that the contract had no effect because it was contrary to a section of the Family Home Protection Act 1976 since the wife had not consented in writing to the sale. The defendants were using the provision to try to avoid the sale. On a strict reading of the section it could be argued that the contract had no effect due to a lack of formal consent of the other party. (There is a sworn declaration on a printed form which signifies consent.)

However, the Supreme Court ruled that the provision concerning 'prior consent in writing' did not apply where **both** parties had entered into the contract for sale at the outset as the part of the Act relied on could not have been intended to apply where both husband and wife had both signed the contract, which clearly meant both parties had knowledge of and consented to the sale.

Murphy v. Bord Telecom Eireann [1989] ILRM 53

Article 119 EC (which is now Article 141) contains the principle of equality of pay for men and women engaged in equal work.

The Irish legislation on this area was the Anti-Discrimination (Pay) Act 1974 which provided for equal pay for 'like work' or work of equal value.

The applicant did work of a **greater** value than that of a male colleague, and initially under the domestic procedures for enforcing rights and using the literal approach it was argued that she could not claim.

Questions were referred to the European Court of Justice for a preliminary ruling. The ruling was given and the ECJ stated the Article must be interpreted to cover the situation where the worker is performing work of a higher value than the male comparator.

The High Court applied the preliminary ruling and stated that the purposive or teleological approach to interpretation should be adopted as this would ensure the supremacy of EC law and the effectiveness of Article 119 in the national context. As the **purpose** of the EC Article was to prevent disparities in pay between the sexes for equal work it must be interpreted as covering the case of a person who is engaged in work of a higher value than that of a person with whom a comparison is to be made.

3.3.3 The Interpretation Act 2005

Section 5 provides that where a provision is obscure, ambiguous or absurd, a purposive approach will be applied by the courts.

Section 6 provides that when interpreting legislation, a court may make allowances for changes in the law, social conditions, technology, the meaning of words used and 'other relevant matters'.

TASK

The aim of this Task is to consider the importance and the difficulties of interpretation.

Assume that under Section 1 of the Drugs Act 2008 (a fictitious statute):

'It is a criminal offence to possess a controlled drug with intent to supply to another.'

Alex is arrested after having been found with a quantity of drugs
(which are classified as controlled) that a neighbour and hardened
criminal, Barry, had left in Alex's car and was returning to collect
later. When the Gardai search Alex's car, the drugs are found. Alex
protests that they are not his and he was forced to keep them by
Barry, a notoriously violent dealer in the area.

Questions:
1. Do you think Alex could be charged with the offence of
    possession with intent to 'supply'?
2. What words or phrases need to be defined in this Section?
3. Do you think retaining the drugs and giving them back to an
    individual could constitute 'supply'?

Key Points:
1. Again, there is no 'right' answer to this question.
2. Clearly, the term 'controlled drug' needs definition within the
    legislation.
3. How would you define the term 'supply'? In other contexts we
    talk of supply of goods and services and electricity, etc. for
    payment. There was no payment on these facts, but rather
    retention of the goods and collection by the owner. If Alex
    retained the drugs and intended to give them back to Barry when
    he came to collect them, could the prosecution argue Alex had 'an
    intent to supply'?

This very issue has arisen in a number of important cases on the UK,
and judges there have ruled that a literal interpretation of the world
'supply' can cover retention of goods and returning them later
(whether or not there is payment). Using this reasoning the
prosecution could argue that Alex intended to return them and he
therefore intended to supply them.

   If a person is forced to retain or store controlled drugs through
fear of violence to themselves or their family, the defence of duress
could be argued by the defendant.

4 EU Law

The main types of EU legislation are set out in Article 249 EC.

Articles of the Treaty

These form part of the national legal system of each member state as
soon as a state joins the EU. Example: Article 141 EC (equal pay for

men and women for equal work or work of equal value).

Regulations

An EC Regulation forms part of the national legal system as soon as it is passed by the EC. It is does not require any national implementing measure. It is **directly applicable**.

Directives

A Directive sets out the aim and policy to be achieved by every member state. A Directive has a deadline for implementation and each member state must enact laws or alter existing laws (transpose the Directive) to achieve the EU aims. They are used to harmonise standards throughout the EU.

Example: the Working Time Directive 93/104 EC set out the maximum working week and holiday entitlements, etc. It allowed the member states until 23 November 1996 to implement the Directive. Ireland implemented the Directive in the Organisation of Working Time Act 1997.

Decisions

These are binding on the persons, states or undertakings to whom they are addressed. They are usually issued by the Commission and are of great significance in competition law.

4.1 Incorporation of EU law in Ireland

In Ireland the position relating to EU law is governed by Article 29.4.7 of the Constitution. Laws made by the EU may automatically become part of Irish law without there being any need for the Oireachtas to pass them formally into law. However, constitutional changes in the EU require a referendum.

Where there is a conflict between the law of the EU and Irish Law (including Constitutional provisions) EU law is superior and takes effect.

5 Human Rights Law

See Chapter 9 for a discussion of the European Convention on Human Rights Act 2003.

Summary

There are five main sources of law in Ireland.

Constitutional law is the highest form of national law. It has a special status, as any changes to the Constitution require a special legislative procedure, including a referendum of the people. Legislation that is contrary to the Constitution is invalid. The High Court and Supreme Court have jurisdiction to consider constitutional issues and interpret terms of the Constitution.

Legislation is law made by the Oireachtas and can be categorised as primary (Acts) or secondary (Statutory Instruments).

Legislation is interpreted and applied by the courts using established principles of statutory interpretation.

The legal principles decided by the courts in judgments may form binding precedents which must be followed by courts of equal or lower status, unless there are good reasons to depart from or distinguish the precedent. The relevant legal reasoning that decides the case is known as the *ratio decidendi*. Other parts of the judgment are referred to as *obiter dicta*. These precedents form another source of law in Ireland.

European Union law is an increasingly important source of law in Ireland. EU law takes a number of forms, including Articles of the Treaty, Regulations, Directives and Decisions. Due to the binding principle of the supremacy of EU law, it takes priority over even constitutional law in Ireland.

The final, and most recently incorporated source of law in Ireland is the European Convention on Human Rights, which guarantees fundamental rights to those who live in Ireland (and elsewhere in Europe).

QUESTIONS

1. Ireland has a 'common law' legal system. What does this mean?
2. Name two other countries that have a common law legal system.
3. Outline three differences between civil and criminal law.
4. List the sources of law in Ireland.
5. Explain the role of statutory instruments in the Irish legal system.
6. The Irish Constitution is a major source of law in Ireland. List three areas of citizens' rights covered by the Constitution.
7. List the three main types of law created by the institutions of the European Union.
8. How does EU law become part of Irish law?
9. Explain, giving examples, the methods a court may use to

interpret unclear or ambiguous words contained in a statute.

10. Give a brief description of the hierarchy of the courts in Ireland.
11. What is the rule of precedent? Give an example of a case which has been followed in later cases.
12. Outline the relationship of the various sources of Irish law to each other. In the event of a conflict between the sources of law, which law takes priority or is supreme?
13. List the types of secondary legislation created by the institutions of the EU.

REFERENCES

Byrne, R. and McCutcheon, J. (2001). *The Irish Legal System* (4th edn). Butterworth.

Doolan, B. *Principles of Irish Law* (6th edn). Dublin: Gill & Macmillan.

Law Reform Commission (2000). *Report on Statutory Drafting and Interpretation — Plain Language and the Law*, LRC 61–2000.

3

THE INSTITUTIONAL FRAMEWORK IN IRELAND AND EUROPE

At the end of this chapter you should be able to demonstrate an understanding and appreciation of:

- Legislative procedure in Ireland.
- The operation of the court system in Ireland and the role of alternative dispute resolution (ADR) systems.
- The institutional framework of the European Union and the roles of the European Commission, European Parliament and the Council of the European Union.
- Some important terminology and classifications in the legal systems, such as inquisitorial and adversarial systems.
- The origins of the Council of Europe and its institutional structure as distinct from the European Union.

You should also be able to navigate and identify relevant information from websites such as Europa.

1 The Legislative Process in Ireland

The legislative process is set down by the Constitution. It is important to have an appreciation of the stages of legislation as this is fundamental to the operation of democracy and the drafting and amendment of Bills, which may become Acts.

The way in which a Bill (proposed legislation) is presented and debated in the Oireachtas is outlined in Articles 20–25 of the Constitution.

1.1 Legislative procedure: how Bills become Acts

Below is a summary of procedure for the passing of ordinary Bills. There are differences in procedure if the Bill concerns changes to the Constitution or if it is a **Money Bill** (concerning finance or taxation elements covered by Articles 21 and 22). Money Bills must commence in the Dáil. The Seanad cannot amend or reject a Money Bill.

The legislative procedure is divided into stages.

TASK

As an introduction to this topic watch the excellent short video of the work of the Oireachtas which is available on the Houses of the Oireachtas website. This ten–minute video gives an overview of the legislative procedure, including the important work of the Committees which scrutinise and debate prospective legislation.

First Stage: Permission is sought by a Minister in either House to introduce a Bill which is then circulated to members. (Note: Money Bills can only originate in the Dáil.)

Second Stage: This consists of a debate on the main principles contained in the Bill. Amendments may be put forward. When these are agreed the Bill is considered in Committee.

Third Stage: Also known as the Committee Stage. The Bill is discussed in detail. There are different types of Committee. There could be a Committee of the whole house or a Select Committee (comprising a number of TDs who discuss the detailed provisions of the Bill).

Fourth Stage: Also known as the Report Stage. Amendments tabled in the Third Stage are considered.

Fifth Stage: This is the last stage, when the Bill is given final consideration before it is passed. When the Bill is passed by both Houses it goes to the President for her/his signature and becomes an Act (Article 25 of the Constitution).

TASK: TRACK THE PROGRESS OF A BILL

Go to the website of the Houses of the Oireachtas. In the left-hand margin select Bills 1997–2008.

First look at the progress of an uncontroversial piece of legislation — the Citizens Information Bill No. 48 of 2006. You will see that it was a government-sponsored Bill and that it was enacted. Look at the dates of the Stages of the Progress of the Bill. At the second stage there were a number of discussions before it was referred to Committee Stage. The Committee, Report and Final Stage were considered together by the Seanad and the Bill was passed and became the Citizens Information Act No. 2 of 2007. (The site also gives you sight of the Bill and often a very useful Explanatory Memorandum, which explains the purpose of the Bill.)

If you look at some other Bills in 2006, for example the Civil

Unions Bill 2006 (Bill No. 68 of 2006), which was sponsored by Deputy B. Howlin, or the Privacy Bill (Bill No. 44 of 2006) sponsored by Senator Mary O'Rourke, you will see that they have had a much slower passage and have not yet become law. Many Bills never achieve enactment due to lack of political will, competing legislative priorities, being overtaken by events or lack of parliamentary time. Government-sponsored Bills have a much better chance of being enacted due to the dominance of the Government in the Dáil.

Even so, the progress of many Bills can be slow. For example, the Building Control Bill of 2005, which regulates the energy rating of houses and commercial buildings and the professions of building surveyors and architects, only became law in April 2007 as the Building Control Act of 2007.

1.2 The Dáil has the main legislative power

Although the Dáil is known as the lower house it has the main legislative power.

Question: Why does the Dáil have more power than the Seanad?
Key Point: This is because the Dáil is representative of the citizens and is directly elected, whereas the Seanad is a small second chamber comprised partly of nominees and partly of elected representatives.

If a Bill is voted on by the Dáil the Seanad generally has 90 days to consider the proposal (it has less time for a Money Bill). If it is passed without the Seanad making any amendments it goes to the President to be signed into law. If the Seanad amends the Bill it is returned to the Dáil for consideration.

If the Seanad rejects the proposal it lapses (fails to progress) unless the Dáil overrules the Seanad. The Dáil can therefore effectively ignore the objections of the Seanad.

1.3 Reference of a Bill to the Supreme Court (Article 26)

A Bill may be referred to the Supreme Court by the President (provided it is not a Money Bill or a Bill to amend the Constitution) if he or she considers the Bill may contravene the Constitution. This has occurred on a number of occasions.

1.4 Bills to amend the Constitution

These must commence in the Dáil. A referendum is required to pass an amendment.

1.5 Fast-track Bills

In theory, under Article 24, the process can be accelerated in the case of urgent bills for public peace or security. This provision has never been used.

2 *The Court Structure in Ireland*

OVERVIEW

- The court structure.
- Link with the rule of precedent (Chapter 2).
- The status of the European Court of Justice.
- Using the Courts Service website.

2.1 *The development of the modern court structure*

The court system in Ireland and its terminology are easier to understand if you have an overview of the origins and development of the system.

TASK

Access the Courts Service website (www.courts.ie). Read the short Introduction under 'The Courts'. Note that the present court system was established by the Constitution and Articles 34–37 cover the area of administration of justice. The section on the history of law is also very useful to read.

In Chapter 2 we looked at the doctrine of precedent and saw that court hierarchy is important to this doctrine because courts must apply relevant *rationes decidendi* of higher courts in a relevant situation, unless there are reasons to depart from an earlier precedent.

2.2 *The structure of the court system*

There is a link on the Courts Service website to a diagram of the structure of the Irish court system. On the home page of the Courts Service website click on 'The Courts', then on 'Introduction', where you will find a link to 'Structure of the Courts Chart'. You should make notes on this diagram and note the arrows denoting the appeal route and the different jurisdictions of the various courts. This diagram illustrates the hierarchy of the courts in Ireland. (Note: although it is not shown in the diagram, the European Court of Justice (ECJ) could be placed at the top of the daigram. It gives binding judgments on matters of EU law which the Irish Supreme Court, High Court, etc. are obliged to follow due to the supremacy of EU law (see Chapter 2).)

- *European Court of Justice* (ECJ): Judgments on EU law matters are binding on all Irish courts.
- *Supreme Court*: Hears civil and criminal appeals and constitutional issues.
- *Court of Criminal Appeal*: Deals with appeals by persons convicted on indictment.
- *Special Criminal Court*: A criminal court with three judges and no jury, which tries cases where the ordinary courts cannot effectively secure the administration of justice.
- *High Court*: Has full jurisdiction to determine all criminal or civil matters and may determine issues of constitutionality of law. Hears appeals from the Circuit Court in civil matters.
- *Central Criminal Court*: The criminal division of the High Court; hears serious crimes.
- *Commercial Court*: Jurisdiction to hear disputes of over €1m.
- *Circuit Court*: Hears criminal and civil cases. It has limited jurisdiction based on locality. Hears family law matters of divorce and judicial separation and criminal cases on indictment — jury cases. An appeal court from the District Court.
- *District Court*: Civil and criminal cases. Has limited jurisdiction. No jury — a single district judge in criminal cases. Hears family law issues of domestic violence, maintenance, custody and access.
- *Children Courts*: Hears criminal matters relating to charges against children under 16 years.
- *Small Claims Court*: Attached to the District Court.

2.3 Overview of the courts

2.3.1 Supreme Court

This is the highest court in Ireland. Its main business is to hear appeals from the High Court. Generally it consists of three judges, but in cases of exceptional constitutional importance seven judges may sit. It does not hear witnesses but decides cases on the basis of transcripts of the oral evidence and the documentation that was presented to the lower court.

The Supreme Court also hears issues of law referred to it by a judge of the Circuit Court or High Court.

The Court may be referred a Bill by the President for a decision as to whether the Bill is contrary to the Constitution under Article 26.

A Supreme Court decision is a decision of the majority of the judges. Each judge may give a separate judgment, including a dissenting judgment (except in cases regarding the constitutionality of a law, where a single judgment will be given).

2.3.2 Court of Criminal Appeal

The court hears appeals from defendants convicted on indictment in the Circuit Court or Central Criminal Court where the appellant (the person who is appealing) obtains permission to appeal from the trial court or the Court of Criminal Appeal itself. The court consists of one Supreme Court judge and two High Court judges. Appeals on the grounds of a miscarriage of justice can be made to the court under the Criminal Procedure Act 1993. The Director of Public Prosecutions can refer cases to the court if s/he is of the opinion that the sentence imposed by a court is too lenient (Criminal Justice Act 1993).

2.3.3 High Court, Central Criminal Court, Commercial Court

The High Court has jurisdiction to determine all matters of law and facts in relation to civil and criminal matters. This is known as unlimited jurisdiction. It also has jurisdiction to hear cases challenging the constitutionality of a law. The High Court is known as the **Central Criminal Court** when hearing criminal cases.

It is an appeal court from the Circuit Court on civil matters and can review decisions of some tribunals.

In criminal cases it has the power to award bail if denied or restricted by the District Court.

The High Court hearing civil actions sits in Dublin and in other areas, for example Cork, Dundalk, Kilkenny and Sligo.

Cases are heard and decided by a single judge. A Divisional Court with three judges may decide a case if the President of the High Court decides this is appropriate. The High Court is the appeal court from the Circuit Court on civil matters.

The Central Criminal Court hears all murder and rape trials. It hears criminal trials under the Competition Act 2002. The court sits in Dublin and in other regional centres such as Cork, Limerick and Ennis. The case is heard by a single judge with a jury of twelve.

The **Commercial Court** is a division of the High Court and hears commercial cases of over €1 million. It was established to make the process of commercial litigation more transparent and speedy and imposes a case management system and timetable on cases.

2.3.4 Circuit Court

For judicial business Ireland has eight circuits. A judge is assigned to each circuit (though Dublin and Cork are assigned more judges). There are a number of court venues in each circuit area. The Circuit Court has limited and local jurisdiction.

Civil jurisdiction is generally limited to cases where the claim is less than €38,092, unless all the parties in the case consent to the court hearing the case.

It has **criminal jurisdiction** to hear all cases except murder, rape, aggravated sexual assault and some others. The court has jurisdiction if the court is in the area of the arrest, where the offence was committed or where the defendant lives. The trial is heard by a single judge and a jury.

It has **family law jurisdiction** in divorce, judicial separation, custody and access orders, etc.

It hears **appeals** from the District Court and also from other courts such as the Labour Court and the Employment Appeals Tribunal. Generally this consists of a full rehearing.

2.3.5 District Court

There are 23 districts and judges permanently assigned to each district. Generally a case will be heard in the district where the offence was committed or where the defendant was arrested or resides. The District Court undertakes four main areas of work.

Civil jurisdiction: limited to claims of less than €6,348.

Criminal jurisdiction: it tries summary offences by judge alone. It can hear indictable offences where the accused, the DPP and the judge agree that the offence is of a minor nature.

It can sentence the accused for certain indictable offences after the accused pleads guilty and the DPP consents and the judge accepts the guilty plea. For indictable offences the judge will consider the Book of Evidence and any submissions and if satisfied there is a sufficient case to answer will send the accused to the Circuit or Central Criminal Court for trial.

Family law: the District Court has wide powers in this area, including issues of custody, access, maintenance and domestic violence. These hearings are not open to the public.

Licensing: deals with liquor and lottery licences.

2.3.6 Children Court, Juvenile Court

There are specific rules for the protection of child defendants. The District Court can try a child or young person for any offence (except murder or manslaughter), provided that if the offence is indictable the child's parents (or the young person themselves) have been told of the right to trial by jury and they have agreed to be tried by District Judge instead.

Children for these purposes are defined as those under the age of 16. Dublin has a separate Children Court which sits daily. In Cork, Waterford and Limerick there are also Children Courts. In other places charges against children are heard at different times or days from ordinary District Court sittings in Juvenile Courts.

2.3.7 Special Criminal Court

Authority for the creation of this court is under Article 38.3 of the Constitution. This court is designed to secure the effective administration of justice. Cases can be transferred from the ordinary criminal courts to the Special Criminal Court. It is used in cases where the offence is 'scheduled'. These include offences with a subversive element, firearms offences, offences under the Offences against the State Act 1939. It sits with three judges and has no jury.

There may be an appeal to the Court of Criminal Appeal from a judgment.

3 Adversarial and Inquisitorial Judicial Systems

These terms describe different methods that are used for gathering evidence, court procedure, case presentation and the role of the judge.

The Irish legal system is founded on the adversarial model.

The **adversarial system** can be viewed as a type of legal 'contest', in which the lawyers present legal argument and evidence to the judge (and jury). The judge can be seen as a form of referee enforcing the rules of court procedure and evidential rules as well as making the final judgment in civil and summary criminal cases.

The **inquisitorial system** is found in the countries where law and procedure is based on the old Roman law model of civil law. In the inquisitorial system the judge plays a much more active role in collating and sifting evidence. The judge will **investigate** matters. In serious criminal cases, for example, there will be collation and preparation of evidence by a judge to see whether there is enough evidence to charge and proceed. Another judge will conduct the trial.

Although the parties are represented by their own lawyers it is the judge who controls and manages the presentation of the case.

Note: in the Irish and English adversarial systems there are aspects where judges are becoming more active in giving directions for the conduct of pre-trial and trial procedure.

Other forms of dispute resolution may adopt an inquisitorial system.

4 Alternative Dispute Resolution Methods (ADR)

OVERVIEW

- Reasons for creation of ADR mechanisms.
- Different forms of ADR in civil and criminal matters.
- Personal Injuries Assessment Board (see also Chapter 4).

The court process has a number of drawbacks. It can be costly and time-consuming to pursue civil litigation. The adversarial approach of the 'legal contest' and point scoring with tough negotiation may be appropriate in some contexts but can tend to escalate and extend disputes concerning negligence actions, marriage breakdown, financial provision and custody arrangements. In commercial settings the adversarial approach may inflate costs, and the general costs rule that the 'winner' is awarded costs, which are paid by the 'losing' side, can have the effect of entrenching the parties in litigation and further increase costs and cause delays. There are procedural devices to encourage settlement out of court and the parties are free to settle at any time.

There is always a risk with civil litigation, and the emotional stress of ongoing court proceedings and uncertainty of outcomes should not be underestimated.

There have always been different methods of settling disputes apart from litigation and the court process. These are known as alternative dispute resolution (ADR) and we will briefly consider some different types and examples.

4.1 Arbitration

Arbitration is a method of resolving a dispute other than by taking court action. It has a long history as a means of resolving commercial disputes. The parties to a dispute appoint an independent third party, an arbitrator, to decide the issue and the parties agree to follow the arbitrator's decision. Often a commercial contract will contain an arbitration provision so that a matter at issue will automatically be referred to arbitration. Typically these will appear in construction contracts, commercial contracts and partnership agreements. The advantages of using arbitration instead of lengthy and expensive litigation in the courts include saving time, lower costs and the lack of publicity.

The Arbitration Acts 1954–98 govern the arbitration process. The procedure is private. The arbitrator may be an expert in the particular field of dispute (for example construction, shipping or energy contracts). The findings of the arbitrator are final. A disappointed party cannot generally appeal the decision unless the arbitrator has made an error of law.

4.2 Mediation

Mediation aims to resolve disputes through an agreement between the parties rather than by investigation, analysis and formal decision. A mediator aims to facilitate the parties negotiating an agreement between themselves. It is a voluntary process which either party can terminate at any stage. The meetings are confidential and voluntary.

The Equality Tribunal is an independent body which hears and mediates disputes or complaints of alleged discrimination under the equality legislation. It adopts a more inquisitorial role. Although it is a mediation process the decisions it reaches are legally binding.

The Family Mediation Service aims to help a separating couple (married or unmarried) reach agreements on arrangements concerning parenting, the family home and property and financial arrangements. It may result in a written document being drawn up which sets out the details of the agreement between the couple and this can facilitate the drawing up of a Deed of Separation by a lawyer.

4.3 Conciliation

This is similar to mediation. It is a voluntary and confidential ADR process in which the parties agree to work with an independent conciliator. The Labour Relations Commission describes the process as a 'facilitated search for agreement between disputing parties'. In the area of employment law, conciliation between employers and employees or trade unions may resolve industrial disputes and restore a working relationship between the two bodies. In individual employment disputes relating to unfair dismissal, for example, a conciliator known as a Rights Commissioner may help to resolve the dispute. The Labour Relations Commission was established in 1990 to promote good industrial relations practices. It offers services to employees, employers and trade unions. An Industrial Relations Officer (an independent professional external mediator) will be appointed to assist employers and employees to resolve industrial disputes.

TASK

Look at the website of the Labour Relations Commission and read the section on the Conciliation Division, addressing the following questions:
1. Is conciliation as a process successful in most cases?
2. What types of employees can use the services of the LRC?
3. What does the process cost the parties?
4. If the parties cannot reach agreement in the conciliation process what are the options for the parties?
5. Who is said to be in control of the conciliation process?

Question: Having read the material on the LRC, identify three advantages of conciliation over court action or litigation
Key Points: You may have identified: ease of access and informality; that legal representation is not required; the possibility of a speedy resolution; the service is free; the parties are in control of the process and can withdraw at any time; the availability of the Labour Court to deal with any issues if the process cannot be resolved by conciliation.

4.4 ADR in the criminal sphere

The concept of ADR in the criminal area being used to resolve an issue without the court system is a relatively new concept in Ireland.

Question: From your knowledge of criminal law can you identify any ways in which the criminal process and consequences may have disadvantages for the victim and for a convicted person? (You may find it useful to refer to information on sentencing options in Chapter 6.)
Key Points: A finding of guilt in a criminal trial results in a criminal record for the accused and may result in imprisonment. This may impact on his or her future employment prospects and chances of rehabilitation. The rate of recidivism (repeat offending) after imprisonment is high. The formal criminal process, sentencing and incarceration may lead to further criminal conduct.

The criminal process may be particularly inappropriate for young and vulnerable people. The sentencing process may result in an individual having very limited opportunities for education or rehabilitation. For the victim the court process may be intimidating and may result in no real explanation of the conduct of the accused, apology or reparation for loss or damage.

In the case of serious physical assaults or homicide ADR may seem inappropriate since there can be no effective 'resolution' of these type of offence. The traditional resolution of criminal cases is in the sentencing of offenders following a formal criminal prosecution and trial process. The sentencing of an offender traditionally seeks to achieve a number of aims, including retribution (to punish the offender), rehabilitation (to help reform the offender and prevent reoffending), or to deter the individual or others from committing the same sort of offence.

The court is also able to award reparation (compensation for victims) in some cases where the offence involves loss of property or personal injury by making a compensation order under the Criminal Justice Act 1993. The court will take the financial means of the convicted person into account.

Restorative justice
This method is victim-focused and aims to prevent the perpetrator from reoffending. It is often termed victim-offender mediation and involves the perpetrator and victim meeting in a safe, structured and professional environment in the presence of a trained mediator.

TASK
Go to the Department of Justice, Equality and Law Reform website and type 'restorative justice' into the search facility. Read the short extract and introduction to the concept and the establishment of the new Commission on Restorative Justice in Ireland.

Question: Are there any schemes offering restorative justice in operation at the moment?
Key Points: Pilot projects were established in Nenagh and Tallaght. A description of the project is given on the website. The Restorative Services:

> ... encourages and facilitates both victims and offenders to participate in a mediation process, leading in most cases to an

agreed contract which can include personal commitments and reparation by the offender. They have pioneered the Offender Reparation Programme, whereby persons convicted of offences agree a programme of reflection, reparation and restoration. This is an innovative approach and the work done is documented to the court and their final penalty is commensurately lenient.

In these systems the restorative justice system runs parallel with the existing court system and can have a favourable impact on the position of the victim and on the final outcome for the convicted person.

Restorative justice models that are designed to be used instead of the court system operate elsewhere in Europe. They can be especially appropriate in the youth justice field. They have been established in some areas of Northern Ireland by the Public Prosecution Service.

4.5 Personal Injuries Assessment Board (PIAB)

4.5.1 Background

The Personal Injuries Assessment Board is an independent body established by the Personal Injuries Assessment Board Act 2003. The function of the board is to assess the amount of compensation due to a person who suffers a personal injury and who claims the injury was caused by the fault of another. All claims for personal injury (i.e. workplace, motor and public liability accidents) including claims concerning the use or occupation of land or buildings must be submitted to the PIAB.

It does not deal with medical negligence cases. It can be seen as a form of ADR because the resolution occurs outside the court process. If both parties agree to the assessment made by the PIAB an Order to Pay will be issued and this has the same effect as an award of the court and can be enforced by the other party.

The PIAB was established as a response to the perception of a growing 'compensation culture' in Ireland and to escalating legal costs and time delays in the court process. Anyone who seeks to make a claim for a personal injury must make a claim to the PIAB. The assessment is provided without the need for the majority of current litigation costs, such as solicitors', barristers' and experts' fees. These fees often amount to over forty per cent of the cost of the claim and are generally paid by the unsuccessful party in proceedings, often an insurance company.

The board is comprised of people with legal, insurance and

medical expertise to assess compensation. There is also an independent panel of medical experts.

4.5.2 Outline of procedure

The applicant must submit a claim to the PIAB with relevant documentation. The respondent (the person against whom the applicant is claiming) will be notified of the claim. If the respondent does not consent to the PIAB assessment (for example because s/he disputes they are liable for the incident in the first place) the PIAB will issue the applicant with an **Authorisation**, which allows the applicant to take the matter to the courts.

TASK

Using the PIAB website, research the following information. (Hint: The Guide for Injured Parties (reached from the Forms and Publications tab) is a useful starting point.)
1. What is the time limit for making a claim?
2. Who makes the assessment and on what information is it based?
3. What types of damages can be awarded?
4. Can the figure reached by the PIAB be challenged by the applicant or the respondent?
5. Are the parties free to settle the claim between themselves without the intervention of the PIAB?

Key Points:
1. The time limit for making a claim is two years from the date of the injury (there are some exceptions, e.g. for those under 18). It is advisable to lodge an application well before the two-year period.
2. Two qualified assessors make an assessment based on medical and financial evidence of loss and the Book of Quantum.
3. General damages cover pain and suffering, loss of life enjoyment and loss of opportunity caused by the accident.
   Special damages cover the specific expenses incurred by reason of the accident.
4. The claimant has 28 days to decide whether to reject or accept the assessment. The respondent has 21 days. If either party rejects the assessment an Authorisation to proceed with court action will be issued.
5. The parties can settle the case at any time during the PIAB process.

4.5.3 Costs of the PIAB process

The initial application form must be submitted with €50 and a medical report. If a respondent consents to the PIAB assessing damages the respondent pays a set sum to the PIAB for processing costs and towards a medical report.

There is no provision in the PIAB process whereby the respondent pays the costs of the applicant's legal advice. If there is rejection of the PIAB offer by the claimant and the personal injury action is taken to court then if the court awards less than the PIAB assessment the court may order the claimant to pay all or part of the defendant's costs.

5 The Institutions of the European Union and European Union Law-making

OVERVIEW

- The origins and development of the European Union.
- Functions and roles of the institutions of the EU.
- Types of EU law — Articles, Regulations, Directives and Decisions.
- The European Union website.
- How EU law binds Ireland.
- Concepts of supremacy of EU law and direct effect.

5.1 The origins of the European Union

The first European community created was the **European Coal and Steel Community** (ECSC) in 1951, the principal object of which was to tie the economies of Germany, France and Italy (belligerents in World War II) together in the heavy industries of coal and steel and to foster co-operation between them.

The **European Economic Community** (EEC) was established in 1957 by six countries (Germany, France, Italy, Belgium, the Netherlands and Luxembourg) by the Treaty of Rome. The aim of the EEC was to secure peace and to promote prosperity by the establishment of a common market.

Question: What do you understand by the term 'common market'?
Key Points: A common market aims to allow the 'factors of production' of goods, services, capital and workers to move freely without restriction within the geographical boundaries of all the member states.

The EEC also established a Common Agricultural Policy (CAP) to regulate the agricultural market throughout Europe. In the 1970s the EEC began to develop social polices and regional policies, extending its type of activities.

Ireland became a member of the EEC in 1973. As the geographical area of the EEC was expanding, so was the scope of activities in which the EEC was engaged, and it began to include more social (e.g. employment) policies and environmental policies.

Note on terminology: You will see that law which comes from Europe is often referred to as European Union (EU) law and also as European Community (EC) law. This is because originally the European Economic Community (EEC) was based on three different treaties (an economic treaty (EEC), a treaty regulating the coal and steel market (ECSC) and a treaty regulating atomic energy matters (EURATOM)). The European Economic Community was the most important. The EEC became the European Community after the Treaty of Maastrict in 1993.

The Maastrict Treaty of 1993 created the concept of the European Union being founded on the three pillars of:
1. European Community (EC) law
2. justice and home affairs
3. foreign affairs and security co-operation (CFSP).

These two last pillars were the policies which were to be developed on the basis of co-operation between the member states and to form the foundations of the European Union. The two terms can both be used. This book will generally use the term European Union law. When referring to the legal provisions under the EC Treaty such as Articles, Regulations, etc., the correct citation is Article 49 EC, Article 141 EC (not Article 49 EU).

5.2 A timeline of the European Union

It is important to be aware of the developmental steps and the gradual enlargement of the European Union.

1951: The Treaty establishing the European Coal and Steel Community (ECSC) came into force. This set the scene for the Treaty of Rome. This Treaty expired in 2002.

1957–8: Creation of the European Economic Community and the Treaty of Rome. Originally six signatory states: France, Germany, Italy, Belgium, Netherlands and Luxembourg. Establishment of a common market, Common Agricultural Policy and common commercial policy were the main areas of focus. The Treaty also established the European Atomic Energy Community EURATOM (jointly known as the European Communities).

1970s: EEC develops social, employment and regional policy.

1973: Denmark, Ireland and UK join.

1981: Greece joins.

1986: Single European Act. Introduction of the concept of the internal market (deadline 1991). EC begins to become more involved in environmental and employment rights.

1986: Spain and Portugal join.

1991–3: The Maastrict Treaty or the Treaty of European Union (TEU) came into force in November 1993 after protracted negotiations. This introduced the concept of European Monetary Union (EMU) and the euro. It changed the name of the EEC to the European Community. It created the three-pillar structure of organisation with inter-governmental co-operation on justice and home affairs issues (now called the area of freedom, security and justice AFSJ) and on foreign and security policy (CFSP). The three pillars together are known as the EU.

1995: Austria, Finland and Sweden join.

1997: Amsterdam Treaty introduces institutional reform and renumbers the provisions of the Treaties.

2002: Euro introduced.

2003: The Nice Treaty came into force after Ireland had rejected the first referendum on ratification. The Institutions were reformed and there was a consolidation of the Treaty, anticipating the growth of the EU to 25 member states.

2003–2007: The Convention on the Future of Europe drafted a Constitution for Europe which was agreed by heads of state in 2004. The Constitution was rejected by referendums in France and the Netherlands and was permanently suspended. The Czech Republic, Cyprus, Estonia, Hungary, Latvia, Lithuania, Malta, Poland, Slovakia and Slovenia all join.

2007: Two new members (Bulgaria and Romania) accede. A total of 27 states and 490 million EU citizens now comprise the Union.

2007–2008: The Reform Treaty is agreed by member states in Lisbon and signed in December 2007 (not ratified at the time of writing).

TASK

You will find an excellent introduction to the evolution and growth of the policies of the European Union on the Europa website: select 'Gateway to the EU' and type 'History of the EU' in the search box. This will bring up a number of options. Look at the animated map that should appear and then click on the top bar of this page to select 'History of the EU'. This gives an excellent overview of key stages and personnel, with video clips.

5.3 The institutional structure of the EU

OVERVIEW

- European Parliament
- Council of the European Union
- European Court of Justice and Court of First Instance
- European Commission
- European Council
- Court of Auditors
- Other bodies: Economic and Social Committee; Committee of the Regions.

5.3.1 The European Parliament

TASK: THE EUROPEAN PARLIAMENT

This task introduces you to the only democratically directly elected institution of the EU through the main authoritative source of information on the EU (the Europa website). You should become familiar with the layout of the site and use it to access information on European institutions. The Europa website is the official portal to the European Union. It is updated regularly and contains proposed legislation, law, news and reports on the work of the EU. You will be using the website frequently.

Go to the Europa website and click on 'Gateway to the European Union'. In the centre of the screen click on the 'Institutions' tab and then on 'Parliament'.

Using the information provided answer the following questions. (Note: The Introductory section gives a good overview of key facts and links to other information.)

1. How many Members (MEPs) are there in the European Parliament?
2. Who is your MEP?
3. The European Parliament is said to have three main functions or powers. Can you identify these?

Key Points: The EP has **legislative** power (the power to make laws) which it shares with the Council of the European Union. It has **budgetary** power over the EU's budget (it can veto certain aspects). It has **supervisory** power over the Commission (it can take a vote of censure/no confidence in the Commission as a whole and remove the Commission), and Reports must be made to the Commission by the Council of the European Union.

Membership

The Parliament is elected for a five-year period. The number of MEPs varies from state to state. Ireland has 13 MEPs. The maximum number of MEPs for the states with larger populations is 99 (Germany).

Locations

The European Parliament operates from two bases, Brussels and Strasbourg. The primary base is Brussels. In Brussels there are Parliamentary Committee meetings, which scrutinise draft EU laws, meetings of the political groupings and some plenary sessions. There are twelve two-day plenary sittings in Strasbourg.

Political groupings

The MEPs do not sit in national party groups, but in European Parliamentary groupings, so for example the European People's Party (EPP) is a centre-right party and the largest political grouping. The second largest is the Party of European Socialists. There is also the Alliance of Liberals and Democrats for Europe, the Green/Free Alliance and other smaller parties.

5.3.2 The Council of the European Union

Membership

There is one Council in institutional terms, however in functional terms the Council sits in nine different configurations and at different times and places according to the type of subject matter under discussion. (For example, the General Affairs and External Relations Council, made up of foreign affairs ministers; the Justice and Home Affairs council, comprising ministers of justice and home affairs; the Environment Council; the Agriculture and Fisheries Council.) Each Council is attended by the relevant minister from each of the member states or by an ambassador. (The Press Releases section of the website tells you about current Council sessions, some of which are televised.)

Functions

The Council of the European Union represents the governments of the EU. Its primary role is to make EU legislation and it shares legislative power with the European Parliament when using the co-decision legislative procedure (see below). It does not have power to initiate legislation (that power is held by the European Commission, which develops proposed legislation). The Council takes decisions on the basis of **qualified majority voting**, which means that each member state has a number of votes according to the population of the member state (weighted voting).

The work of the Council is prepared by an influential group called the Council of Permanent Representatives (COREPER), which comprises the member states' ambassadors.

Presidency

The Presidency of the Council is held successively by each member state for a period of six months (Article 203 EC). The order of succession is set out in the Treaty. The President is responsible for organising the work of the Council. There is also a political aspect as the priorities and political will of the President may result in new policies or action being initiated.

Locations

Headquarters are in Brussels but Councils meet throughout Europe.

Note on terminology: The Council of the European Union (which used to be called the Council of Ministers) is a different organisation from the European Council (which consists of the heads of state of each member state — see below).

5.3.3 The European Court of Justice (ECJ) and the Court of First Instance (CFI)

Functions

To enforce the law under the EC Treaties and secondary legislation. They have developed EC law by interpreting and defining phrases within the Treaty and secondary legislation. The CFI and ECJ do not operate a rule of precedent, but there is a generally consistent line of case law. The ECJ, in its function of giving preliminary rulings, has developed the fundamental principles of EU law such as supremacy, direct effect and state liability for breaches of EU law.

Location
They are both located in Luxembourg.

CFI membership
One judge from each member state. The CFI sits in Chambers of Judges of three or five judges.

CFI jurisdiction
The Court of First Instance has jurisdiction to hear:
• Direct actions brought by natural or legal persons against acts of Community institutions (addressed to them or directly concerning them as individuals) or against a failure to act on the part of those institutions. This is a form of European judicial review where a person or a company can challenge the grounds on which a decision is made. This is the only time an individual or company has direct access to the CFI. A recent example was Microsoft's case against a Commission decision on competition law principles. There are strict procedural requirements and limits to this type of action.
• Actions brought by the Member States against the Commission and certain actions brought by the Member States against the Council.
• Actions **seeking compensation for damage** caused by the Community institutions or their staff.
• Actions based on contracts made by the Communities that expressly give jurisdiction to the Court of First Instance.
• Actions relating to **Community trademarks**.

The rulings made by the Court of First Instance may be appealed to the ECJ on a point of law within two months of the ruling.

ECJ membership
The Court of Justice is composed of 27 judges and eight advocates general. The judges and advocates general are appointed by common accord by the governments of the member states for a renewable term of six years. They are chosen from among lawyers whose independence is beyond doubt and who possess the qualifications required for appointment in their respective countries, to the highest judicial offices, or who are of recognised competence. The ECJ is assisted by eight advocates general, who give opinions to the ECJ.

ECJ jurisdiction

The ECJ decides cases brought against member states by the Commission or other member states.

Its most important function is to give binding, advisory **preliminary rulings** to the courts of member states who request a ruling on any aspect of EU law.

It has developed key principles of European Union law by a consistent line of case law in some areas (such as supremacy of EU law, the scope of free movement of goods and workers legislation, concepts of indirect discrimination, etc.).

It hears appeals from the Court of First Instance.

5.3.4 The European Commission

Membership

The Commission presently comprises 27 Commissioners, one from each member state. Each Commissioner is nominated by their national government in consultation with the President of the Commission. The Commission must be approved by the European Parliament. Once appointed they are independent of the appointing member state. They act in the best interest of the European Union. They have a five-year term which coincides with the term of the European Parliament.

Functions

The Commission has a number of functions. It is the 'civil service' of the EU, but has much more extensive powers than an ordinary civil service. It is the only institution which has the right to propose new EU legislation — a **legislative function**. It enforces EU law — it can take defaulting states or organisations to the European Court of Justice — and it acts as the 'guardian of the Treaties'. This can be seen as an **executive** function. In competition law areas the Commission has the power to fine undertakings or states (as it did in the Microsoft case). This can be seen as a **quasi-judicial** function. The Commission is largely responsible for managing EU policies such as environmental, energy, agricultural, internal market and regional policies. It also manages the EU budget, which is also an **executive** function.

Organisation

The Commission is split into Directorates General, each of which has a policy area. The head of each is the Director General.

Location

Brussels. It has a large civil service (about 25,000) supporting its work.

President of the Commission

The presidency is held for a five-year term. Past presidents have largely been responsible for driving policy developments in the EEC–EC and now EU. The Commission has been termed the 'motor of European integration'. Presently José Manuel Barroso is the President; he holds the office from 2004 to 2009.

TASK: THE EUROPEAN COMMISSION

Use the Europa website access the home page of the Commission. Click on 'Who's Who' in the left-hand margin and find out which Commissioners are responsible for:
- internal market and services
- trade
- competition
- agriculture and rural development.

5.3.5 The European Council

This institution is distinct from the Council of the European Union. The European Council consists of the presidents or prime ministers of the member states, together with the President of the European Commission. It holds high-level policy meetings and also discusses attitudes to events on the international scene. These meetings are generally highly publicised and are held in Brussels.

5.3.6 The Court of Auditors

This institution audits the revenue and expenditure of the EU. It is independent of the other institutions. It has a supervisory function and issues reports on the Budget and use of expenditure. It aims to secure 'best value for money' for the European citizens.

6 The Types of EU Law

The primary law is set out in the EC Treaty. The Treaty (Article 249) provides for secondary legislation to be made by the institutions of the EC.

The **Articles of the Treaty** form part of the national legal system of each member state as soon as a state joins the EU. The Irish

Constitution provides for the incorporation of the Treaty and secondary legislation.

EC Regulations are directly applicable. They enter into the law of the member states automatically without the need for implementing legislation.

TASK

Find Regulation 1612/68 Freedom of Movement for Workers using the Europa website.

There are a number of ways to access this legislation. If you click on 'Documents' you will be on the Eur-Lex page. Then go to the 'Legislation in Force' heading in the left-hand margin. Click on this and a 'Directory of Legislation' will appear. You need to select the topic area you are interested in — the freedom of movement for workers. Scroll down the legislation and you will come to Regulation 1612/68 EC. There are a number of headings showing the amendments. It is the consolidated text that is the up-to-date version of the Regulation.

A **Directive** sets out the aim and policy to be achieved by every member state by a certain deadline. Each member state must enact laws or alter existing laws (transpose the Directive) to achieve the EU aims.

TASK

Locate Directive 90/314 EC on Package Holidays. This is a consumer protection measure and is in the directory relating to Environment, Consumers and Health Protection.

Decisions are binding on the persons, states or undertakings to whom they are addressed. They are usually issued by the Commission and are of great significance in competition law.

6.1 Primary and secondary law of the EU

6.1.2 Law contained in Treaty provisions

The highest form of EU law is that found in the EC Treaties. This is the primary law of the EU. The Treaties are broken down into Articles. These Articles set out the principal policies and laws of the EU. They are not comprehensive, as the detail of the policies is given in secondary legislation. The EC Treaty is known as a framework document. It leaves the other institutions of the EU to develop and implement the detailed law needed to put the policies into effect.

TASK

This task aims to make you familiar with accessing up-to-date information on the EC Treaty, to introduce you to Eur-Lex and the search facilities on the site. Below is a step-by-step guide, but once you have used the site a few times and become familiar with it you will be able to access information by a number of different routes.

Go to Europa and click on 'Gateway to the European Union'.

You will see in the centre of the screen a number of tabbed options. Click on 'Documents' and you will find a page entitled 'Where to find EU Documents — An Online Library'.

Click on Eur-Lex, the portal to EU law. This will take you to the Welcome page, which gives you information on what is contained in this portal. You will find it useful to read the selection of materials available.

In the left-hand margin click on Treaties. Select 'European Union — Consolidated Versions of the Treaty on European Union and of the Treaty Establishing the European Community'. This is the up-to-date, comprehensive Treaty.

It is a huge document and the relevant section is on pages 37–186.

The Preface sets out the origins and purpose of the European Community. Part I of the Treaty sets out the aspirations of the nations establishing the original EEC and the Principles of the European Community.

Scan through the Contents of the Treaty to appreciate the breadth of topics which are covered by the Treaty, from agriculture to free movement of persons, services and capital, visa and asylum matters, transport, competition, tax, employment, environment, etc.

Find the following important Treaty Articles and summarise the principles within each Treaty Article. Articles 2, 3, 10, 17, 18, 21, 25, 26 and 28.

Key Points:

Articles 2 and 3 EC set out the economic aims of the EU.

Article 10 EC imposes an obligation on all member states to comply with the Treaty. This is a key provision of the Treaty.

Article 17 EC establishes the concept of citizenship of the Union.

Article 18 EC cover the rights of the European citizen to move and reside within the EU, but note the important words, 'subject to the limitations and conditions laid down in this Treaty'. The right of citizens is not an absolute right; it can be limited on narrow grounds by a member state.

Article 21 gives a right to petition the European Parliament and to apply to the Ombudsman.

Articles 25 and 26 cover the prohibition on custom duties (duties imposed on goods by virtue of crossing a national boundary) and the concept of free circulation of goods.

Article 28 is a prohibition on quantitative restrictions and measures having equivalent effect. The phrase 'equivalent effect' does not have a simple definition, and there have been hundreds of cases in this area. The basic principle is that member states cannot impose numerical quotas and they cannot impose unfair restrictions or barriers that impede goods entering from other countries within the EU. We shall look at this again in Chapter 8.

6.2 The legislative processes of the EU

There are two main methods of enacting legislation in the EU: the **co-decision** procedure; and the **co-operation** procedure. These procedures are set out in Article 251 of the Treaty. Each policy area covered by the Treaty will specify whether the co-decision or co-operation procedure is to apply.

6.2.1 Co-decision

This is now the most important procedure and puts the directly elected European Parliament on the same footing as the Council of the European Union. It is often described as a 'trilogue' (a conversation between the Parliament, Council of the European Union and the Commission). The Parliament and Council of the EU, acting on a proposal of the European Commission, adopt legislation jointly. It is now the normal procedure for all EU legislation (exceptions include agriculture and fisheries, taxation, trade policies, state aids and competition law legislation).

The stages of the passage of legislation are known as readings, and there can be up to three readings. The final and third reading can also include a conciliation process if the EP and Council of the EU cannot agree. In practice many legislative proposals can be agreed between the parties after the first reading. If there is continued disagreement about the form and content of proposed legislation, at the third reading a Conciliation Committee comprised of delegations from the Commission, Council of the EU and the EP will be convened. The aim of the committee is to reach agreement on a joint text.

6.2.2 Co-operation procedure

Under this procedure the Parliament can amend the Council of EU's common position, but the final decision rests with the Council. Unlike the co-decision procedure (above) the EP does not have a power to veto legislation.

6.3 The Status of European Community Law

The EU Treaty and secondary legislation made by the institutions regulates an enormous range of activities. Inevitably discrepancies between EU legislation and an individual member state's legislation arise from time to time.

This issue caused constitutional conflicts when it first arose as the EC Treaty did not specifically deal with the issue of whether EC law or national law took precedence. The conflict was exacerbated by the concept of direct effect which was being developed by the European Court of Justice. Direct effect enables certain provisions of the Treaty and secondary legislation to be invoked and relied upon by individuals before a domestic court to enforce rights under EC law.

In a number of cases the European Court of Justice felt its way to an unequivocal assertion of the supremacy of European Community law over any form of conflicting national legislation.

The reaction of the legal and political systems of the member states to the assertion of supremacy illustrates the wide range of constitutional traditions embraced by the European Community. Only in recent years have the legal systems of some of the 'major players' in the European Union fully endorsed the position, and debate over the encroaching power of the European Court of Justice is ongoing. The important topic of supremacy of EU law is looked at in detail in Chapter 8.

7 The Council of Europe

This is an intergovernmental political organisation which was established in the aftermath of World War II. It is entirely distinct from the European Union and has no direct connection with it. (There is exchange of information and meetings scheduled between the Council of Europe and the European Union, but these are for exchange of information and co-operation; they are not institutionally linked.) It has its headquarters in Strasbourg. The Council of Europe has a number of aims:

- protecting and strengthening pluralist democracy and human rights and the rule of law
- seeking solutions to problems facing European society
- promoting awareness of a European cultural identity
- promoting democratic stability within Europe by promoting political and constitutional reform.

7.1 The institutions of the Council of Europe

7.1.1 Committee of Ministers

The Council of Europe operates through the Committee of Ministers, which is the main decision-making body. It comprises the foreign affairs ministers of all member states. They have a meeting (or session) once a year in Strasbourg. They appoint a Permanent Representative and a Deputy Permanent Representative.

The meetings of the Permanent Representatives are held every week. They appoint 'Committees of Experts', who may be scientists, academics or politicians, to carry out inter-governmental activity in certain fields such as: human rights, social and economic questions, combating terrorism balanced with respecting human rights, cultural matters, information technology issues, bioethics, environmental issues.

The Committee of Ministers also monitors compliance with undertakings of the member states.

7.1.2 The Parliamentary Assembly of the Council of Europe (PACE)

The members who make up PACE come from the parliaments of the 47 member states of the Council of Europe. PACE meets four times each year for a week-long session to discuss issues, request reports and raise initiatives.

The Assembly also monitors whether member states are honouring their obligations under the Council of Europe Treaties.

The Parliamentary Assembly co-operates and liaises with other international bodies (such as the European Parliament of the EU).

There are various committees, including an international committee of experts who make spot checks in places of detention to ensure that signatory states abide by Conventions.

The Assembly has secured over 150 legally binding Treaties and Conventions, mostly concerned with matters that have no economic element, such as the Social Charter 1961, which guaranteed a number of rights at work.

7.1.3 The European Court of Human Rights

The most significant work of the Council of Europe is the creation and monitoring of the European Convention on Human Rights and Fundamental Freedoms 1950.

It has an international committee of experts to make spot checks in places of detention to ensure that signatory states abide by the prohibition of torture or inhuman and degrading treatment. (For more detail on this see Chapter 9.)

The European Court of Human Rights is the court that enforces the European Convention on Human Rights and Fundamental Freedoms. It is based in Strasbourg. It is a completely different court from the European Court of Justice (the court of the EU), which is based in Luxembourg.

TASK

The aim of this task is to familiarise you with the Council of Europe website and to give you an overview of the work of the Council.
Go to the website for the Council of Europe, click on 'The Council of Europe in Brief', then on 'Facts and Figures', and find out:
1. The current number of members of the Council of Europe.
2. Whether any countries presently have 'application status'.

Summary

Legislation in Ireland is made under the legislative procedure set out in the Constitution. The Dáil has the main legislative power. The court system is organised on a hierarchical basis and the rule of precedent operates to ensure consistent application of principles of law.

In the European Union the main legislative procedures are the co-decision and co-operation procedures. The European Parliament shares legislative power with the Council of the European Union in the co-decision procedure. The Commission has a number of roles. It initiates, applies and enforces legislation. It can also issue decisions. The European Court of Justice and the Court of First Instance are the judicial arm of the EU.

The Council of Europe is a European institution which pre-dates the European Union and its focus is on non-economic areas such as social, welfare, educational and human rights issues. It aims to promote democracy in Europe and constitutional reform.

QUESTIONS

1. How is a Money Bill defined under Article 22 of the Constitution and how does legislative procedure differ from that relating to other Bills?
2. Explain the hierarchy of the courts in the Irish legal system.
3. Identify the relevant courts applicable in these scenarios:

> Annette has a claim against a travel agent for a holiday that was incorrectly described. She calculates that the expenses she incurred amounted to €4,000. In which court could she commence an action?

> Brian has been charged with serious criminal damage under the Criminal Damage Act.

4. What does the acronym ADR mean? Give a brief outline of two forms of ADR with appropriate examples.
5. List the main institutions of the EU. Do the institutions have separate functions or are their competences overlapping?
6. Who currently holds the Presidency of the Council of the European Union?
7. Which EU institutions are involved in passing legislation?

REFERENCES

Cost of the Compensation Culture Working Party: www.actuaries .org.uk/files/pdf/giro2002/Lowe.pdf.

Labour Relations Commission: www.lrc.ie.

FUNDAMENTALS OF TORT

At the end of this chapter you will be able to:
- Explain the nature of tort and outline different types of tort, including assault and battery and trespass to land.
- Identify the origins of the modern law on negligence and key developments including liability for misstatements.
- Apply the principles of negligence liability to a set of facts.
- Understand the concepts of vicarious liability and contributory negligence.
- Locate important cases and become familiar with important terminology and principles of negligence.
- Understand key principles concerning remedies for negligence.
- Evaluate and apply the statutory torts created by the Liability for Defective Products Act 1991 and the Occupiers' Liability Act 1995.
- Be aware of relevant remedies in tort law.

The chapter is divided into three parts: torts generally; the tort of negligence; specific applications of the law of tort and statutory torts.

1 Torts Generally

OVERVIEW OF THE LAW OF TORT
- Civil wrong.
- Trespass to land.
- Trespass to the person: assault; battery; false imprisonment.
- Defamation.

1.1 Definition of tort

A tort is a civil wrong for which a plaintiff can sue in the civil courts to obtain a remedy. Over the centuries the law has given rights to persons by creating various types of tort. These principles were generally created by the courts and the system of precedent. Each case, however, is decided on its facts.

There are relatively few Acts which affect this area of law. Examples of relevant statutes include the Civil Liability Act 1961, the Occupiers' Liability Act 1995 and the Liability for Defective Products Act 1991 (see section 3 below).

1.2 Types of tort

Below is a snapshot of some important torts. Remember, these can give rise to civil actions. Some may also give rise to separate criminal prosecutions (see Chapter 1).

1.2.1 Trespass

This is one of the oldest forms of civil liability and the oldest form of tort law. Trespass comprises a number of separate torts. There can be a trespass to the person (assault, battery and false imprisonment). There can also be trespass to goods or land of another person.

Trespass to the person
Assault: someone is intentionally put in fear or threat of a battery.

Battery: unlawful physical contact, which can be defined as when someone intentionally and without the other's consent or other lawful justification applies force directly to the person. This can cover a wide range of actions, from a minor push to being shot or stabbed. It also covers a situation where a doctor operates without the patient's consent.

You will notice that, although assault and battery are separate torts, they often occur in the same incident, e.g. a threat (spoken or otherwise) of immediate violence is followed by violence. These are two **distinct** torts, but you will often read or hear that an individual was sued for assault, when in fact they were sued for assault **and** battery.

(Note: there may also be a separate **criminal prosecution** for an assault; see Chapter 6.)

Trespass to goods: the goods of a person are unlawfully disturbed or destroyed by another either intentionally or carelessly.

Trespass to land: an intentional or unintentional entering on land, remaining on land or causing anything to contact land without permission or other lawful justification. An individual who is in lawful occupation (the owner or a tenant) can sue for trespass. 'Land' covers the soil, trees, buildings, underneath the soil (subject to mineral rights) and airspace up to a certain height.

There are circumstances under which entry to land or premises will not amount to a trespass.

Question: Can you think of situations in which you might be allowed on land or premises which are not your own?

Key Point: You could be lawfully on land if the landowner has given consent, which may be express or implied consent. You may have a contractual licence to enter premises (e.g. if you have paid for a ticket to a concert). The contractual licence gives you a limited right to access the land.

Question: Brian is in a crowded sports shop when he decides to practise his golf swing. Unfortunately, on his follow-through he hits a customer, Ann, on the chin, breaking her jaw. Do you think this could constitute a tort (civil wrong)?

Key Point: This could constitute negligence (see section 3, below). If Brian was an impoverished golf player could you think of anybody else Ann might sue? She might argue that the shop, by failing to supervise customers adequately, was negligent.

The shop is more likely to carry insurance, too, and therefore may be able to pay a claim for compensation.

1.3 The tort of false imprisonment

This occurs when a defendant intentionally and without any lawful justification detains a person or restricts a person's liberty within an area. Actual physical restraint is not required but the defendant must believe that she or he is restrained.

If an individual is told by the Garda that she or he is under arrest, then unless there is lawful justification for the arrest, this may amount to false imprisonment.

1.4 The tort of defamation

The tort of defamation aims to protect a person from someone publishing a defamatory statement about them. A defamatory statement is a false statement that adversely affects a person's reputation. The publication must be such as to injure the plaitiff's reputation in the mind of a reasonable reader, viewer or recipient of the publication.

It is traditionally categorised as either:

- *Slander*: defamation by communication in a non-permanent form such as an unrecorded verbal statement or a gesture made in the presence of others; or
- *Libel*: defamation by communication in a permanent form such as publication in a book, newspaper or internet form. Radio and television broadcasts are treated as permanent publications for this purpose.

A defamation case is one of the few civil actions when a jury may hear a civil action.

The law on defamation in Ireland is contained in the Defamation Act 1961. It has been the subject of criticism and reform proposals for over twenty years. The most recent proposal, the Defamation Bill, was introduced in the Senate in 2006 and has yet to be fully debated by the Dáil.

1.5 The tort of nuisance

This tort is also an ancient form of law. It has a renewed importance today as it is often used in claims concerning the protection of the environment from pollution and other elements. It protects rights to enjoyment of land and/or premises.

The tort of nuisance can be defined as an act (or an omission) that causes an unreasonable interference with, or an annoyance to, or a disturbance to a person who seeks to exercise his/her rights relating to land.

There are two forms of nuisance, **public** and **private**.

If the right disturbed or interfered with belongs to an individual as a member of the public it is termed a **public nuisance**. Generally only the Attorney General can bring such actions. Permanent obstructions on a highway or objects that render the use of the highway dangerous are examples of public nuisance.

If it is a right connected with the rights of ownership or occupation or assertion of other rights connected with land (e.g. an easement or right of way) it is termed a **private nuisance**.

There are many similarities between nuisance and trespass: and both were created by the law to protect the enjoyment of land.

There are difficulties with the definition of nuisance in Irish law. The fundamental difference between nuisance and trespass is that nuisance is often said to be an indirect form of invasion of land.

Example: A city council decides to build an incinerator. While building the incinerator the neighbouring land is hit by flying stones and dust which land on the neighbouring owner's property. The stones will be a direct hit or an invasion of his land and fall within the tort of trespass to land.

The dust, if it does not settle, which creates poor visibility and atmospheric conditions, is more likely to be a nuisance.

The person who creates the nuisance (noise, dust, etc.), for example a builder, may be liable. The **occupier**, if s/he authorises its commission or fails to take action to stop an encroachment onto neighbouring land, may also be liable.

2 The Tort of Negligence

OVERVIEW

- The duty of care: breach of duty of care; causation; damage or loss.
- Possible defences to negligence actions.
- Contributory negligence.

2.1 Negligence: the most important tort

Many torts can be committed through carelessness rather than intentionally. The courts have developed the tort of negligence, which can be described as civil liability for a failure to take proper care in the circumstance to avoid causing damage or injury which is foreseeable. The basis of the modern tort of negligence is the key case of *Donoghue v. Stevenson [1932] All ER Rep 1*. This case is still cited in cases today. The reasons why it is so important are:
- it created the principle that manufacturers of products owe a duty of care to their ultimate consumers; and
- it set down guidelines for the courts to decide whether other categories of business/person may owe a duty of care to others.

The Facts: On 26 August 1928, P drank a bottle of ginger beer, manufactured by M, which her friend, B, had bought from a shop, S. The bottle contained the decomposed remains of a snail which could not be detected through the opaque glass. P alleged that as a result of drinking and seeing the snail she suffered from shock and severe gastroenteritis. She brought proceedings against the manufacturer.

The judge anticipated that this case would prompt a number of negligence claims by individuals. The judge set down the principle that only people who are owed a **legal duty of care** can sue for negligence, in one of the most famous statements of law.

You must take reasonable care to avoid acts or omissions which you can reasonably foresee would be likely to injure your neighbour. Who, then, in law, is my neighbour? The answer seems to be persons who are so closely and directly affected by my act that I ought reasonably to have them in contemplation as being ... affected.

This is termed the ' neighbour principle' in negligence law.

The *Donoghue v. Stevenson* principle was adopted by the Irish courts and became part of Irish law after the case of *Kirby v. Burke & Holloway [1944] IR 207.*

Task A

This short task focuses on the facts of this key case and the relationships between the various parties in a typical consumer transaction.

Draw a diagram to represent the facts of *Donoghue v. Stevenson* using the labels B, P, S, and M.

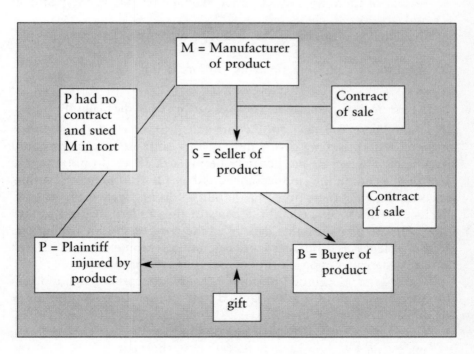

- S was the café — seller of the ginger beer
- P consumed the ginger beer, was injured and was the plaintiff
- B bought the ginger beer
- M manufactured the ginger beer

Note that there was no contract between the café and P, who drank the ginger beer, because P had not bought the beer; she had been given the beer by her friend. If she had paid S herself there would have been a contract and she could have sued the shop directly for breach of contract. There is no direct contractual link between M and B or P. The plaintiff (P) sued the café for breach of duty in negligence.

2.2 The elements of negligence liability

To prove negligence the plaintiff must prove on a balance of probabilities all the following elements:

1. the defendant owed the plaintiff a duty of care to avoid causing injury to persons or property; and
2. there was a breach of that duty by the defendant; and
3. breach of the duty caused injury, damage or loss to the plaintiff; and
4. the damage or loss must be of a type recognised by law.

We need to look at these elements in more detail.

2.2.1 Element 1: there must be a duty of care owed to the plaintiff

In *Donoghue v. Stevenson* the court stated that as individuals or as business enterprises we owe a duty of care to those people we could reasonably foresee or predict may be injured. If we do not exercise reasonable care in the circumstances and as a result the person suffers loss or damage there may be liability for negligence. This case, decided in the 1930s, is still the basis of the modern negligence law. The concept of **reasonable care** is at the core of law of negligence. Reasonableness is a flexible standard, and a reasonable response to a situation depends upon all the surrounding circumstances.

The law has developed through case law and precedents and in a number of situations it is recognised that a duty of care is owed. For example:

- Car drivers owe a duty of reasonable care to other road users, pedestrians and passengers travelling in their car.
- Doctors owe a duty of reasonable care to their patients.
- Manufacturers owe a duty of reasonable care to consumers.

- Employers owe a duty of reasonable care to employees.

Question: Can you think of any other situations where a duty of care may be owed?

Key Points: You may have considered the situation in which landowners owe certain duties to those using their property.

Other professionals such as electricians, accountants and surveyors owe a duty of care to their clients. Solicitors owe a duty of care to their clients for non-advocacy work. Prison services owe a duty of care to prisoners. Schools owe a duty of care to their pupils.

Whether or not a duty of care is owed is still the starting point for all negligence actions. There are continuing debates about the scope of the duty.

In some situations the courts have held that no duty of care is owed because of the lack of connection or proximity between the persons in the events or the fact that the events were unforeseeable. The courts have said there may be public policy grounds why a duty of care should not be imposed. We will consider a case on this point in Task B.

2.2.2 Element 2: there must be a breach of the duty of care

To be liable for negligence the plaintiff must prove that the defendant did not exercise reasonable care in all the circumstances. This involves the court assessing the facts and circumstances surrounding each case and deciding whether the defendant's conduct has fallen short of the 'reasonable person' test.

The test is objective. The required standard of care is based on the reasonable person, not the individual attributes or situation of the defendant.

The courts look at what would have been reasonable at the time of the incident, and not with the benefit of hindsight. The test is one of knowledge and general practice existing at the time. It is always easy to be 'wise after the event'. What the law requires is that an individual acts in a manner which is reasonable at the time of acting.

A higher standard of care may be expected where the defendant knows or should know a person is at special risk and that any injury may be severe.

Paris v. Stepney Borough Council [1951] AC 367
A note about this authority: this is an older case from England, decided long before health and safety law became part and parcel of

organisations. It is still a relevant authority for the principle in negligence that if there is a greater risk, the reasonable person would take greater care.

The facts: The employers failed to provide safety equipment including goggles to an employee who worked on vehicle maintenance and panel beating. The employee lost the sight of an eye through injury from a steel chipping. At the time it was not customary to supply protective goggles to workers in this type of work. However, the employer knew that this employee had already lost his sight in one eye.

The court ruled that the gravity of the injury, blindness, was foreseeable and that in the circumstances a reasonable employer would have exercised a higher standard of care and provided goggles for this employee.

The employer had not acted as a reasonable employer in the circumstances and there was a breach of a duty of care and liability for negligence.

Fitzsimmons v. Bord Telecom and ESB [1991]

An employee was killed when attempting to move a fallen cable which was in contact with an electric overhead power line.

The court ruled there was a foreseeable risk of harm and the gravity of injury (electrocution) was great. The standard of reasonable care was high in the circumstances and there had been a breach of the duty. Liability was imposed on both defendants.

In summary, if the risk is high the defendant should take steps to guard against it. If the gravity of any possible injury or damage is severe the standard of care that a reasonable person would exercise is higher. For example, driving in heavy rain or fog increases the risks associated with poor visibility and increased stopping distances. Reasonable drivers would reduce speed.

Special expertise cases

A person who has a special skill or expertise must use the standard of care expected by members of that profession. If the defendant complies with a practice which is commonly accepted in his/her profession or trade this will be strong evidence that there has been exercise of reasonable care.

In medical negligence cases the tests for establishing negligence in diagnosis or treatment is slightly different. The plaintiff must prove that the defendant was guilty of failure such that no medical practitioner of equal specialist or general status and skill would be guilty of if acting with ordinary care. This test was laid down in the important case of *Dunne v. National Maternity Hospital [1989] IR 9*.

That judgment recognised the need to balance the requirements of advancing medical science with the law of negligence. In particular the frequency of unsustainable legal claims meant that it was undesirable to set a 'lax' standard of care for the purpose of assessing what is and is not medical negligence. It will not be enough to prove that a doctor deviated from an approved and general practice: it must also be proved that the course of treatment was one which no other medical practitioner would have followed if s/he had been taking the ordinary care required from a person of his/her qualifications.

TASK B: THE SCOPE OF THE DUTY OF CARE

The aim of this task is to practise navigating the BAILII website and to read an important recent case on the subject of duty of care. This will help you develop an understanding of the elements of the tort of negligence. You will consider policy issues surrounding the tort of negligence and practise your summarising and writing skills.

Locate the case of *Breslin v. Corcoran [2003] IESC 23* on the BAILII website by typing 'Breslin v. Corcoran' into the search box. It is a good idea to refine your search, so in the database box below select 'Ireland' and then click on 'Search'. (Refining your search means narrowing the range of topics that the search engine scans so that you will not have thousands of options to run through.) Make sure you identify the correct case because the earlier case of *Breslin v. Corcoran and Anor* decided in 2001 by the High Court is also listed. The decision was appealed and it is the decision made on appeal in 2003 that you need to locate.

Read through the judgment and use the questions below to help you focus on the most important parts of the judgment. This is a relatively short judgment. Do not worry if you do not understand large parts of it. By working through the judgment and the text below you will soon get to grips with the key points.

Terminology: The phrase *novus actus interveniens* is used in this case. This phrase is relevant to the third element necessary to prove negligence (see below) — that the negligence of the defendant *caused* the loss or damage. If something other than negligence is responsible for the loss or damage the defendant has a defence. In this case one of the defence arguments was that it was the thief of the car who caused the loss/damage, *not* the negligence of the owner of the car who had left the keys in the ignition.

1. When was the judgment given and by which court?
2. Who were the two defendants in the case?
3. What did the judge in the High Court award?
4. Summarise the facts of the case in fewer than 80 words.
5. Identify the key legal principle being argued here in fewer than 50 words. (Note: refer to paragraphs 7 and 8 of the judgment in particular.)
6. Summarise the final judgment of the court in fewer than 100 words.
7. Explain, in under 50 words, whether you agree with this judgment.

Key Points:
1. 27 March 2003 by the Supreme Court.
2. The two defendants were Noel Corcoran (1) and the Motor Insurers' Bureau of Ireland (MIBI) (2).
3. The plaintiff succeeded against the MIBI (the second defendant). All liability was attached to the MIBI and the damages were agreed at £65,000.
4. Noel Corcoran (the first defendant) left his car unlocked outside a shop with the keys in the ignition. A person took the car and drove it off at speed. The car ran into a pedestrian (the plaintiff) at Talbot Lane and injured the pedestrian.
5. The key legal issue was whether the carelessness of leaving a car in a street with the keys in the ignition amounts to negligence. The car owner may argue that although there is an obvious risk of the car being taken, the illegal taking of the car by a third party is a new act (a *novus actus interveniens*) and the car owner should not be liable for the actions of the third party.
6. The question of whether or not a duty of care is owed to the plaintiff in new or unusual circumstances depends upon all relevant circumstances. (See paragraph 10 of the judgment.)
   Even if a duty of care is established a person will normally not be liable for the tort of negligence, even where s/he has been careless, if the harm/damages has been caused by another (a third party) for whom s/he is not vicariously responsible.
7. Whether an individual should face negligence liability for the criminal acts of another is the key point here. In this situation, the victim of the joyrider will be compensated by the Motor Insurers' Bureau, so the victim will have a remedy.

The court was anxious that the boundaries of negligence and particularly the existence of a duty of care were becoming ever larger and that boundaries to the tort of negligence had to be set.

2.2.3 Element 3: the breach of duty must cause the loss or damage

This is known as the **causation principle**. It is often straightforward for the plaintiff to prove that the defendant's failure to exercise reasonable care caused a loss. This is often termed the 'but for' test: would the loss have occurred 'but for' the negligence of the defendant?

In straightforward cases, such as road traffic accidents, the negligent driving of one person will have **caused** the injuries and financial losses (such as loss of earnings) of the injured party. There will be no issue over causation. In some situations the defendant may argue there was a new factor, which broke the chain of causation, as mentioned in Task B above and the issue of *novus actus interveniens*.

In some cases causation can be problematic. If an employee has worked for a number of employers and has contracted an industrial disease the causation issue is a problem. How can an employee prove that the breach of care of one or more specific employers by exposing him or her to hazardous environments, by failure to provide safe systems of work, etc., caused the particular loss?

The issue is whether the defendant's negligence caused the loss, or whether it would have happened in any event.

Barnett v. Kensington and Chelsea Hospital [1969] 1QB 428
The plaintiff's husband was unwell and went to a casualty department. He was sent home without seeing a doctor. Some time later, he died of arsenical poisoning. His widow sued the hospital for negligence.

The issue in question was whether the negligence of the hospital caused the widow's loss. The plaintiff has to prove this link. After hearing expert evidence the court ruled that due to the type of poisoning, even if the patient had been seen by the doctor, the type of poisoning could not have been discovered and the antidote delivered in time. Therefore the negligence of the hospital did not cause the death, which would have occurred in any event. The hospital was accordingly not liable in negligence as the plaintiff had failed to prove causation, the third element.

2.2.4 Element 4: the damage or loss must be of a type recognised by law

The measure of damages in tort aims to put the injured person in the position they would have been in had the tort not occurred. Of course it is impossible to restore a seriously injured plaintiff to their position prior to an accident, so financial compensation is the only option.

The amount of damages is termed the **quantum.** The quantum will depend upon all the circumstances of the case. Damages are awarded as a one-off lump sum payment to compensate and anticipate all losses, be they past, present or long into the future. In the UK serious injuries can be compensated by a series of staged payments (called a structured settlement), which can have a number of advantages. This option is not yet available in Ireland.

Typically the amounts of loss are quantified and categorised under certain heads of damage. They cover losses incurred up until the date of trial and for the future.

2.3 Damages

Damages are split into two broad categories:
* **Special damages** are damages that are quantifiable (e.g. loss of earnings, hospital bills, etc.)
* **General damages** are damages that are by their nature less easily quantifiable and more subjective. They include elements for pain and suffering, loss of amenity and enjoyment of life, future health problems, etc.

Not all types of loss are recognised by the law of negligence, for example the claimant cannot receive compensation for upset or inconvenience. Rules developed by case law govern the types of loss that may be claimed. Generally the loss claimed cannot be too 'remote' from the incident.

Normally the types of loss recognised as being capable of being claimed in the tort of negligence are:
* physical damage to the person or property of the plaintiff
* consequential economic damage
* nervous shock and psychological damage.

Example: Declan is 50 and is injured by an accident at work caused by faulty scaffolding. He suffers a fractured femur and is hospitalised for one week after an operation to pin his leg. He is a self-employed contractor and is forced to take three months off work. His doctor tells him he is likely to suffer knee and ankle problems in the future and that he should consider retiring from his job early.

Question: What types of losses will he claim?

- Pain and suffering at the time of the accident (including post-operative pain) up to the time of trial.
- Financial losses sustained up to the trial such as loss of earnings.
- Future pain and suffering.
- Future losses.

2.3.1 Claims for nervous shock and psychological injury

The courts in the UK and Ireland have been faced with a number of negligence cases arising from tragic incidents such as the Hillsborough disaster in 1989, and fatal car accidents, which have caused injuries to people who were not immediate victims of the accident but witnessed the aftermath and suffered as a result. This is now often termed post-traumatic stress disorder (PTSD). The courts have found that in certain situations a **duty of care** may be owed to relations who are in close proximity to such an accident and that nervous shock could be seen as a reasonably foreseeable result of the injuries to family members caused by the defendant's negligence. They are in a 'neighbour relationship' with the person who has committed a tort.

Alcock v. Chief Constable of Yorkshire Police [1991] 4 All ER 907

The Hillsborough stadium disaster happened during the FA semi-final between Liverpool and Nottingham Forest in 1989. Poor crowd control by the police resulted in a massive crush which resulted in the deaths of 96 people and injuries to 400. The defendant (the Chief Constable) admitted negligence liability to those who were physically killed or harmed at the stadium. The issue that the highest court in England (the House of Lords) heard was whether those who had suffered psychiatric injuries from the shock of witnessing the events at the stadium, on television or from identifying the bodies of the victims should be able to claim for nervous shock and psychiatric damage. The court ruled that certain categories of secondary victims who were closely related to those who had died or been injured could claim, provided that there was a close connection (proximity) in time between the witnessing of the aftermath and the incident.

McFarlane v. EE Caledonia Ltd [1994] 2 All ER

The plaintiff saw the explosion of the Piper Alpha oil rig from on board a rescue vessel. The plaintiff had not been involved in the rescue effort himself and had not been directly in danger. He had witnessed terrible deaths by burning. The Court ruled that for policy reasons he could not be owed a duty by the oil rig company.

Recent cases in Ireland

In *Kelly v. Hennessy [1995] IESC 8* the Supreme Court considered the claim of damages for nervous shock and psychological damage. The defendant, who drove negligently, caused severe personal injuries to the husband and daughters of the respondent. The respondent suffered psychological harm upon hearing of the accident and witnessing her severely injured family in hospital and watching their suffering and partial recoveries. This is an area of law which is still evolving. There was an appeal to the Supreme Court on a number of grounds which were set out in the judgment (paragraph 5).

Task C

This task involves reading an extract from an important Supreme Court case (*Kelly v. Hennessy [1995] IESC 8*) on the extent of the duty of care which may be owed to the family of primary victims of negligence. It will introduce you to some legal issues raised by post-traumatic stress disorder.

Locate this judgment using the BAILII website.

Note on terminology: The original plaintiff (Anne Kelly) is referred to as the **respondent** in the appeal case as the original defendants (the appellants in this case) appealed against the original judgment of the High Court and the Supreme Court heard the appeal. The appellant is taking an appeal case against the respondent.

Focus on the judgment of Mrs Justice Denham (para 70 onwards), who gives the facts of the case and the applicable law.

Questions:

1. What were the facts that gave rise to the claim?
2. What did the trial judge award (note para 79)?
3. How does Mrs Justice Denham define a primary and a secondary victim?
4. Identify three cases used by the judge as providing guidance on the state of the law (or persuasive cases rather than binding precedents).

Key Points:

1. The plaintiff/respondent was the wife and mother of three people

who were very seriously injured in a road traffic accident. The accident was caused by the negligence of the defendant. She was informed of the accident by her niece. She immediately became ill, went to Jervis Street and saw her family, who were in a very serious condition. The plaintiff/respondent suffered post-traumatic stress disorder at that time and continued to suffer permanent psychiatric illness.

2. The trial judge awarded pain and suffering damages for nervous shock of £35,000 suffered to the date of the trial and £40,000 for pain and suffering in the future.
3. A primary victim is somebody who is a participant in the accident or event. A secondary victim is a non-participant, but somebody who is injured as a consequence.
4. The judge relied on cases from Australia (*Jaensch v. Coffey [1984] 155 CLR 549, para. 16*) and the UK (*McLoughlin v. O'Brian [1983] 1 AC 410*). She also cited a case in Ireland which was decided on similar principles: *Mullaly v. Bus Éireann [1992] IRLM 722*.

2.4 Contributory negligence

This is claimed when the defendant argues that the plaintiff was partially responsible by failing to exercise reasonable care for his/her own safety and has contributed to his/her injury.

The defendant may be able to disprove negligence or argue that the plaintiff partially caused his/her loss or injury.

The essential issue is whether the plaintiff/claimant exercised reasonable care in respect of his/her own safety, as we have a duty of care towards ourselves as well as others.

Under the Civil Liability Act 1961 the courts have a duty to allocate the proportion of loss. The court apportions the fault as it thinks just and equitable having regard to the respective degrees of fault on the plaintiff and defendant where the damage results partly from the defendant's wrong and partly from the plaintiff's wrong. If the court is unable to determine the relative fault then liability may be apportioned equally.

Question: List two examples of a plaintiff being injured due to negligence and in which issues of contributory negligence may often arise in practice.

Some suggested examples: Failure to wear a seat belt in a car or a helmet on a motorcycle severely increases the risk and gravity of injury. The Supreme Court ruled on contributory negligence in seat belt cases in *Sinnott v. Quinnsworth [1984] ILRM 523.*

In a road traffic collision if the plaintiff was speeding (*Callaghan v. Bus Atha Cliath [2000] IEHC 88*).

In addition, situations in which employees take short cuts in working practices, ignoring health and safety procedures and causing injuries to themselves could result in a finding of contributory negligence.

People suffering injuries while intoxicated, which contributes to the severity of the injury: *Judge v. Reape [1968] IR 226.* A passenger accepted a lift from a drunk driver. The passenger was also drunk. A collision occurred. The Supreme Court ruled that 'a person who knows or should know that the driver is by reason of the consumption of alcohol not fit to drive, and who nevertheless goes as the driver's passenger, is not taking reasonable care for his safety and must therefore be found guilty of contributory negligence.'

2.5 Liability for negligent misstatements

We have looked at situations when a person can be found to be negligent due to their actions or inactions. There can also be liability for financial losses that are caused by a defendant relying on statements that are made negligently. The statements can be written or oral. This type of negligence liability is restricted by the courts for some obvious policy reasons.

Rory meets some people at a football match. One of them (Diane) is a dentist and they discuss wisdom teeth and dentists generally while watching the match. She gives Rory some general advice and mentions a couple of colleagues. Rory becomes a patient of one of these colleagues. Unfortunately he is wrongly diagnosed and suffers additional treatment and extra costs.

Question: Should Rory be able to sue Diane for her general advice and recommendations?
Key Points: You probably thought, correctly, that the primary remedy should be against the dentist who incorrectly diagnosed Rory. If that dentist is untraceable then Rory may try to seek a remedy from Diane. The law on this area has developed to restrict the occurrence of this type of liability. For policy reasons it is important that whatever we write or speak should not be a matter for potential litigation. The

courts have limited this type of liability to situations in which there is a 'special relationship'.

If there is a relationship between the maker of a statement and the recipient, where it is justifiable that the recipient relies on the statement, the maker is under a duty to take reasonable care to ensure the advice/information is correct.

Hedley Byrne v. Heller & Partners [1963] 2 All ER 575
Facts: This concerned the request for a credit reference statement from a bank concerning a client. On the strength of the reference the company entered into a contract. When the contract was not honoured the plaintiff sued to recover from the maker of the credit reference statement.

The court ruled that although on the facts there was no liability (as the maker had validly excluded liability) the court accepted the principle that a negligence action could be a potential remedy for misstatements that were made without reasonable care. The person who makes the statement must usually do so as an expert/professional and it must be likely that the statement will be relied upon by another person.

> *Scenario*: You are the human resources director of a medium sized-software company. You have been asked for a reference about an employee, Nigel, a notoriously poor time keeper who has a disciplinary record for unauthorised company car use. You would be pleased to see him leave your organisation.

Question: What are the company's legal obligations when giving a reference?
Key Point: There is no legal obligation on an employer to provide a written or oral reference. However, if an employer does provide a reference, it must be accurate or the maker could be liable for a negligent misstatement.

Spring v. Guardian Assurance plc [1994] All ER 129
Facts: Spring worked as a sales manager for an insurance broker, selling policies on behalf of Guardian Assurance. When his potential employer received a bad reference (the House of Lords called it 'the kiss of death'), the potential employer decided not to employ Spring. Spring sought damages from Guardian Assurance for economic loss. The House of Lords ruled that an employer who provides a reference concerning an employee or former employee to a prospective

employer owes a duty of care to the employee regarding the preparation of the reference and may be liable to the employee/former employee in damages for any economic loss suffered as a result of negligent misstatement.

The duty of the employer is to take reasonable care in giving a reference and in verifying the information on which it is based. It is generally accepted that the *Spring* case is likely to apply in Ireland.

Employers are under no duty to give a full and comprehensive reference. However, the reference must not be false or inaccurate and it should not be misleading by being selective of the facts or by giving a false impression.

If a reference is inaccurate, it is clearly foreseeable that the employee may suffer financial loss as a result of failing to obtain new employment.

In addition, an employee who suffers loss as a result of an inaccurate reference may also be in a position to bring an action in defamation if the statement is untrue.

2.5.1 The use of disclaimers

In order to try to prevent an issue of liability arising, disclaimers are often written into documents and used in websites too.

Go to the Irish Statute Book website. Before you access the site you have to accept the disclaimer:

> Whilst every effort has been made to ensure the accuracy of the information/material contained on the web site, the State and Attorney General, its servants or agents assume no responsibility for and give no guarantees, undertakings or warranties concerning the accuracy, completeness or up to date nature of the information provided on the web site and do not accept any liability whatsoever arising from any errors or omissions.

Look for other disclaimers in documents you read or sign.

Question: Do you think disclaimers will be effective in preventing any claim arising?

Key Points: A disclaimer is a form of exclusion clause (as it seeks to prevent or exclude liability in tort).

Task D

Review the area of negligence generally and negligent misstatements in particular by reading an important recent Supreme Court case on the area. Locate *Walsh v. Jones Lang Lasalle Ltd [2007] IEHC 28* on the BAILII website and use the following questions to focus on the key points raised in the case, which concerned the misdescription of commercial property.

1. Where was the misstatement published and what was the plaintiff's basis of claim?
2. What was the nature of the 'small print' referred to as a 'waiver' in the brochure? (Refer to para 1 of the 'Relevant Facts'.)
3. Identify three cases the court considered as relevant in deciding the issues in this case. (There are more than three cases.)
4. Did the court find there was a 'special relationship' of reliance on the brochure on these facts?
5. Did the court consider that the waiver was effective to prevent liability to the plaintiff?
6. Was the loss and damage claimed by the plaintiffs (the lost rental income and anticipated capital appreciation figures) a reasonably foreseeable type of loss caused by the negligence?
7. Explain why the judge did not find there was any contributory negligence on the defendant's part in failing to measure the premises.
8. How were damages assessed?

Note: The Supreme Court decided another important case (referred to in the *Jones* case) in this area in *Wildgust & Anor v. The Governor and Company of the Bank of Ireland & Anor [2006] IESC 16*. This case is more factually complicated than the Jones case above. You can access the *Wildgust* case on the BAILII or Courts Service websites if you are interested in this area of liability.

2.6 Bringing a negligence claim within the limitation period

A limitation period is a time limit that is set in order to prevent individuals from suing long after the alleged tort (or other breach of legal obligation) has occurred. The claim is said to be 'statute barred' if it is not brought within time.

In tort cases generally an action must be commenced within three years of the date when the tort occurred or when all elements of the tort can be established.

In personal injury actions generally (for negligence, nuisance or breach of duty) an action must be brought within two years of the date when the cause of action accrued or from when the relevant knowledge (if later) became known to the plaintiff. These limits were altered by the Civil Liability and Courts Act 2004 (see the section on the PIAB in Chapter 3).

Note that the court has a discretion to extend the limitation period in appropriate cases.

There are a number of complex exceptions to these general principles. For example, the time limit does not apply to persons under the age of 21, those who have a serious mental incapacity and those who have suffered psychological injury as a result of being a victim of sexual abuse (Statute of Limitations (Amendment) Act 2000).

TASK E: PROBLEM QUESTIONS ON NEGLIGENCE

Problem questions are often set on the area of negligence. You are not expected to deliver a judgment like those you have read in the examples above. The main aims are to:

- show that you understand the key principles of negligence
- be able to apply the principles sensibly to the facts of the case.

> Dan is driving his customised car along a narrow country road at about 50kmph. It is dusk and raining. He fails to notice a cyclist, Jon, who has a dim, flickering rear light on his bike. Dan manages to swerve onto the other side of the road and avoid Jon, who is so shocked he drives into the ditch and breaks his arm. Rory, the driver of an oncoming vehicle, manages to stop just in time, but suffers whiplash as a result of braking violently.

Assume you act for Jon. Explain how the law of negligence could apply in this situation. Focus on the following points:

1. Explain the concept of the duty of care and the neighbour principle, using the principles of *Donoghue v Stevenson*.
2. Was there a breach of the duty of care in all the circumstances of the case, such as we know them? Did Dan act as a reasonable driver would?
3. Did the breach of the duty of care cause the loss to Jon? What would you anticipate Dan's advisor would argue?
4. What type of loss or damage was caused to Jon?

Note: Go through the four stages of establishing negligence liability set out in *Donoghue v Stevenson* — use this case as the framework for your answer.

Key Points:
1. Road users owe a duty of care to other road users. Consider whether Dan is the only road user who owes a duty of care.
2. You should point out that the standard is objective, i.e. what would a reasonable driver have done in these circumstances?
3. What would you anticipate Dan's advisor would argue?
4. Clearly the loss would include physical injuries and pain and suffering, loss of income, damage to bike, and nervous shock if relevant in Jon's situation. Jon, the plaintiff, must prove all these elements on the balance of probabilities (i.e. was it more likely than not that the assertion was correct?) in order to be able to prove negligence.

You should anticipate that Dan will argue that it was Jon's negligence (in being unlit at night) that caused the accident, and this will certainly be raised as a defence.

2.7 Vicarious liability

Definition: This is a form of indirect liability where a person or organisation can be financially liable for the actions of another.

2.7.1 Vicarious liability situations

Under the Partnership Act 1890 a partner is liable for the actions of a co-partner. A vehicle owner is liable for the tortious conduct of a person driving their vehicle with their consent under the Road Traffic Act 1961.

The area where the principle is most apparent is in the employment relationship. An employer is generally liable for the torts committed by employees while at work and in the course of employment.

Vicarious liability is an important principle in practice and the concept was created by the courts for a number of reasons:
- It is unrealistic to sue an individual employee for a tort which has been committed (e.g. negligence, defamation or assault) as generally employees will not have the financial means to pay damages.
- An employer will usually have financial resources and should be insured to cover liability.
- If an employer faces liability for the torts of staff it will encourage proper supervision of employment practices by the employer.

A particularly extreme of an employer being liable for the torts of an employee in the UK illustrates the principle.

Mattis v. Pollock (t/a Flamingo's Nightclub) [2003] IRLR 603
Facts: The defendant owned a nightclub and employed a doorman. The claimant was involved in a dispute with the doorman. After the incident the doorman returned home and armed himself with knives. He returned to the area of the club and stabbed the claimant, severing his spinal code and leaving him paralysed.

The claimant argued that the owner of the nightclub and employer was vicariously liable for the tort of the employee (tort of battery).

The court ruled that the nightclub owner was liable as the assault by the employee was so closely connected with what the employer authorised or expected of the doorman (i.e. the use of force).

Note that the employer is generally not vicariously liable for the actions of independent contractors. There is some uncertainty in the law in this area at the moment as to how to categorise who is an employee and the circumstances where a employer may be liable for the torts of independent contractors.

Often it is obvious that an individual is an employee if he or she has a written contract of employment. If the employee is negligent at work the employer will be liable. However, more people are now working as 'consultants', 'freelance' workers, etc. This gives the advantages of flexibility and different tax rules for employees. For employers it is less expensive to employ due to less administration, fewer employment rights, etc. The cases that come before the courts that turn on whether person can be classed as an employee or independent contractor generally arise because a person has been injured or denied rights at work and/or is seeking employment or social welfare rights on the basis they were an employee.

An example of this is:

Henry Denny & Sons (Ireland) Ltd v. Minister for Social Welfare [1997] IESC 9
Facts: A demonstrator in a supermarket claimed she was an employee for the purpose of the Social Welfare Acts. She had signed a contract which stated she was not an employee. The Supreme Court looked at previous case law on the area and suggested that the principal 'test' for whether somebody is an independent contractor is whether they are in business on their own account or working for another. The fact that she was under the management control of the supermarket, had clothing and equipment provided for her and overall 'the facts or

realities of the situation on the ground', meant that she was correctly classified by the Social Welfare appeals officer as an employee.

The area of vicarious liability at work is developing. This is an area where there is uncertainty in the scope of the law. Judgments from the Irish courts have suggested that employers may have vicarious liability for independent contractors, depending on the level of control the employer has over the worker.

In addition to being an employee the conduct that gives rise to the liability must have some connection with the employees' functions. The *Mattis* case above is an illustration of this: the bouncer was engaged to use force; the court noted that the employer knew of his reputation; and the altercation which led to the revenge attack arose at work.

Another important case on this area from the UK is *Lister and Others v. Hesley Hall Ltd [2001] UKHL 22*.

The claimants were boarders at a school for maladjusted boys and were the victims of sexual abuse by a warden of the house.

They claimed against the employer. The House of Lords ruled that a broad test of the scope of employment had to be adopted for the purpose of vicarious liability and the torts of this employee were closely connected with his work, and the employer was liable.

Patrick, John and Jim work for a pharmaceuticals company Druggs plc. As a prank they bundle Donal into an industrial tumble dryer, used for sterilising lab clothing, and keep him there for five minutes. This is against company rules. Donal is claustrophobic and suffers a panic attack which requires hospitalisation. He is off work for three months due to stress.

Question: Could Druggs plc be liable to Donal?

Key Points:
There are a number of possible torts committed here. If Donal was in fear of immediate physical force there will be an assault. There was a deliberate application of force — a battery. The tort of false imprisonment is also relevant here.

Donal may claim that Druggs plc is vicariously liable for the torts of their employees. Druggs will argue that this action was outside the course of the employment and totally contrary to employment policy and in breach of their contracts of employment.

Question: If you were hearing the case explain how and why you would decide the case: for or against the employers?

3 Specific Applications of the Law of Tort and Statutory Torts

3.1 Common law duties owed by an employer to an employee

Even before the watershed case of *Donoghue v. Stevenson* the courts had ruled that employers must exercise reasonable care towards their employees.

The courts had implied terms into the contract of employment to the effect that an employer owed a contractual duty to take reasonable care for the safety and well-being of employees. However, there were serious limitations to the effectiveness of this avenue of redress for employees.

The factors for negligence liability outlined in *Donoghue v. Stevenson* are clearly capable of applying to an employment situation. An employer/employee relationship triggers a duty of care situation.

To prove negligence the plaintiff must prove on a balance of probabilities *all* the following elements:
1. the defendant owed the plaintiff a duty of care to avoid causing injury to persons or property; *and*
2. there was a breach of that duty by the defendant; *and*
3. breach of the duty; *and*
4. injury, damage or loss to the plaintiff.

Note: Employers also owe employees duties imposed by statute and secondary legislation under health and safety legislation. The area of occupational health and safety has grown rapidly over the last ten years, driven in particular by EU developments and the expanding tort of negligence.

This section focuses on the application of the principles of negligence in an employer-employee context.

This duty of reasonable care has been historically divided into four main areas, which frequently overlap.

3.1.1 Duty to provide a safe place of work
An employer owes a reasonable duty to ensure that the work premises/location are safe.

Latimer v. A.E.C. [1953] AC 643
The plaintiff slipped on a wet factory floor following the flooding of a factory. He sued his employers, who had done everything they could to minimise the risk apart from closing the factory. The court ruled

the employers had not broken the standard of reasonable care, as the cost of factory closure was greater than the risk of slipping. Any reasonable employer in the circumstances would have done the same thing.

This duty covers premises, access and the workplace being safe as well as the quality of the light and air in the working environment.

3.1.2 Safe system of work

Walsh v. Securicor (Ireland) Ltd (unreported)
The plaintiff was driving a security van for his employers between Cork and Cobh and was injured during an armed raid. A police escort had been provided, but this was ruled not to be a sufficient precaution in the circumstances to absolve the employer of negligence. The court noted that a failure to alter the timings of deliveries (same time every week for seven years) was negligent. A high standard of conduct was expected in cases of extreme risk.

McDermid v. Nash Dredging & Reclamation Co. [1987] HL
Facts: The plaintiff was untying the cable attaching tug to dredger. The system of work required the captain to wait until the plaintiff knocked twice on the wheelhouse door, to ensure the plaintiff was clear of the hawsers. The captain failed to do this and the plaintiff was seriously injured as he was dragged overboard by the hawser. The Court ruled there was a failure to ensure a safe system of work.

Stress at work
The issue of overloading an employee and causing levels of stress so as to occasion injury is a growing area of litigation, as is the issue of bullying and harassment at work. Safe systems and procedures at work, if followed, may prevent liability arising.

3.1.3 Safe equipment

An employer must not provide unsafe equipment or tools to employees. Inadequately maintained tools may cause injuries. (This common law duty is bolstered by wide-ranging statutory duties.)

3.1.4 Safe workforce

The employer has a duty to exercise reasonable care to select competent staff, particularly if the job exposes others to hazards. Similarly, if an employee acts in breach of safety standards or in a way that endangers others a reasonable employer would take disciplinary steps to prevent this.

3.2 The Liability for Defective Products Act 1991

OVERVIEW
- Origins and purpose of the Act.
- Strict liability placed on producers of the product.
- Key definitions.
- Applying the Act.

This is a relatively short Act (with fourteen Sections and a Schedule). You should access the Act through the Irish Statute Book site and read the relevant sections in full with these notes. When you come to apply the Act in the task you will need to refer to the specific sections of the LDPA 1991.

3.2.1 Purpose of the Act

The Act was passed to implement EC Directive 85/374, commonly referred to as the Product Liability Directive. EC Directives aim to harmonise (or approximate) the laws of member states. The Directive is set out in the Schedule to the Act. Read through the Preamble to the Directive, which sets out the purposes of the Directive. The Directive places liability for damage caused by defective products on the producer in order to protect consumers and to ensure standards of safety across the single market. The Act was amended to cover agricultural products in 2000 following Directive 1999/34.

All member states had to implement the Directive within three years of the notification (Article 19).

It is important to note that the Act does not replace the existing remedies in tort for negligent manufacture or for breach of contract (see section 11 of the LDPA). The Act **adds** to consumers' existing remedies. Although it is a form of consumer protection law (dealt with in Chapter 7) it is more appropriate to deal with the Act here as it imposes liability in tort.

3.2.2 Main provisions

Under Section 2 the producer is **strictly liable** in tort for damage caused wholly or partly by a defect in the product. Strict liability means that the plaintiff does not need to prove that the producer was at fault or negligent.

There are limited defences available to a producer to avoid liability under Section 6.

The Interpretation section (s.1) defines key terms in the Act.

Liability is on the producer
The **producer** is:
- the manufacturer of a finished product, raw material or a component of a product; *or*
- the initial processors of agricultural products or produce; *or*
- a person who holds himself out to be the producer by putting his mark or name on the product (often referred to as 'own branding'); *or*
- the importer into the European Union; *or*
- a supplier of the product who fails to identify the producer of the product (a so-called 'forgetful supplier').

The damage must be caused by a defect in the product
Damage is defined as death or personal injury or loss of or damage to any item of property other than the defective product itself. The property must have been used for private use. The Act does not cover damage to business property.

A **defective product** is defined in s.5 LDPA 1991 as a product which 'fails to provide the safety which a person is entitled to expect, taking all the circumstances into account'.

There are some **defences** for the producer under Section 6. The main defences are summarised below. If the defendant can prove one of these defences there will be no liability under the Act.
- If a producer proves that it did not put the product into circulation (s. 6(a)).
- It is probable the defect did not exist at the time the product was put into circulation (s. 6(b)).
- The product was not manufactured by the producer for sale or distribution (s.6(c)).
- The state of scientific and technical knowledge at the time the goods were put into circulation was such that the defect could not be discovered (the 'state of the art defence') (s. 6(e)).

Small financial claims cannot be made under the Act. Claims under €500 will not be awarded damages under the Act. The consumer would have to use different legal claims.

Questions:
1. *How long after the event can a plaintiff sue under the Act?*
   The limitation period is three years after the cause of action or when the plaintiff should have become aware of the damage, defect and producer's identity. So, for example, if a person becomes ill in 2007 but it only becomes apparent in 2010 that the illness is due to a defect in a pharmaceutical product, time will begin to run from the date of knowledge that the illness was attributable to the defective product in 2010, and not from the first date of illness.
2. There is a long-stop provision which prevents claims under the LDPA being brought ten years after the product is put into circulation (s.7(2)(a)).
   Can a producer exclude liability by a contractual term for breach of this Act?
   Section 10 prevents any contracting out.

Provisions of the Act are to be interpreted to conform with the EC Directive s.1(3) LPDA

A and Others v. National Blood Authority and Others
[2001] EWHC 446

This was a case heard in the High Court in England, which was brought under the Consumer Protection Act 1987 (passed to implement the Product Liability Directive 85/374 and which contains very similar provisions to the LDPA 1991).

Facts: An action was brought by a number of people infected by the hepatitis C virus following blood transfusions given to them during medical treatment from 1988 to 1991. The product in question was blood.

The Act was interpreted in line with the spirit and purpose of the Directive. The case pivoted on two issues.

First, whether the blood was defective. The definition of a defective product, 'when it does not provide the safety which a person is entitled to expect, taking all circumstances into account', was analysed by the court. The judge focused on consumer expectations. As no warnings or information about the risks had been given the public could not be said to have been informed or accepted that some batches of blood could be defective and contain harmful viruses. The consumer expectation was that the product was safe.

Second, the defendants argued that they had a defence in that 'the state of scientific and technical knowledge at the time ... was not such as to enable the existence of the defect to be discovered'. Although the risk of hepatitis C in blood products was known at the time, the defendants relied on the absence of an effective screening test for the particular batches of blood products which were the source of the damage caused to the plaintiffs. The judge rejected this defence and said that as the relevant defect was a **known risk** and the goods were supplied despite the fact that the producer is unable to identify whether the defect will occur in any of the products the defendants could not rely on this defence.

The defendants were found liable to the plaintiffs for breach of the Act.

PROBLEM QUESTIONS

These questions ask you to apply provisions of the LDPA to different scenarios. You should read the Act and apply the key sections to the facts.

A. A Ltd have been developing a prototype scooter which runs on biofuel. Three weeks ago, ten of the prototypes were stolen. Barry bought one of the scooters after seeing a newspaper advertisement. He paid €600 to S. Unfortunately the scooter overheated last week and caused burns to Barry's ankles and ruined his new trainers worth €200.

Question: Advise Barry whether he could sue A Ltd under the Liability for Defective Products Act 1991.

Key Points: Under Section 2 of the Act the producer shall be liable in damages in tort for damage caused wholly or partly by a defect in the product. The Act imposes strict liability. The producer cannot escape liability by showing it exercised reasonable care.

Barry has suffered damage due to a defect in a product. He has suffered personal injury and damage to property (Section 1).

However, A Ltd has a defence under Section 6 of the Act. A Ltd will be able to prove that the scooters were stolen and therefore the producer (A Ltd) did not put the goods into circulation under s.6(a). In addition the product (prototype) was not manufactured for sale or distribution under s.6(c).

> B. Lornlite Ltd import new sit-on lawnmowers from the US manufactured by USit Corp. Donal bought a lawn mover from his local shop Elp Ltd three months ago. One day he lent his lawnmower to Anne, his neighbour. While she was using the machine the steering mechanism broke and the machine drove down a steep bank and crashed. The lawnmower was a write-off and Anne broke her ankle badly and was unable to work for six weeks (she is a self-employed personal fitness adviser) and lost six weeks' pay.

Questions:
1. Advise Anne as to whether there is liability under the Liability for Defective Products Act 1991 and which person(s) could be liable.
2. Could Donal use the Act to claim back the cost of the lawnmower from Elp Ltd?
3. If Anne and Donal lived in Finland and the same purchase and incident had happened there, would they have any remedies under EU law?

Key Points:
1. The lawnmower is a product under the Act (s.1). The product appears to be defective under section 5 as it has failed to provide the safety which a person is entitled to expect. The lawnmower was new and was being used appropriately and the steering failed. Under section 4 Anne must prove the product was defective and it caused the damage. She should ensure Donal preserves the machine. She could get an independent engineer's report to do this to prove the defect.

Anne has suffered damage under section 1. She has suffered personal injury and also financial loss due to her absence from work.

The producer is liable for damages in tort for damage caused by the defective product under section 2. If Anne requests the supplier (Elp Ltd, who sold the machine to Donal) to inform her of the producer of the machine Elp Ltd may notify her of Lornlite Ltd who are importers into the EC (s.2(c)). Lornlite Ltd will be the producer under the Act. If Elp Ltd fails to notify Anne of the producer then Anne could proceed against Elp Ltd (under s.2(3)). There does not appear to be any defence under section 6 that the producer could rely on.

The producer will be liable for damages in tort for Anne's injuries and losses as a result.

2. Under section 1 (b) the definition of 'damage' which can be claimed under the LDPA 1991 excludes 'the product itself' so Donal cannot use this Act to claim the cost of the lawnmower, which is a write-off.

   Donal will have to use his remedies in contract law to claim the cost of the lawnmower. (We shall look at this in detail in Chapter 5.)

3. If the same events occurred in Finland they would be covered by the Finnish law that implements the Product Liability Directive 85/374. Member states of the EU are obliged to implement Directives by the due date and therefore there will be similar remedies available to the person injured by a defective product anywhere in the EU.

3.3 Occupiers' Liability Act 1995

LEARNING GOALS

- To understand the reasons for the creation of the statutory tort.
- To explain the scope and application of key sections of the Act, to undertake a case study and to appreciate the issues surrounding the Act.

OVERVIEW

- The concept of 'occupier' and 'premises'.
- Duties owed by the occupier to types of 'entrant'.
- Concepts of reckless disregard.
- Minimising liability.
- Case law.

3.3.1 The purpose of the Occupiers' Liability Act 1995

Before this Act the tortious liability of landowners for injuries or damage caused by dangers on the land was governed by the principles created by the courts. The old common law rules were uncertain and confused, particularly with regard to the duties owed towards a trespasser. There had been persistent lobbying by landowners seeking a clarification of the law.

The Act sets out the possible civil liabilities in tort of the occupiers of premises (defined in the Act) for injury or damage caused to persons or their property due to any danger existing on the property.

The level of care owed depends upon the type of entrant. The OLA categorises different entrants as visitors, recreational users or trespassers.

3.3.2 The scope of the Act

TASK

Locate the Occupiers' Liability Act 1995 (OLA) on the Irish Statute Book site and then consider the following issues.

QUESTIONS

1. How would you define the word 'premises'? Compare this with the definition under the OLA 1995.

Key Points: Under Section 1 premises include land, water and any fixed or moveable structures on the land. Vessels, vehicles, trains, aircraft and other means of transport are also premises. This statutory definition is much wider than the usual meaning of premises.

2. How would you define an occupier? Who is classed as an occupier under the Act?

Key Points: An occupier is defined as a person exercising such **control** over the state of the premises that it is reasonable to impose upon that person a duty towards an entrant. There may be more than one occupier. Again the statutory definition is wider than the normal meaning of somebody who lives or works in the premises. Under the Act there can be more than one occupier, so an owner of a property, who has control over the property, may be classed as an occupier as well as the tenant.

3.3.3 Duties owed to visitors under Section 3 OLA

An occupier owes a visitor a duty to take such care as is reasonable in all the circumstances to ensure that a visitor to the premises does not suffer injury or damage by reason of any danger existing thereon.

Who is a visitor to a premises?
- Someone who enters the premises at the invitation or with the permission of the occupier or as of right (such as an official or member of the gardai).
- A member of the occupier's family.
- Someone who enters at the express invitation of the occupier's family or for social purposes or by reason of an express or implied term in a contract.

3.3.4 Duties owed to recreational users and trespassers under s.4

A 'recreational user' is someone who enters the premises for the purpose of engaging in a recreational activity (basically an outdoor activity) without a charge, whether or not this is with the occupier's permission or implied invitation.

A trespasser for the purposes of the OLA is any other user other than a visitor or recreational user.

Under s.4 recreational users and trespassers are owed a duty by the occupier that the occupier does not injure them intentionally or act with **reckless disregard** for them and their property.

What is reckless disregard?

Some guidelines are given in the Act itself. All the circumstances of the case must be considered:

- Whether the occupier knew or had reasonable grounds for believing that a danger existed on the premises.
- Knowledge of a person's presence on the premises and the vicinity of the danger.
- Burden of eliminating or guarding against the danger.
- Character of the premises, e.g. the tradition of open access.
- Conduct of the entrant and the level of care that could reasonable be expected of entrants.
- Nature of warnings.
- The level of supervision given or reasonably to be expected.

Although the legislation made no specific provisions in respect of children the courts may be more ready to find a reckless disregard exists in respect of child entrants. Children have a propensity towards risk, they tend not to heed warnings (even assuming they are able to read them), and they tend to be attracted by dangerous machinery, building sites and potentially risky locations.

3.3.5 The use of notices/warnings

The Act provides that notices or warnings may exclude or restrict the duty owed to visitors.

Any notice purporting to restrict or exclude liability must be reasonable and reasonable steps must be taken to bring it to the attention of the visitor. An occupier is generally presumed to have taken reasonable steps to bring a notice to the attention of a visitor if it is prominently displayed at the normal means of access to the premises.

But even a notice will only reduce the duty owed to visitors to that owed to recreational users/trespassers. The duty not to intentionally harm/act with reckless disregard cannot be excluded.

However, the existence of notices and warnings will be a relevant factor in assessing whether an occupier has acted with reckless disregard.

Notices should therefore:
- deny access if relevant (e.g. at building sites, premises after closing hours, etc.)
- be prominently displayed
- be legible
- warn of any dangers.

3.3.6 Liability of occupiers for negligence of independent contractors

An occupier of premises is not liable to an entrant for injury or damage caused to the entrant or property of the entrant by reason of a danger existing on the premises due to the negligence of an independent contractor employed by the occupier if the occupier has taken all reasonable care in the circumstances. These reasonable steps include such steps as the occupier ought reasonably to have taken to satisfy himself or herself that the independent contractor was competent to do the work concerned, unless the occupier has or ought to have had knowledge of the fact that the work was not properly done.

3.3.7 Duties under the OLA towards those entering for the purpose of committing an offence

Occupiers are not liable for injury or damage unintentionally caused to persons entering their premises for the purpose of committing an offence or who commit an offence while there, unless the court decides otherwise in the interests of justice.

Summary

The area of tort law protects a wide range of interests and rights. The law of trespass is the oldest form of tort law, and one still highly relevant today to protect rights to bodily security and property rights. The modern law of negligence started with the seemingly trite facts of *Donoghue v. Stevenson*. It changed the legal landscape. It created the 'neighbour' principle of negligence law and the concept of an expanding duty of care. The negligence concept has changed the way in which individuals and businesses anticipate and respond to situations. It made 'reasonableness' the key word in negligence. The tort of negligence has been used to give remedies to secondary victims (as well as primary victims) of incidents caused by negligence.

Although the law of negligence remains primarily a case-based subject, dependent upon precedents and persuasive authorities to guide its development, there have been legislative developments. The area of product liability in consumer safety is now a European Union issue and an early consumer protection measure was the Product Liability Directive, which Ireland implemented in 1991 as the Liability for Defective Products Act. The tortious liability of occupiers of land was clarified by the Occupiers' Liability Act 1995.

PROBLEM QUESTIONS

1. Alan and Bertie break into a glasshouse in order to steal some prize orchids. While searching the glasshouse a rotten support collapses and a sheet of glass falls onto Alan, injuring him severely. Would the occupier of the premise have any liability under the Occupiers' Liability Act 1995?

2. Clive is a surveyor who is late for an appointment. He enters a development and a sign says 'Access prohibited. Contact the Site Office opposite.' Clive is in a rush. He ignores this sign and he slips on wet boarding and breaks his ankle.
Explain whether there may be any liability under the Occupiers' Liability Act 1995.

3. Alice and Brendan are on holiday in Kerry and see a sign, 'Ancient Burial Site — Admission €6 — Apply at Farm'. They decide to look around. They pay the farmer. While they are walking on the hillside after severe rain a stone falls off the hillside and Alice sustains damage to her eye.
Discuss whether the farmer may be liable under the Occupiers' Liability Act 1995.

4. Annette goes to a concert, paying €45 for the ticket. While she is in the lobby a light fitting falls onto her head, causing a gash that requires stitches. Would there be liability under the Occupiers' Liability Act 1995?

TASK

This task involves reading one of the few reported important cases on the operation and application of the Occupiers' Liability Act 1995. Locate the Supreme Court case of *Weir Rodgers v. The S.F. Trust Ltd*

[2005] IESC 2 using the BAILII website. This important case concerned the scope of the Occupiers' Liability Act 1995, in particular section 4 of the Act and the duty owed to recreational users of premises. Read the case focusing on the questions below.

1. What was the plaintiff claiming for?
2. What did the judge in the High Court award?
3. Summarise the facts of the case in under 100 words.
4. What type of duty is owed to recreational users of premises?
5. In what way did the respondent allege the occupier had shown a reckless disregard?
6. How are recreational users defined in the Occupiers' Liability Act 1995?
7. Mr Justice Geoghegan refers to some important English and Scottish authorities (cases) to support his judgment. Name one of these cases and give the full reference.
8. Summarise the decision in *Weir Rodgers v. The S.F. Trust Ltd* in fewer than 50 words.
9. Do you agree with this judgment? Explain your answer in under 100 words.

Key Points:

1. She was seeking damages for injuries sustained when she fell down a steep cliff. The occupier/owner of the land was a company formed by the Franciscan Order.
2. After taking into account contributory negligence of 25 per cent the High Court awarded €84,666.
3. The respondent (this is the name given to the original plaintiff, Geraldine Weir Rodgers, when there was an appeal against the High Court judgment) fell down a cliff at Coolmore, Rossnowlagh in County Donegal. She fell down the slope, ended up in the water and was rescued by a friend. She sustained fractures to her left shoulder, elbow, hip and pelvis and injuries to her ankle and foot.
4. Under Section 4 of the Occupiers' Liability Act 1995 occupiers owe recreational users a duty:
   (a) not to injure the person or damage the property of the person intentionally; and
   (b) not to act with reckless disregard for the person or the property of the person.
   The Act sets down the circumstances that can be looked at in assessing whether the occupier had acted with reckless disregard (see page 5 of the extract of the case).

5. The respondent claimed that the occupier was liable due to a failure in fencing the area and/or in failing to put up warning notices.

   On appeal (in the Supreme Court) the judge pointed out the difficulties of assessing what was meant by the phrase 'reckless disregard' in Section 4. He considered that the High Court judge had looked at the ordinary standard of negligence, rather than considering the concept of 'reckless disregard'.

6. A 'recreational user' is one who enters premises for the purpose of engaging in a recreational activity without a charge, whether or not this is with the occupier's permission or implied invitation.

7. A number of cases were referred to:

   Tomlinson v. Congleton Borough Council [2003] 3 All ER 1122
   Stevenson v. Corporation of Glasgow [1908] SC 1034
   Corporation of the City of Glasgow v. Taylor [1922] 1 AC 44
   Hastie v. Magistrates of Edinburgh [1907] SC 1102.

8. For liability under Section 4 an occupier must act with reckless disregard. On these facts there was no reckless disregard as the dangers were obvious to the entrant.

9. There is no 'correct' answer to this. Issues you could raise are whether landowners should be under a duty to fence off land and to restrict public access to 'dangerous areas'; if so, how would you define a 'dangerous area'? Should all potential hazards attract notices? What would this do to our landscape? Many might view this judgment as one of common sense and limiting possible claims from accidents occurring in a natural landscape.

REFERENCES

Moore Walsh, K. (2002). *Make that Grade Irish Tort Law*. Dublin: Gill & Macmillan.
Mullis, A. and Oliphant, K. (1997). *Torts* (2nd edn). Macmillan Press.
Quill, E. (2004). *Torts in Ireland* (2nd edn). Dublin: Gill & Macmillan.

5

FUNDAMENTALS OF CONTRACT LAW

Learning Goals

At the end of this chapter you should be able to explain and apply important concepts of contract law, including:
- The definition of a contract.
- Different types and forms of contract.
- The necessary elements to form a binding contract.
- The difference between express and implied terms.
- The consequences of breach of contract and available remedies.
- The importance of key case law in this area.

The principles of contract law underpin the modern commercial world. Every aspect of commerce is regulated by contract. Sales of goods, employment contracts, sales of land, loan contracts and service contracts are all governed by contract law. Contract law has developed over the centuries by decisions of the courts. Legislation has been introduced which affects some aspects of contract law (we shall look at some terms implied by statute in Chapter 7).

Certain types of contract have been the subject of European Union legislation. The EU has legislated for the protection of European consumers from unfair terms in contracts. There are contractual requirements in relation to the fulfilment of package holidays contracts. There are detailed European Union rules as to the awarding of public service contracts and the tendering process (procurement rules).

These types of rules aside, the law on contract is still mainly contained in precedents or case law examples applied by the courts: it is a case law-based subject.

It is important to note that generally the same rules govern the formation of a contract, whether the goods or services contracted for are worth €100 or €10 million.

Overview
- Definition of a contract.
- Methods of entering into contracts.
- Oral and written contracts.
- Elements of offer: acceptance; consideration; intention to be contractually bound; legal capacity; lawful purpose.

1 Introductory Issues

1.1 Definition of a contract

A contract is a **legally binding agreement** between persons or companies (the parties to a contract) to do some act or to not to do some act where the intention of the parties is to create a legal agreement.

Question: When did you last enter into a contract?
Key Points: You may have identified a contract where you spent an appreciable amount, such as the purchase of a mobile phone or airline ticket. You are likely to enter into many contracts every day. Buying a magazine, a LUAS ticket, a coffee or gym membership are contracts. We often do not discuss the terms of the contract or the price; but these are still binding contracts.

1.2 Different methods of entering contracts

Contracts can be made orally or in writing. Individuals and businesses frequently enter into oral contracts. If you order a meal in a restaurant you are orally making a contract to pay for the food provided.

If you order an airline ticket online you are presented with written terms and conditions and a series of tick boxes. Even though you may not read these terms and conditions you are entering into a **written** contract.

Question: Identify an advantage of a written contract over an oral contract.
Key Points: One of the main reasons contracts are put in writing is for reasons of certainty and to prove the terms of the agreement.

Example: B Ltd considers it has an oral contract with Machines Ltd to manufacture a printing machine and deliver it by 12 September 2007. Machines Ltd fails to deliver on the day, saying, 'We agreed a three-week margin.' B Ltd's response is, 'The delivery date of 12 September was final and you are in breach of contract.' How would each company prove its argument? It would rest on one person's word against another. This is not a satisfactory situation for any commercial undertaking. A written contract ensures the parties must consider each term before contracting and there is written **proof** of the terms.

The general rule is that a contract does not have to be in writing to be binding. A contract may be orally agreed or may even be implied by the **conduct** of the parties. Obviously in a commercial setting most valuable contracts will be in writing as businesses prefer certainty and order in their business dealings and they will have legal departments and advisors.

There are certain types of contract that the law says must be in writing (which includes in electronic form) to be enforceable. These include loan contracts and contracts concerning land. Note that certain types of contract (consumer credit and distance selling contracts to consumers) require additional written formalities and notices to be binding.

1.3 Electronic contracts

Contracts are increasingly made electronically. The Electronic Commerce Act 2000 (ECA 2000) deals with certain aspects of electronic contracts. The Act and regulations made on foot of the Act were passed to comply with EU Directives in this area. As contracts became more frequently concluded online and across borders it became necessary to impose some common European standards in the area.

Note that many provisions of the ECA contain the phrase 'unless otherwise agreed'. This enables the parties to reach their own agreement as to what rules should apply to any contract they conclude, i.e. whether electronic acceptance will be accepted, etc.

1.3.1 Electronic Commerce Act 2000

Section 19(1) provides that:

> ... An electronic contract shall not be denied legal effect, validity or enforceability solely on the grounds that it is wholly or partly

in electronic form, or has been concluded wholly or partly by way of an electronic communication.

(2) In the formation of a contract, an offer, acceptance of an offer or any related communication (including any subsequent amendment, cancellation or revocation of the offer or acceptance of the offer) may, unless otherwise agreed by the parties, be communicated by means of an electronic communication.

This Act implements the Electronic Signatures Directive (1999/93/EC) and some parts of the Electronic Commerce Directive (2000/31/EC). The Act provides for the legal recognition of electronic signatures, electronic writing and electronic contracts (but there are some exceptions).

1.4 Standard form contracts

Consumers and businesses often contract on standard form contracts. These are prepared, standard contracts setting out the terms on which they contract with their customers. Often there is no room for negotiation when a customer is faced with a standard form contract; it is a 'take it or leave it' situation. For example, a customer has to accept the standard terms of supply of electricity on ESB's terms. Individuals are not in a position to negotiate discounts.

Question: Consider what type of standard form contracts you have entered into.

Key Points: Buying an airline ticket, the hire of a car, a contract involving transport all involve standard terms. Look at the back of a ticket and you may see a reference to 'standard terms and conditions'.

2 The Elements of a Binding Contract

For an agreement to constitute a binding contract all the following elements need to be present:

- A contractual **offer** by one party.
- **Acceptance** of the offer by the other party leading to an **agreement**.
- **Consideration**. This is a term with a specific legal meaning of 'money or money's worth'.
- An **intention to create legal relations**.

- **Capacity to contract.**
- **Lawful purpose** of contract.

2.1 Contractual offer

An offer is a statement (which can be written or oral) that indicates a party is ready to be bound to a contract if another party accepts the offer.

It can be difficult to recognise a contractual offer and it needs to be distinguished from other situations. For an offer to be contractual it must be **clear** and **certain**.

An example of a contractual offer would be. 'I will sell you my bike for €200 cash.' This offer is clear and certain.

Question: You request a quotation for house double glazing. G Ltd send you a written quotation stating: 'Quotation: Cost of double glazing approximately €15,500 (plus VAT).' Do you consider this would be a contractual offer?

Key Points: This is unlikely to be a binding contractual offer, but rather the start of negotiations about price, time of contract and other aspects. However, a quotation with words that make it clear that it is a contractual offer will amount to such (e.g. 'subject to immediate acceptance' as in the case of *Dooley v. T L Egan & Co Ltd (1938)*). It will often be a debateable issue whether a quotation is a binding offer.

2.1.1 Offers distinguished from invitations to treat

For the offer to be contractual it must not be an 'invitation to treat'. This is an old phrase used by the courts but still very relevant today. An invitation to treat is meant to convey the starting of negotiations. It could be seen as a step inviting a formal contractual offer from the other party.

Generally there are four common types of invitations to treat situations:

- auctions
- an invitation for tenders
- display of goods for sale
- advertisements are generally invitations to treat, not offers (but there are exceptions).

→ It was decided by the High Court - Dooley v T Egan that a quotati

Displays of goods in a shop are invitations to treat, not contractual offers

A display of an item in a shop window is not a contractual offer to sell at the price indicated but an invitation to treat, inviting the customer to make an offer to buy the item, which the shopkeeper may then accept. Even if the goods are displayed as 'special offers' this is a promotional term and does not make the display a contractual offer.

The authority for this point is the case of *Pharmaceutical Society of GB v. Boots Cash Chemists Ltd [1953] 1 All ER 482.*

Facts: Boots were prosecuted for breach of regulations requiring the 'sale' of certain medicines to take place under the supervision of a registered pharmacist. Boots operated a self-service system and a pharmacist at the cash desk supervised the purchase at the checkout, not at the point of selection of the goods.

The issue in this case was at what point were the goods *sold*?

The court ruled that the display of goods on supermarket shelves was not an offer but merely an invitation to treat. The offer occurred when the customer gave the goods to the person at the checkout. The taking of money by the pharmacist was acceptance. Therefore the *contract of sale* did occur *under the supervision* of a pharmacist and Boots were not in breach of the Regulations.

Question: Bridget goes into a furniture store and sees an expensive-looking rug, which she thinks may have been wrongly priced at €100 instead of €1,000. She carries it to the checkout desk and hands over €100. The cashier realises it has been wrongly priced and says that she cannot sell it to her at €100. Suzanne tells her that under contract law the shop must sell it to her at this price. Is Suzanne correct?

Key Points: The displayed rug is only an invitation to treat. By taking it to the cash desk Bridget is making an offer to buy it at that price. The cashier has rejected that offer and contractually she is entitled to do this.

(*Note*: misleading or false pricing, when it is deliberate, may have consequences for the seller under the Consumer Protection Act 2007; in addition, knowingly and dishonestly obtaining goods at a lower price may have criminal consequences.)

An offer can be made to a number of people at one time, for example an offer in a newspaper. The next case is one of the most famous in contract law and, although the facts may seem rather old-fashioned now, the case is still highly relevant as it contains key points about contractual offers.

Carlill v. Carbolic Smoke Ball Co. [1893] 1 QB 256
Facts: The Carbolic Smoke Ball Company placed advertisements in newspapers promising to pay £100 to any person who, having used the defendant's smoke ball product, caught 'influenza, cold or any disease caused by taking cold'. Mrs Carlill bought the smoke ball preparation, used it as the directions indicated and then caught influenza. She sued for the promised £100.
Issue: Was the advertisement a contractual offer or was it just an extravagant statement made as part of a publicity stunt?

The court decided that this was a contractual offer made to everyone. The company was contractually bound to anyone who accepted that offer and Mrs Carlill recovered £100.

In the 1990s the Hoover company advertised a free flights offer promising free flights to Europe and the US to purchasers of Hoover products costing over £100. The company was inundated by people wanting to take up the offer. The contractual offer was massively popular and Hoover were contractually bound to honour their advertisement. It cost them many millions.

To control the cost and scale of take-up of advertisements, companies advertising on the radio or in newspapers or on the internet will now typically make the offers **conditional** by including words such as 'While Stocks Last', 'Subject to Terms and Conditions', 'See in store for terms of this offer'. This means the offer is conditional and terms can be changed to match demand, etc., to prevent the Hoover scenario.

2.1.2 The duration of a contractual offer

The long-standing rule of contract is that an offer can be revoked (ended) by the offeror at any time up until the offer has been accepted. The revocation of the offer must be brought to the attention of the offeree.

Some types of contractual offer may be required to remain open for a certain time if consideration (see below) has been provided.

For example, S offers B an option to purchase a piece of land before 17 October 2008, provided B sells him a plot of neighbouring land. In this case S may be contractually bound to keep the offer/option open and if he revokes the offer he will be in breach of contract.

2.1.3 Termination of a contractual offer

In addition to an offeror revoking the contractual offer (see above) there are other circumstances when an offer may lapse:

- after a specified time or, failing a specified time, after a 'reasonable time'
- if it is rejected (see the *Hyde v. Wrench* case below).

2.2 Acceptance of a contractual offer

OVERVIEW

- Valid acceptance of a valid offer creates a contract (provided all other elements are present).
- The acceptance must match the offer.
- Acceptance must generally be communicated to the other party.
- The timing of effective acceptance.
- Postal acceptance and other forms of acceptance.
- Offers which may be accepted by conduct.

2.2.1 The acceptance must match the offer

For a contract to come into existence a contractual offer must be accepted by the other party. Acceptance may be oral, written (including electronically) or inferred from conduct, e.g. the delivery of goods may be acceptance of an offer to buy.

Example: Marie calls up her usual local oil supplier. She wishes to order 1,000 litres. She leaves a message on the telephone asking for delivery the next day. The oil is delivered next day and an invoice left at her house. There has been acceptance of the contractual offer by delivery, even though there was no direct communication between the parties.

If the 'acceptance' does not mirror the terms of the offer it is not a valid acceptance to form a contract, but merely another step in the contractual negotiation. An old case illustrates this point and the key point of law is the same nearly 170 years later.

Hyde v. Wrench [1840] 3 Beav 334

1. The defendant offered to sell land to the plaintiff for £1,000 (a contractual offer).
2. The plaintiff replied he would pay £950.
3. The defendant refused to sell so the plaintiff wrote that he would pay the original price of £1,000.
4. The defendant still refused to sell and the plaintiff sued for breach

of contract and argued that he had accepted the initial offer and had a binding contract.

The court ruled that the offering of £950 was a counter-offer or, to put it another way, a rejection of the first offer.

The plaintiff had made an offer to buy for £950, which replaced the original offer, and this had been rejected.

In a business setting there may be so much negotiation or haggling, with offers and counter-offers, that the actual terms of the contract may be difficult to identify. Many businesses do business on the basis of 'standard forms'.

These are pre-printed contracts with appropriate blanks (and often contain clauses excluding liability for breach of contract), which may be sent to customers with quotations, acceptance notes, price lists, contractual documents and delivery notes. The other party may send back their own form of standard form contract which has different terms. There can be difficulties over which standard form governs the contract.

If there is a **request for further information** this may have no contractual effect.

This is a common situation in the business setting where requests for further details on contractual terms, etc. happen as a matter of course.

Stevenson v. McLean [1880] 5 QBD 346
1. The defendant offered to sell iron to the plaintiff at a sum per ton at a cash price.
2. The plaintiff replied asking whether the defendant would be prepared to accept the per ton price for delivery over a period of time — i.e. for credit terms.
3. When the defendants did not reply the plaintiffs replied accepting the first offer.

The Court ruled this was not a counter-offer but merely an enquiry asking for a variation in the contract terms. The plaintiff had accepted the offer and the defendant was contractually bound to sell according to the offer.

Acceptance is judged in an objective sense. The court will assess whether a reasonable person would interpret a response as being an agreement to buy the goods at a price (followed by an enquiry as to method or flexibility of payment) or whether the response was a rejection of an initial offer and a counter-offer requiring acceptance by the other party. What the court is looking for is the concept of agreement between the parties.

2.2.2 Acceptance must normally be communicated to the offeror

Generally acceptance is only valid on communication (i.e. on receipt by the offeror). However, one old and important rule is an exception to this.

If the post is a reasonable method of communication the postal rule states that acceptance is effective on proper posting (and not on receipt of the letter).

Household Fire Insurance Co. v. Grant [1879] 4 Ex D 216
Grant offered to buy shares in a company. A letter of acceptance and allotment of shares was posted but never reached Grant. Grant refused to pay for the shares and was sued.

The English Court of Appeal ruled that the contract was complete when the acceptance letter was posted.

The reason for the decision was to give commercial certainty. Businesses needed to know when a contract was concluded, i.e. at the time of posting. Otherwise there would be too much uncertainty concerning whether acceptances had been received and the time when the contract came into being.

Telephone, fax or email/web offers are not subject to this general rule governing the timing of acceptance.

The general rule can also be excluded by an express term of the offer. If a contractual offer states, 'This offer will be valid for seven days from the date of this letter. Acceptance must be in writing and must be received by the seller at the premises of STU at Factory Walk, Rosseath by that date to be effective', the express terms of the offer state that the acceptance must reach the offeror to be effective. The postal rule will not apply in this situation.

In some situations the instantaneous receipt rule may apply and the contract is only complete when the offeror receives the acceptance. In the latter event, the contract is formed when and where the receipt occurred.

2.2.3 Electronic commerce

Under the Electronic Commerce Act 2000 an acceptance of an offer may, unless otherwise agreed by the parties, be communicated by means of an electronic communication (s.19(2) ECA 2000).

The time at which electronic communication is taken to have been sent is outlined by Section 21 of the Electronic Commerce Act. Where an electronic communication enters an information system, or the first information system, outside the control of the originator, then, unless otherwise agreed between the parties, it is taken to have been sent when it enters such information system or first information system.

Under s. 21(2) if a designated information system has been defined then it is taken to have been received when it enters that system (unless otherwise agreed). If no designated system is specified then, subject to contrary agreement, it is taken to have been received when it comes to the attention of the addressee.

The terms of the offer contained on the web or in the email will often displace these presumptive rules contained in the ECA 2000. The interface between traditional contract principles and the realities of instantaneous electronic communication still leave a number of issues to be resolved definitively by the courts.

Acknowledgement of receipt of electronic communication

Note that Section 20 of the ECA provides that if the originator of an electronic communication states that receipt of the electronic communication is required to be acknowledged, then until the acknowledgement is received no legal rights or obligations between the parties arise and the originating communication will be treated as if never sent (unless the parties otherwise agree).

In summary, although there is legislation governing electronic signatures and contractual aspects there is still uncertainty over the scope and application of the legislation, particularly as there is little case law on the area and much of the Act contains the provision of 'unless otherwise agreed'.

2.2.4 Silence will not amount to an acceptance

Acceptance cannot be imposed on the other party as there has to be an agreement for a contract to be formed. There has to be an act or communication on the part of the offeree to indicate acceptance.

Felthouse v. Bindley [1862] 142 ER 1037

F wrote to his nephew offering to buy his horse for £30 and included the words, 'if I hear no more about him, I consider the horse is mine'. The nephew did not reply. The horse was sold by an auctioneer to another person. F sued, trying to recover the horse.

The court ruled that F's offer to buy the horse had only been mentally accepted, there had been no **communication** of the acceptance and therefore no binding contract had occurred.

2.2.5 There can be acceptance by an act of the offeree

There can be cases where an offer can be made to 'the whole world' or a potentially large number, typically by way of a newspaper advertisement. In this type of situation the law does not require communication of acceptance. It treats the conduct or performance of the contract as sufficient for acceptance. You may see these types of contracts referred to as 'unilateral contracts'. A simple example would be 'Reward of €1,000 for finding diamond ring lost on the beach.'

In *Carlill v. Carbolic Smoke Ball Co.* Mrs Carlill **accepted** the offer of a £100 payment if she became ill after having used the preventative medicine **by buying and using the smoke ball**. She did not need to communicate her acceptance to the company.

Kennedy v. London Express Newspapers [1931] IR 532
Facts: A newspaper offered free accident insurance to registered readers. The plaintiff's wife had registered with a newsagent in Clonmel. A bus killed her and her husband claimed under the scheme.

The Supreme Court held that the free insurance was an offer made to the whole readership. The plaintiff's wife had accepted the offer by the act of registration. There was a binding contract.

2.2.6 Preventing a binding contractual offer: 'subject to contract'

This is a common phrase often used in the sale of land or buildings when the parties may not wish to be finally bound until matters such as finance, planning, surveys are resolved. In such cases the phrase may be used and it may operate to prevent a contract coming into existence until a formal contract is drawn up and signed (*Boyle v. Lee and Goyns [1992] ILRM 65 SC*). However, if a binding contract has already come into existence a letter or a statement which is later added stating that the arrangement is 'subject to contract' will not undo the contract.

TASK

The purpose of this task is to develop understanding of the elements of the law of contract by reading an important case on the subject.

The importance of determining when a contract is formed will be considered.

Locate the Supreme Court case of *Declan Kelly v. Cruise Catering and Kloster Cruise Ltd [1994] IESC 3* using the BAILII database. Read the judgment and your notes on contract and consider the following questions.

Note on the case: This is a case brought on appeal on an important procedural matter concerning the serving of legal papers on defendants outside Ireland (outside the jurisdiction). For our purposes we are concerned with the other key point discussed in the case — **when the contract was made** — and this is discussed in the first part of the judgment.

QUESTIONS

1. Who gave the judgment in the case?
2. Summarise the facts that gave rise to the case in under 100 words.
3. When does acceptance of the contract occur if contracts are made by post? Which numbered paragraphs of the judgment contain this rule of contract?
4. To which case/precedent did the judge refer when giving the judgment?
5. Where was the contract made in this case?
6. Apart from contracts formed by post, list two other means of forming a binding contract.

Key Points

1. Mr Justice Blayney gave the judgment.
2. The plaintiff was injured while working as a waiter on a ship owned by the defendant in 1991. The accident occurred while the ship was sailing off Mexico. The plaintiff argued that the accident was a result of the defendant's breach of the contract of employment.
3. Acceptance of the contract occurs in contracts made by post as soon as the letter is posted. Paragraphs 7–9 refer to the principle.
4. The case of *Entores Ltd v. Miles Far East Corporation [1955] 2 QB 327.*
5. The contract was made in Dublin.
6. Contracts can also be made orally or electronically (by email).

2.3 Consideration

A contract is a legally enforceable bargain between two or more parties. 'Consideration' is an example of a word that has developed a specific legal meaning. Consideration in this context does *not* mean a chance to view and consider the terms of the contract. It means 'money or money's worth' and is often described as involving a benefit received by a party or some detriment suffered by a party which makes the contract enforceable.

In the normal contractual situation the consideration is generally the **price**. A promise alone is not a contract; there must be another element. For example, I promise to give you my bike. If I change my mind, you cannot sue me for the bike. You have provided nothing in return for my promise of a gift. In contractual terms you have provided no *consideration*.

However, if I promise to sell my bike to you for €150 and you agree, this is a contractual promise as you have promised consideration (cash) in exchange for the promise to sell the bike.

2.3.1 Contracts by deed

Certain contracts which have no consideration can be enforceable if made by a deed. Examples of this type of contract include deeds of separation, deeds of covenant and deeds of gift.

2.3.2 Forms of consideration

As well as money consideration the courts recognise other types of consideration that may support a contract.

Example: Craig promises to let Barry live in his house rent-free while he is on holiday for three months provided Barry feeds and walks his dogs. This house-sitting contract contains consideration. Barry obtains a promise of free accommodation for the promise of looking after the pets.

An interesting recent case concerning a free flights promotion illustrates the width of the concept of consideration.

O'Keeffe v. Ryanair Holdings plc [2003] 3 IR 228
Facts: The plaintiff bought a Ryanair flight. When she arrived at the airport she was told she could be its millionth passenger and asked if she agreed to participate in a publicity event. She was announced publicly as the millionth passenger and informed that she, together with a nominated person, would have unlimited Ryanair travel for

life. When the defendant restricted the flights she sued for breach of contract. Ryanair argued that there was no enforceable contract as the free flights were a gift.

The court found the plaintiff had provided consideration by giving up her privacy and anonymity by participation in the promotion of the prize as requested by the Ryanair and a binding contract had been created.

2.3.3 Consideration must be sufficient (but need not be adequate)

This rather confusing statement of an old legal principle means that the consideration provided must be of some value as far as the law is concerned but the consideration need not reflect the true price or market price of the transaction.

The law of contract is not designed to protect people from making a bad bargain. The principle of 'buyer beware' or *caveat emptor* can still be applied to modern-day contracts.

There are statutory provisions that protect consumers and others in certain circumstances (see Chapter 7). However, the price paid for goods, in the absence of fraud, misrepresentation or undue influence, is generally still the responsibility of the parties.

2.3.4 The giving of consideration involves giving something which is not already owed under the general law or by contract

An old seafaring case is the authority for this proposition. You may notice that many of the key principles of contract law were decided when litigation primarily concerned land, horses and ships.

Stilk v. Myrick [1809] 170 ER 1168
Facts: The plaintiff was part of the crew of a ship. During the voyage two men deserted and the captain promised the remainder a salary increase if they did not desert. The Captain later refused to pay the increase. The sailor sued.

The court ruled that the plaintiff was **already** contractually obliged to complete his voyage and not to desert and there was therefore no new consideration for the promise of extra pay. There was no contract to pay him this extra no-desertion bonus.

Glasbrook Bros v. Glamorgan [1925] AC 270
Facts: The owners of a mine requested additional police protection for the mine during the General Strike. They later refused to pay for

the protection stating that there was no valid contract. They argued that no consideration had been provided by the police as the police had not conferred any benefit on them; they were merely doing their job of maintaining public order.

The Court ruled that the police had provided more protection than was necessary under their general duties. This 'extra' element was valid consideration and there was a contract.

In modern cases the courts have been ready to find consideration in situations so as not to deprive the parties of rights. A case from New Zealand (another common law country with similar contract law principles) illustrates this.

Attorney General of England and Wales v. R [202] 2 NZLR 91
Facts: An SAS soldier signed an agreement not to publish information relating to his service in the Special Air Services. Failure to sign this agreement would result in a transfer. After serving in the Gulf, R sought to publish a book. The plaintiff applied for an injunction on the ground of breach of contract.

One of the arguments made by R in seeking to resist the injunction was that there was no binding contract as no consideration had been given in return for his promise not to publish.

The court held that by the Ministry not returning him to his unit (which they had been entitled to do before signature of the confidentiality agreement) they had provided consideration.

In an important but complex case the English courts have shown a willingness to interpret the concept of consideration widely.

Williams v. Roffey Bros & Nicholls (Contractors) Ltd [1990] 1 All ER 512
Facts: The plaintiff was a carpenter (and subcontractor) who agreed to do carpentry work for the defendants, who were building contractors. The defendants were the main contractors in refurbishing a block of London flats. The main contract contained a penalty clause.

Due to delays in work the defendant offered the plaintiff a further sum of over £10,000 to get the work done on time. The defendants did not pay the agreed extra amount. They argued there was no consideration. The judge said the principle in *Stilk v. Myrick* still represented the law, but that the application of principle could be 'refined', as where there was a real benefit which had been gained by the defendants (the reassurance that the contract would be completed and the penalty clause not invoked) this could amount to consideration. The court made it clear that there was no duress or fraud in this case which exacted the promise of the extra sum. Accordingly this was a valid contract.

Question: Donal voluntarily paints a crumbling cottage as part of a Clean up your Streets project. A month later a wealthy local shopowner, Ed, publishes a newspaper advertisement to pay for projects completed before the Clean up your Streets annual competition as this will 'attract trade and business to the neighbourhood'. Could this be a binding contract?

Key Points: A newspaper advertisement may amount to a binding contractual offer, depending upon the wording of the advertisement. *Carlill v. Carbolic Smoke Ball Co. [1893] 1 QB 256* is an authority which states that a contractual offer can be made to the whole world. The precise wording of the advertisement will be important. Donal may argue that he has accepted the offer by painting the cottage (by his conduct), as in *Kennedy v. London Express Newspapers [1931] IR 532*. Ed will argue that there was no valid consideration as the painting was completed prior to the contractual offer and the consideration element of the contract was therefore in the past, as in *Stilk v. Myrick (1809) 170 ER 1168*.

2.3.5 Some exceptions to the requirement of consideration

The requirement for consideration to be present in every contractual relationship (except where a contract is created by deed) led to some potential injustices. The situation where a person who had contractual rights but agreed to waive (or relinquish) rights or debts has created a number of different lines of case law.

In particular the principles of **equity** have been used to mitigate the harshness of the rules of consideration and to prevent exceptional types of arrangement failing due to the lack of contractual consideration. The courts have used the principle of **estoppel** to protect people who have relied upon a waiver of existing legal rights from the person changing their mind and later suing to recover their legal rights.

This is a complex area. The main points to focus on are the requirements of consideration (and the wide definition that can be given to the term); note that there are exceptional cases where the courts may use other principles to enforce contractual promises.

2.4 An intention to create legal relations

There must be an intention to be legally bound for a contract to be formed. What the courts assess is whether a reasonable person would infer that there is an intention from the course of conduct, negotiations, etc. between the parties. In a commercial setting the courts will generally find there is an intention to be bound, as contracts are the basis of the trading world. However, if the agreement arises in a family or domestic context there is often no intention to create legal relations. Generally family or social agreements are presumed not to be binding.

Question: Daniel agrees to drive his brother Rory to the airport 50km away at 4am if Rory gives him a concert ticket. Rory gives him the ticket. The night before Rory's flight Daniel decides he is too tired and tells Rory to get a taxi instead. Do you consider they intended their agreement to be legally binding?

Key Points: Although offer, acceptance and consideration are present this family arrangement is unlikely to be seen as intended to have legal consequences and will not be a contract. Some types of contract between family members are clearly drafted with the intention of being binding, such as settlements between spouses on marriage breakdown.

The court will look at the circumstances of the arrangement to see if a contractual relationship was intended.

Simpkins v. Pays [1955] 3 All ER 10

Facts: Three women shared a house. They took part in a weekly coupons competition. They agreed to send their entries on the same coupon and to share the prize money. They all contributed to the stake money. One week they won £750. Two of the victors denied the plaintiff her share. The court held there was an intention to create legal relations and a binding contract.

Question: Are you are part of a lottery syndicate? If so, what are the terms of your agreement if you win or fail to pay your stake?

A court may accept an express statement by the parties that they do not intend the agreement to have legal consequence.

Rose and Frank & Co v. Crompton & Bros Ltd [1925] AC 445

Facts: This concerned an agreement made between the defendant (a British manufacturer) and a US distributor. The defendant terminated the agreement without giving the required notice and was sued. The contract contained an 'honour clause' which stated:

> This arrangement is not entered into, nor is this memorandum written, as a formal or legal agreement, and shall not be subject to legal jurisdiction in the law courts either of the United States or England, but is only a definite expression and record of the purpose and intention of the parties concerned, to which they honourably pledge themselves with the fullest confidence — based on past business with each other — that it will be carried through by each of the parties with mutual loyalty and friendly co-operation.

The court ruled that this clause showed that the parties did not intend the contract to be legally binding.

2.5 Capacity to enter into a contract

Both parties to a contract must have **capacity** to enter a contract for the contract to be legal and enforceable.

The general rule is that all persons can enter into a binding contract. There are categories of people who do not have capacity or only have a limited capacity to contract:

- minors (people aged under 18)
- people suffering from a mental incapacity
- people who are drunk.

2.5.1 Minors

In legal terms minors are those who are under 18 years of age (Age of Majority Act 1985).

Contracts with minors

The policy of the law is to protect minors in their contractual dealings with other persons. The Sale of Goods Act 1893 section 2 provides that minors may enter into binding contracts for 'necessaries'.

Necessaries are defined in the Act as 'goods suitable to the condition in life of [a minor] .... and to his actual requirements at the time of the sale and delivery'.

This is an example of an old Act that is still in force today. Our concepts of what is necessary for under-18s have significantly changed. Many of the old cases were about the purchase of horses and clothing. Now we take for granted that people aged under 18 buy expensive electronic equipment, mobile phone services, etc.

Under the old common law rules contracts that were beneficial for the minor were enforceable, and these rules remain. A minor may enter contracts of apprenticeship, education or employment or for the minor's benefit. So a minor may enter into a contract for music lessons or gym membership.

Doyle v. White City Stadium [1935] 1 KB 110

Facts: Jack Doyle, a minor and a trainee boxer, obtained a licence to box from the regulatory board. The terms of the licence provided that if he was disqualified for a deliberate foul blow then he would lose his right to most of the purse.

Doyle was disqualified and he claimed that as he was a minor the terms of the licence contract did not bind him.

Court ruled that as the contract was generally beneficial for him it was a valid and enforceable contract.

De Francesco v. Barnum [1890] 45 Ch D 430

Facts: A minor entered into a contract as an apprentice dancer. The terms of the contract were strict and limited her right to work elsewhere, and she could not marry during her apprenticeship. The court ruled that the contract was unreasonably harsh and not beneficial to the minor. It was unenforceable.

Loan contracts

Section 1 of the Infants Relief Act 1874 provides that loan contracts to a minor are void. There is uncertainty about the precise scope of this provision. It does not apply to sale of goods contracts for necessaries supplied on credit terms, and such contracts may be seen to be **voidable**. This means the minor may end the contract. It does not apply to contracts concerning goods supplied by a minor, so a contract entered into by a 16-year-old to sell his petrol scooter to a 19-year-old on instalment terms is not caught by the provision.

Certain contracts with minors which may be valid

Certain contracts made by minors are voidable, i.e. the minor may avoid/repudiate such contracts before s/he reaches the age of 18. Examples of these include contracts to buy shares in a company, contracts involving land.

2.5.2 Other situations involving an incapacity

- Persons of unsound mind.
- Drunken persons.

Contracts made by people suffering from a mental illness may be voidable.

That is, the contract may be binding unless the party to the contract knew at the time of contract that the individual was not capable of entering the contract. If there was such knowledge the contract will be voidable.

The position is also similar if a person is intoxicated at the time of contract. A person who argues that s/he was incapable due to unsound mind or intoxication must prove the fact of his/her incapacity and also that the other party knew of the situation.

3 Contracts that are against Public Policy or Illegal

These contracts are not enforceable. The general rule in contract law is that the parties are free to contract about matters (the freedom of contract principle). However, there are exceptions to this general rule. Certain types of contract may be prohibited under statute or by common law.

Examples of contracts which the courts regard as contrary to public policy and unenforceable include contracts:

- to commit a crime, tort or fraud
- to interfere with the administration of justice
- that seek to defraud the Revenue
- that serve to corrupt public officials
- in unreasonable restraint of trade
- that contravene EU competition law rules
- pyramid selling schemes.

Case law examples of contracts contrary to public policy:
Beresford v. Royal Insurance Co. [1938] 2 All ER 602
Facts: A major took out life assurance. The policy was due to expire on a given date. He became bankrupt. Minutes before the policy lapsed he shot himself in a taxi cab in London. The personal representatives claimed under the policy. The court dismissed the claim for the life assurance policy to be honoured. Suicide was a criminal offence at the time. The court applied the principle that a person must not profit from his crime.

Question: Adam agrees with Barry that Adam will pay Barry €2,000 to 'create' a car crash and that the €2,000 will be paid out of insurance proceeds. Is this an enforceable contract?

Key Point: There may be offer, acceptance, consideration and intention, but the court will not enforce a contract with an illegal purpose. This is on public policy grounds. (This type of arrangement may also have criminal consequences.)

3.1 Contracts in restraint of trade

The phrase 'restraint of trade' is an old one. It means a restriction on the ability of a person or business to trade freely. The law in this area is still highly relevant for employees and also people who sell their businesses. Often employers and new business owners will want to protect their business interest by drafting contracts that prevent employees or former business owners setting up in business in competition with the employer and poaching former clients or customers.

Example: A Ltd is a software developer based in Dublin. It specialises in payroll software. It employs Mike, an expert in the area. He is employed on a salary of €200,000 p.a. and has a number of bonus packages. A Ltd is anxious that he does not leave the company and seek similar employment which would compete with them. A clause is included in the contract: 'The employee agrees that upon termination of the contract he will not be employed by a competitor or a potential competitor of A Ltd for a period of three years after termination.'

This is a clause which attempts to restrain the employee from trading (working) in a certain sector for a period of three years.

For public policy reasons the courts have imposed limitations on this type of clause and the general principle is that employees should be able to work freely and businesses to trade without undue limitation. Balanced against that is the legitimate business interests of employers in preventing their assets (customers, clients, etc.) being undermined by former employees.

Restraint of trade clauses will be enforceable if:

- they protect a legitimate business interest of the employer (a customer case); *and*
- they are reasonable in terms of scope including geographical scope, duration and type of restrictions.

You can read a case on this area on the BAILII website: *John Orr Ltd v. Orr [1986] IEHC 1.*

4 The Terms of the Contract

4.1 Express terms

Terms that are expressly made part of a written or verbal contract are known as **express** terms.

    Example: You go into Wheeler Dealers Limited. You are interested in buying a second-hand Skoda for €9,000. The salesperson tells you the car has 34,000 kilometres on the clock, has one previous owner and is in excellent condition. After a test drive you offer €8,500 for the car and this is accepted by the salesman.

Question: What are the express terms of the contract?
Key Points: The price, the kilometre reading, 'one previous owner' are all express terms.

4.2 Implied terms

There may be other terms of the contract which are never expressly discussed. The parties to the contract may omit terms or do not anticipate future possibilities. In such cases the 'gaps' in the contract may be filled by the courts implying a term into the contract.

    In certain types of contract there are terms implied by statute (**statutorily implied terms**). The most important set of implied terms for buyers about the condition of the goods come under the Sale of Goods Acts 1893 and 1980. In services contracts there is an implied term that services will be undertaken with due diligence and reasonable skill and care exercised under the Sale of Goods and Supply of Services Act 1980 (we look at these in detail in Chapter 7).

    The courts will imply a term into a contract if the implied term is something so obvious to the functioning of the contact that the parties omitted to expressly agree it or when it is **necessary** to make the contract work, or if the court considers the parties would have intended the term.

4.3 Standard form contracts

Consumers and businesses often contract on standard form contracts. These are prepared, standard contracts setting out the terms on which they contract with their customers. They contain express terms.

4.4 Incorporation of contract terms

Terms cannot be added to the contractual relationship after the contract is formed (unless the parties agree to vary the terms and there is consideration). The terms must be part of the contract by the time of acceptance. This is known as the principle of incorporation. Binding terms must be incorporated into the contract at the time of contract (they cannot be 'tagged on' later).

> Marion went into her local dry-cleaners. It had been newly painted and there were no notices or price lists on the wall. She left her wedding dress to be dry-cleaned, ironed and boxed for storage. The sales assistant took her deposit of €20 and handwrote a receipt because the tills were down. The total cost was €100. When she collected the dress it was ruined. The sequins had been damaged and the dye had run. She complained to the manager who told her the standard terms and conditions of the dry cleaning firm were on the wall and on the computer-generated receipt and they excluded any liability for speciality silks such as the material her dress was made of.

Question: Do you consider she may have a claim for breach of contract?

Key Points: Marion entered into a binding contract. There has been offer, acceptance and consideration. The express terms are that the dress is to be cleaned, ironed and boxed for the total cost of €100. There will be implied terms that the services must be undertaken with due diligence and reasonable skill and care exercised under the Sale of Goods and Supply of Services Act 1980 (which we shall consider in Chapter 7).

No express exclusion clauses were incorporated as part of the contract as there was no indication of limitations of liability for silks expressed by the sales assistant, displayed on the walls or any contractual documentation. The limiting clause was not part of the original contract, it was not incorporated and cannot be relied upon by the dry cleaning firm. (We shall see later that even if it had been incorporated, there is legislation protecting consumers from unfair contract terms.)

4.5 A signed contract is generally binding even if unread

L'Estrange v. F. Graucob Ltd [1934] 2 KB 394

Facts: L bought a cigarette vending machine from G and failed to read the document, signing it believing it to be an order form. In fact it was a very restrictive contract. When the machine proved unsatisfactory and unusable L sued. The court ruled that even though the defendant had made no attempt to draw her attention to the clauses and she had not read the document L was bound by the contract.

Moral: Never sign a contract without reading it. This applies to email and web-based contracts too.

(Since this decision legislation has been passed to protect consumers and businesses from unfair exclusion clauses. Consumers are given more protection than businesses.)

5 Exclusion Clauses

These can also be known as exemption clauses or limitation of liability clauses. They are clauses or terms in a contract that aim to release or exempt a party from liability for contract and also tort liability. They may also attempt to limit liability, such as: 'Any liability for breach of contract is limited to €5,000.'

The area of exclusion clauses, while they are widely used, is complex. This section gives a snapshot of some fundamental points in relation to exclusion clauses.

5.1 Identifying exemption clauses

Question: Have you seen any contractual notices or terms which attempt to exclude or reduce potential liability?
Key Points: You may have noticed signs on car parks to the effect that, 'Cars are parked at owner's risk and no liability will be accepted for loss or damage to the vehicle or contents howsoever caused.' Similar notices may be seen in sports clubs. These attempt to exclude contractual and tortuous liability.

TASK

Next time you look at a holiday brochure, use a car park, buy a ticket for an event or enter into a written contract, read through the contract (before signing it) and identify any exclusion clauses.

5.2 Exclusion clauses must be incorporated into the contract

Exclusion clauses, if valid, deprive parties of their rights. Therefore the court has adopted a strict approach in relation to these clauses. To have any chance of validity clauses must be part of the contract (incorporated into the contract) before the contract is accepted. The term must be part of the contractual package and not 'tagged on' later.

5.3 The clause must be clear and cover the relevant type of liability

If there is any uncertainty or ambiguity in the clause the courts will interpret it against the interests of the person seeking to rely on the clause. This is known as the *contra proferentem* rule.

The courts will not allow an exemption clause to defeat the fundamental purpose of the contract.

5.4 Statutory limits on the validity of exclusion clauses

To control the use of exclusion clauses, restrictions were put on their use and effectiveness in the Sale of Goods and Supply of Services Act 1980. This is an important Act because it amended existing legislation on the sale of goods, and created implied terms in relation to the supply of services by a business. The statutory protection for businesses and especially consumers will be considered in detail in Chapter 7.

6 Discharge of Contract

When the contractual parties are released from their contractual obligations under the contract the contract is discharged.

This can occur in a number of different ways, the main ones being:
1. When the contract is properly performed — when all the contractual terms are completed as stipulated, e.g. payment and delivery — the contract is complete.
2. The parties can agree that the contract is discharged.
3. If there is a breach of contract.
4. In exceptional cases a contract may become impossible to perform, frustrated by events out of control of either of the parties. This is rare and will not be discussed further.

A **breach of contract** can occur through a failure to perform a contractual term, or if the other party acts in such a way that they repudiate the contract. Generally only breach of a serious significant term (called a condition of the contract) in the contract will justify the other party ending the contract on the grounds of breach of contract.

Example: Ross has an employment contract with Eric. It is an express term of the contract that Eric will indemnify Ross for any financial expenses or losses incurred by Ross in good faith during the course of his employment. On Thursday Ross makes an error. Eric loses his temper and storms into Ross's office, shouting, 'You owe me a heap of cash due to your mess-up!' Ross could argue that Eric has repudiated the contract by Eric's actions in not abiding by the express term of indemnity in the contract of employment.

Whether or not a term is a condition of the contract will depend upon what the contract states. A court may find that an express term or implied term is a condition of the contact, as in the circumstances it goes to the heart of the contract.

7 Consequences of Breach of Contract

A breach of contract occurs when the express or implied terms of the contract are not complied with. Liability for breach of contract is **strict**. This means that it is no excuse to say, 'My supplier let me down and I cannot deliver on time.' If the parties need flexibility for this type of contingency they will have to rely on wide clauses in the contract or a valid exclusion or limitation of liability clause.

If one of the parties does not fulfil their contractual obligation there can be a number of different consequences.
1. The innocent party can ignore (waive) the breach and the contract will continue.
2. There may be a re-negotiation and variation of contractual terms, e.g. on the price or completion date.
3. A conciliation clause in the contract may be triggered.
4. An arbitration clause may operate in the contract to give a binding determination of the dispute.
5. The contract may be terminated by the innocent party and a remedy sought.

7.1 Remedies for breach of contract

7.1.1 Damages

This is the primary remedy for breach of contract. A breach of the term of a contract gives the innocent party the right to claim damages. However, if no loss has been suffered, damages will only be nominal. A breach of contract occurs when a party to the contract does not fulfil one of the express or implied terms of the contract.

Examples: G Ltd promises to deliver to B Ltd 10,000 litres of oil on 24 October at a certain price. No delivery arrives on that date. G Ltd is in breach of an express term of the contract.

C Ltd sells a table labelled as 'teak' to Derek for €4000. The following week Derek discovers the table is not teak but cleverly stained softwood.

One of the key differences between the law of tort and contract is that liability for breach of contract is **strict**. Fault or the absence of fault or reasonableness is not relevant in breach of contract. So G Ltd cannot excuse the breach of contract by saying 'it was the distributor's fault', 'my employees were on strike', etc.

The judges have developed the law on remedies. Precedents established the rules on the types of remedies available and also the assessment principles of loss.

The most common form of remedy sought is that of monetary compensation or **damages**, but there will be exceptional situations where money alone is not an adequate or appropriate remedy.

The measure of damages

The measure of damages in a contract is to put the party in the position they would have been in had the contract been properly performed. The aim of awarding damages is to **compensate** the claimant, and not to punish the defendant.

The damages claimed must not be too remote from the loss.

In addition, the person claiming must take reasonable steps to mitigate (reduce) their loss.

What is loss?

Loss includes harm or damage to the person or his/her property and/or economic position. So damages can cover personal injuries, damage to property and loss of profits.

The courts have laid down principles which limit contractual damages to:

1. Losses that directly and naturally flow from the breach of contract; and
2. Losses that were in the reasonable contemplation of the parties at the time the contract was formed.

Example: K Theatre Ltd hires Ms C. Lebrity as their star billing for a Christmas show. The contract is for a run of a minimum of two months. Three weeks before the show Ms Lebrity informs them she will be unable to fulfil her contract as she has been offered a part in a Hollywood film.

K Theatre can sue for breach of contract. They cannot claim the entire loss of the show, profits, abortive expenses, etc. They would be expected to reasonably mitigate their loss by using an understudy or employing a replacement actor. They could sue Ms C. Lebrity for damages for extra costs in finding a replacement, the loss of the star billing advertising revenue and loss of profits.

7.1.2 Injunction

An injunction is ordered to prevent or stop the infringement of a legal right. Injunctions as a form of remedy were created by the courts of equity to reduce the hardship that could be caused by the strict rules of common law on damages. There are strict procedural rules relating to the grant of an injunction. If an injunction is disobeyed it can lead to a committal to prison. An injunction will only be awarded where damages would be an inadequate remedy. There is no right to an injunction; its grant is always within the discretion of the court.

7.1.3 Specific performance

This is a remedy for breach of contract which compels the party in breach to complete the contract. It will only be granted by the court where the subject matter of the contract is unique and cannot be acquired on the market from a different seller. It is a discretionary remedy. Typically it can be used in contracts for land (every parcel of land is unique) or unique items such as paintings.

Example: D contracts with G to sell him a famous painting by Whistler for €2m. If D breaks the contract G may not be content to sue for damages. He may want the contract of sale of this unique painting to be enforced.

7.1.4 Pre-assessed or liquidated damages

In certain types of commercial contract (construction contracts being an example) the parties themselves may anticipate the results of a breach of contract and may have a clause in the contract which sets down the damages that will be payable, e.g. for late delivery of contract goods or for failing to complete a job on time. These are known as liquidated damages.

The courts will enforce these types of clause provided the clause is calculated to be a genuine assessment of anticipated losses and not merely a penalty to ensure performance.

8 Time Limits for Contract Claims

The right to sue for rights under contract does not last forever. In order to impose certainty and deadlines the law sets down limitation periods. If an action is not commenced within these time limits it is said to be statute barred. Generally the right to sue for breach of contract ends six years from the date of the breach of contract (the Statute of Limitations 1957 as amended).

In certain situations the limitation period can be extended by the court.

If the contract is by deed, the limitation period is 12 years.

Summary

The area of contract law is a huge area. In this chapter only the fundamental elements can be covered. The key to dealing with academic and real-life contract law problems is to have a structured approach and analyse each element. If you are not sure about one of the stages you can still proceed to deal with the next stage. This is why lawyers argue 'in the alternative' before a judge/arbitrator. For example, 'In the event the exclusion clause is incorporated into the contract, the following provisions of the Sale of Goods and Supply of Services Act 1980 may apply ...'

A suggested approach to some contract issues

1. Are the elements of a binding contract present? Generally this will be clear with the scenarios you are presented with. Briefly outline the elements unless there is a real issue of whether there is an intention to create legal relations, consideration being given, in which case deal with the particular issue in more detail.
2. Identify or classify the type of contract. For example, is it a contract for sale of goods (covered by the Sale of Goods Act 1979) or a contract for work and materials (covered by the Sale of Goods and Supply of Services Act 1980)? (These are discusssed in Chapter 7.)
3. Identify the relevant terms of the contract:
   - express terms (written or oral)
   - implied terms, which may be either:
     - ♦ implied by a relevant statute such as the Sale of Goods Acts (e.g. the term 'merchantability', see Chapter 7); or
     - ♦ implied by the court (e.g. by a course of dealing between long-standing business parties).

4. Identify any breach of the contract. (There may be multiple breaches of the contract.) For example, the goods may not be of the specified quality and were not delivered on time.
5. Check whether there is a valid exclusion clause incorporated into the contract protecting the seller from liability. There is legislation governing the validity and/or fairness of many exclusion clauses. (See Chapter 7.)
6. If there is no exclusion clause or if the exclusion clause may be ineffective or void there is an actionable breach of contract. What are the available remedies?
7. The usual remedy is damages. Explain the principles the court uses to assess whether damages are recoverable, and apply them to the facts.

QUESTIONS

1. Briefly outline the elements required to form a binding contract. Give case law in support of your answer. Your answer should be brief.
2. Explain the law concerning the timing of acceptance of a contractual offer, giving case law authority to support your answer.
3. What problems do you think internet shopping can cause in relation to traditional contractual principles?
4. Define the term 'consideration' in contract law and explain how the courts have adopted a wide interpretation of this term.
5. Explain the difference between express terms in a contract and implied terms.
6. Briefly define the purpose of an exclusion clause.
7. What does the phrase 'strict liability' mean in relation to a breach of contract?
8. Referring to your earlier notes (see Chapter 3), where would a contractual dispute between companies for the following amounts be heard?
   a) €5000
   b) €50,000
   c) €5 million.
9. What is the measure of damages in a breach of contract action?
10. What is an order for specific performance?

REFERENCES

Clark, R. and Clarke, B. *Contract Cases and Materials* (3rd edn). Dublin: Gill & Macmillan.

Doolan, B. *Principles of Irish Law* (6th edn). Dublin: Gill & Macmillan.

Law Reform Commission. *Report on Minors' Contracts*. LRC 15-1985

6

ASPECTS OF CRIMINAL LAW

Learning Goals

At the end of this chapter you should be able to demonstrate an understanding of some principles of criminal law, including:
- Terminology and classification of offences.
- The role of the criminal courts in the legal framework.
- Some defences to criminal offences.
- Aspects of constitutional protection concerning criminal law.
- The location of criminal law statutes and case law.

You should also be able to:
- Apply key principles to a set of facts.
- Research topical debates concerning criminal law.

OVERVIEW

The law and order debate is always near the top of the political agenda in Ireland. The area of criminal law is vast, but this chapter gives a snapshot of some key concepts. In order to discuss terms and apply aspects of the law we shall focus on some specific offences:
- criminal damage, under the Criminal Damage Act 1991
- theft, under the Criminal Justice (Theft and Fraud Offences) Act 2001
- assault offences, under the Non-Fatal Offences Against the Person Act 1997.

In Chapter 1 we looked at distinctions between civil and criminal law. You may like to refresh your memory of these distinctions now. You will recall that generally the law requires some sort of 'mental element' (*mens rea*) to attach criminal liability. Usually the defendant has to **intend** to commit the criminal action or to be **reckless** as to whether the act is committed. In addition, the defendant must have committed a guilty act or omission (*actus reus*).

Example: Bertie lights a fire at the bottom of his garden. He wants it to spread and burn down his neighbour's shed, as the shed is blocking the light from the bottom of his garden. The act of lighting the fire with that intention may make him liable for a number of offences.

1 Some Classifications of Criminal Offences

Under the Criminal Law Act 1997 offences that carry a penalty of at least five years' imprisonment are classed as **arrestable** offences and a suspect may be arrested by a garda without a warrant.

Minor offences are known as **summary** offences and are tried by a judge in the District Court. They carry a maximum sentence of 12 months' imprisonment for one offence.

Non-minor offences are known as **indictable** offences. These are tried by a jury in the Circuit Court or the Central Criminal Court. In certain cases indictable offences can be heard by a District Judge, if both sides consent and the judge considers it a suitable case to be heard summarily.

In special cases connected with certain scheduled offences or with subversive elements the trial may occur in the Special Criminal Court without a jury and with three judges. Refer to Chapter 3 to refresh your memory on the Irish court structure.

2 Burden and Standard of Proof in Criminal Trials

A fundamental difference between civil and criminal law is that the state prosecutes the offence before the relevant criminal court. The prosecution must prove all the elements of the offence beyond reasonable doubt. If one of the elements of the offence is not proved beyond reasonable doubt the defendant is entitled to an acquittal.

In some offences the defendant may have to prove an element of his or her defence, and in such cases the defendant need only prove the defence on the balance of probabilities, as under the Misuse of Drugs Act 1977, when the defendant may seek to prove on the balance of probabilities that he or she did not know that what he or she had in his possession was a controlled drug.

3 The Mens Rea Requirement in Criminal Law

A guilty mind is generally required for criminal liability. In *The People (DPP) v. Murray [1977] IR 360* Walsh J. said:

> It is well established that, unless a statute either clearly or by necessary implication rules out *mens rea* as a constituent part of a crime, a court cannot find a person guilty of an offence against the criminal law unless he has a guilty mind.

The type of mental element that needs to go with the criminal action will vary from offence to offence, a factor which can make criminal law complicated. Words such as 'knowingly', 'intent', 'recklessly' and 'dishonestly' are all used to describe different mental elements. The prosecution must prove beyond reasonable doubt that the defendant had this state of mind at the time he or she committed the act or omission.

The central importance of the mental guilt requirement has been emphasised a number of times by the Supreme Court.

In the Matter of Article 26 of the Constitution and *In the Matter of the Equality Bill 1996 [1997] 2 IR 321* the Supreme Court ruled that a provision which sought to criminalise an employer for discrimination or victimisation of an employee without any criminal intent was contrary to Article 38.1 and Article 40.1 of the Constitution and was therefore unlawful. The Bill was amended to ensure its constitutionality before being enacted as the Equality Act 1998.

In the recent Supreme Court case of *C.C. v. Ireland [2006] IESC 33* the court ruled that s.1(1) of the Criminal Law Amendment Act 1935 was unconstitutional because the offence of statutory rape created by the provision did not allow for any defence of reasonable mistake to be raised by the defendant. Effectively it created a strict liability offence. Mr Justice Hardiman stressed the 'central importance of a requirement for mental guilt before a conviction of a serious criminal offence and the central position of that value in a civilised system of justice'. Legislation enacting the Criminal Law (Sexual Offences) Act 2006 was rushed through the Oireachtas to remedy the defect in the 1935 legislation.

3.1 Strict liability offences

Minor criminal offences can be drafted so as not to require proof of a guilty mind. The prosecution needs only to prove the *actus reus* of these offences. These are known as **strict liability offences** and are generally regulatory offences. These are actions which are prohibited in the public interest and carry a penalty. Examples include traffic offences. It is an offence under Section 3 of the Road Traffic Act 2006 to hold a mobile phone while driving a mechanically propelled vehicle in a public place (there are narrow exceptions and defences in the case of emergencies).

4 Identifying the Elements of Criminal Offences

When looking at criminal offences you need to analyse each element of the offence. Key words may be defined in the legislation. Other words will have been defined by the courts.

Question: Identify the *actus reus* and the *mens rea* of the offence of assault causing serious harm below.

(A reminder: the *actus reus* is the act or omission that forms the subject of the offence.)

Section 4 of the Non-Fatal Offences Against the Person Act 1997:

> 4 (1) A person who intentionally or recklessly causes serious harm to another shall be guilty of an offence.
> (2) A person guilty of an offence under this section shall be liable on conviction on indictment to a fine or to imprisonment for life or to both.

Key Points: The *actus reus* is the act of causing serious harm to another. The *mens rea* of the offence is **intentionally** causing or **recklessly** causing the harm.

Question: What terms of this offence require definition to fully explain the scope of the offence?
Key Points: The concept of serious harm needs to be defined. We need to be clear about what needs to be proved for 'intention' or 'recklessness'.

'Serious harm' is defined in Section 1 of the Non-Fatal Offences against the Person Act as:

> ... injury which creates a substantial risk of death or which causes serious disfigurement or substantial loss or impairment of the mobility of the body as a whole or of the function of any particular bodily member or organ.

Intention is a concept which is not defined in statutes. It is an issue which the jury (in the Circuit Court and Central Criminal Court) or the judges (in the District Court and Special Criminal Court) decide. In the case of a charge of assault causing serious harm (as above) the relevant Circuit Court would hear the action.

The law generally presumes that people intend the natural and probable consequences of their actions.

If a person deliberately sets out to achieve a result they will have an intention; so if a person shoots another they are intending serious harm. The prosecution must prove the defendant has the intention beyond reasonable doubt.

Recklessness can be a more difficult concept. It is not defined in the Act; it is a concept defined by the courts. It is generally defined as acting in a way which creates an unjustifiable risk. It has a subjective element in that the court must be satisfied that the defendant had an appreciation that there was such a substantial risk (*DPP v. Cagney and DPP v. McGrath [2007] IESC 46*). It is not enough for the prosecution to prove that any ordinary person would have appreciated the nature of the risk; they must prove that the **defendant** consciously took an unjustified risk in the circumstances.

4.1 Interpreting and applying criminal law — the offence of assault

Section 2 of the Non-Fatal Offences against the Person Act 1997 (NFOPA 1997) defines the offence of assault.

> 2. (1) A person shall be guilty of the offence of assault who, without lawful excuse, intentionally or recklessly—
>   (a) directly or indirectly applies force to or causes an impact on the body of another, or
>   (b) causes another to believe on reasonable grounds that he or she is likely immediately to be subjected to any such force or impact, without the consent of the other.
> (2) In *subsection (1)(a)*, 'force' includes—
>   (a) application of heat, light, electric current, noise or any other form of energy, and
>   (b) application of matter in solid, liquid or gaseous form.
> (3) No such offence is committed if the force or impact, not being intended or likely to cause injury, is in the circumstances such as is generally acceptable in the ordinary conduct of daily life and the defendant does not know or believe that it is in fact unacceptable to the other person.

TASK A

The aim of this task is to focus on breaking criminal offences into constituent parts and to apply the law to facts.

Consider the factual situations below and apply them to the offence of assault under the Act:

Situation 1: Adam and Brian are playing darts in a pub. They have had a lot to drink. Adam aims a dart at a poster in the pub. Unfortunately he misses and hits Carl in the neck.

Situation 2: Declan is watching his son playing Gaelic football in a junior cup match. He becomes angry with the referee and approaches him, threatening, 'I'll level you if you don't blow up now.'

Situation 3: Julie needs to get into Dublin on the train for an interview. The train is packed but she pushes her way onto the train and shoves Fiona, who stumbles into Greg, breaking his glasses.

Situation 4: Daniel is a rugby player. After a match he is confronted by an opposing team member, Jonathan, who starts to punch him in the shoulder. Daniel hits back to protect himself and knocks out Jonathan's front teeth. Daniel is prosecuted for assault contrary to section 2.

Key Points: There may be a number of alternatives in each scenario. The law is open to interpretation and if every application of the law was clear-cut there would be fewer appeal cases and far fewer lawyers. If you consider the law is open to interpretation, state this view and give your reasons and alternative interpretations. When a prosecuting or defence lawyer prepares a case they need to be aware and anticipate arguments raised by the other side so that they can address the issue.

Situation 1: Adam has indirectly applied force (by the dart) under s.2(1)(a) NFOAPA 1997 to Carl. Although he did not intend to hit Carl the prosecution will argue that he realised there was a risk if he threw a dart in an area other than the dartboard area that he would hit a person. The prosecution may argue that he was reckless in his actions. The fact that he was drunk will not act as a defence. The prosecution must prove the facts of throwing and the mental element beyond reasonable doubt to secure a conviction.

Situation 2: Declan has threatened a referee. Under s.2(1)(b) the threat could constitute an assault as he has caused the referee to believe on reasonable grounds that he is likely to be immediately subjected to force if he does not stop the match. The prosecution will argue that Declan intended to cause this belief by his threats.

Situation 3: Julie has directly applied force to Fiona and indirectly applied force to Greg under s.2(1)(a). However, under s.2(3) Julie will argue that there was no intention or likelihood of causing injury and in the circumstances pushing is generally acceptable in rush-hour conditions and that Julie did not know or believe that it would be unacceptable. The issue will be whether the prosecution can prove that she was reckless in her approach.

Situation 4: Daniel has directly applied force to Jonathan. He intended to hit him, so some elements of s.2(1)(a) are satisfied. However, Daniel may argue that he had a lawful excuse and acted in self-defence. Section 18 of the Act outlines the justifiable use of force.

Task B: The Criminal Damage Act 1991

The aim of this task is to familiarise you with the language and structure of a relatively short criminal statute. Using the Irish Statute Book website locate the Criminal Damage Act 1991 and answer the questions below.

Look at the Arrangements of Sections and you will notice the usual format. Section 1 is the Interpretation section: it contains the definitions and use of terminology in the Act. Section 2 is the main section, dealing with the offence. Section 3 deals with threats to damage property. Section 6 deals with the issue of lawful excuse.

Questions

1. List the various offences you identify under Section 2 of the Act.
2. Identify the definition of 'property' under the Act.
3. What is the definition of 'data' and where is this definition contained in the Act?

Key Points

1. Under Section 2(1) it is an offence without lawful excuse to damage any property belonging to another, intending to damage any such property or being reckless as to whether any such property would be damaged.

   Under s.2(2) it is an offence without lawful excuse to damage any property, whether belonging to another or to her/himself intending or being reckless as to whether any property would be damaged AND intending by the damage to endanger the life of another or being reckless as to whether the life of another would be thereby endangered.

   Under s.2(3) it is an offence if a person damages property (whether belonging to himself or another) with an intention to defraud.

2. Property covers tangible property (things), whether real or personal, including money and animals that are capable of being stolen, and data. The definition is found in Section 1(1) of the Act.

3. Data means information in a form in which it can be accessed by means of a computer and includes a program. Section 1(1).

5 Theft

Under s.4(1) of the Criminal Justice (Theft and Fraud) Offences Act 2001 a person is guilty of theft is he or she:

> dishonestly appropriates property without the consent of its owner and with the intention of depriving its owner of it.

Question: Identify the *mens rea* and *actus reus* of this offence. A tabular form may be useful for this.

Mens Rea/Guilty Mind	Actus Reus/Criminal Action

Key Points	
Dishonestly	Appropriation of property
Intention of depriving owner	Without the owner's consent

Appropriates is defined in Section 4(5) as 'usurps or adversely interferes with the proprietary rights of the owner of the property'.
Depriving: means 'temporarily or permanently depriving' the owner (s.4(5)). So if Adam, a 'joyrider', takes Bernie's car without her consent for a few hours Adam can be charged with theft under the Act.
Dishonestly: without a claim of right made in good faith. This is defined in section 2.
Without consent of the owner: the prosecution must prove that the appropriation happened without the freely given consent of the owner.

5.1 Defence to the charge of theft

There is a defence to a charge of theft under s.4(2) if the defendant can show that he or she had an honest belief that the owner had consented or would have consented if the owner had known of the appropriation and the circumstances surrounding it. This is a defence the defendant must prove on the balance of probabilites and if he/she does this there will not be criminal liability. The presence of reasonable grounds for such a belief is a matter to which the court or jury shall have regard, in conjunction with any other relevant matters, in considering whether the person believed he had consent.

In real life, a criminal trial turns on the nature and extent of the facts and whether a witness or a defendant is believed. In studying elements of criminal law and preparing responses you should deal with the facts as given. If you are told the defendant is asserting something you should deal with the situation if she or he can prove this. You should also deal with the situation if the assertion is false.

> Sean takes Brian's car from Brian's garage one evening while Brian is on holiday. Sean needs to pick up his brother from the airport. He has never been permitted to use the car before but since he has just passed his driving test and has insurance he feels sure Brian will not mind and will not find out in any event.

Question: Advise Sean whether he could be guilty of theft as defined in the Act.

Key Points: Sean has appropriated the car under s.4 as he has taken it. The prosecution must prove all the elements of the offence. The prosecution may be able to show he had an intention to deprive the owner. However, it will be difficult for the prosecution to prove beyond reasonable doubt that Sean was dishonest. Sean will argue that he had a genuine belief that he thought the owner would have given consent given the circumstances.

When reading the situation above your reaction may have been, 'Sean should never have been prosecuted for theft on those facts.' This is true. The facts were given to practise identifying and applying elements of the offence. Whether or not a prosecution is brought is of key importance to a defendant, the victim and society in general. This is the important function of the Director of Public Prosecutions.

6 The Decision Whether or not to Prosecute

Not all criminal offences are detected, reported or solved. If there is an investigation and the Gardaí (or another investigating authority such as the Revenue Commissioners) identify a potential defendant a decision has to be made whether to prosecute and the nature of the charge against the accused.

Task: Access the website of the Office of the Director of Public Prosecutions, select 'Publications', then 'General Information' and then 'Role of the DPP'. Read through this short, informative document focusing on the following issues:
- The factors the DPP's office takes into account in deciding whether or not to prosecute an offence.
- The range of people permitted to contact the DPP's office concerning a case.
- Whether the DPP gives reasons for the decision and whether they can be challenged.

7 Some Elements of the Criminal Trial Process

The procedure in a criminal trial will vary. If the defendant pleads guilty then the court will proceed to sentencing after hearing a plea in mitigation by the legal representative of the defendant. The judge may adjourn the case for reports to be made before making a decision on sentence.

7.1 The prosecution case

If the defendant pleads not guilty there will be a full trial of the issues. The prosecution will open the case and present its evidence. The evidence may be given by eye witnesses, gardai, expert witnesses such as forensic experts or other experts. Documentary evidence such as computer records or receipts may be presented by an appropriate witness. There are procedural requirements in relation to the presentation of such forms of evidence.

7.1.1 Examination-in-chief

The prosecution will ask their witnesses questions. This is termed examination-in-chief.

Leading questions, which are questions which lead to a given response, are not allowed. For example, 'Was the accused, James, running away from the shop at 8.15pm?' could be termed a leading question because it is leading the witness to say 'yes'. The question needs to be framed to elicit answers from the witness in their own words, e.g. 'Please tell the court what you saw while you were driving past the shop on the eleventh of November.'

7.1.2 Cross-examination

Once the prosecution has presented its witnesses the defence has an opportunity to cross-examine. All the parties have a right to cross-examine any witness who was not called by them. The aim of cross-examination is to elicit information that is favourable to the party who is cross-examining, to test the truthfulness of the witness and to raise doubts about the evidence that has been given.

The cross-examining counsel will challenge aspects of the witness's story that conflict with the defendant's version of events. So, for example, the prosecuting counsel may say, 'It is our contention that you could not have seen James on the day in question running from the shop and you must have been confused or mistaken as James was visiting his mother in hospital at the time.' Leading questions may be asked in cross-examination.

7.1.3 Re-examination

The prosecution then have an opportunity to re-examine their witness by asking non-leading questions to clarify or confirm any issues that may have been muddied by the process of cross-examination.

If, at the end of the presentation of the prosecution evidence, the judge is of the view that the prosecution have not advanced enough evidence to prove the technical elements of the offence, the case can be withdrawn from the jury on the grounds that there is no case for the defendant to answer. This is rare, as explained by the judge in *DPP v. Buckley [2007] IEHC 150.*

7.2 The defence case

The defence will then present their case. The sequence of questioning will be the same. There will be examination-in-chief of the defence witness, followed by cross-examination by the prosecution and possible re-examination by the defence.

The defendant may or may not give evidence on his or her own behalf.

7.3 The closing speeches

The prosecution and defence will then give a summary of the key elements of their case to the jury.

7.4 Summing up by the judge

In a jury trial the judge will sum up the evidence that has been presented and the key elements of any disputed evidence. The judge will explain the law to the jury. For example, the judge will explain what the prosecution needs to prove beyond reasonable doubt to secure a conviction. The judge will explain the required mental element for the crime (*mens rea*) and the required criminal act or omission (*actus reus*) of the offence.

7.5 Jury decision

The jury retire to reach a decision. If it is not a jury trial, but a summary trial by judge alone, the judge may or may not retire to reach his or her verdict.

7.6 Verdict

If the verdict is not guilty the accused is free to go. An acquittal is final and the accused cannot be tried again for the same offence. (There are proposals to change this position and to allow an acquittal to be re-opened if there is evidence of inference with a witness or the jury.) If there is a finding of guilt the matter will proceed to sentencing.

8 Some Defences to Criminal Actions

Provocation only exists as a defence to a charge of murder. It cannot be used to defend a serious assault or other crime (though it may be relevant to the sentencing of the offender in these less serious offences).

Legitimate force in relation to a homicide offence. Self-defence and the use of lethal force when a person is killed can operate as a complete or partial defence.

8.1.1 The lawful use of force

The common law recognised that there were circumstances when a person could legitimately use force against another person. The situations in which lawful force was permitted included: defence of oneself; defence of family and other people; coming to the assistance of a police officer; or the prevention of a criminal offence or breach of the peace. These old common law rules were formalised by the Non Fatal Offences Against the Person Act 1996.

TASK

Access the Non-Fatal Offences Against the Person Act 1997 on the Irish Statute Book website and read sections 18–20. Read the following scenario and consider how the law may apply to the facts. This is a controversial area where there will be a range of views and applications.

> Helen is a single mother of three children. She is upstairs one night and hears movement downstairs. Her mobile phone is downstairs. She believes she hears two people. There has been a spate of burglaries in the area for car keys and she hopes they will take the keys and leave. She hears them laughing and one of them seems to be moving towards the stairs. She is frightened that they may be 'high' and aggressive.
>
> She hides behind the door with a heavy bedroom lamp. When one of the men (Jack) begins to walk up the stairs she screams at him and throws the lamp at him. The lamp hits Jack's head. He falls down the stairs and is knocked out and breaks his femur. The other man (Kevin) runs off.

Key Points:

Under Section 18 of the Act the use of force by a person, provided it is reasonable in the circumstances as she or he believes them to be, will not constitute an offence in certain circumstances. Section 18 therefore provides a defence to a possible criminal charge.

Helen may argue that she was acting to protect herself and her family from an injury (s.18(1)(a)) and/or to protect herself or another from a trespass to the person (s.18(1)(b)). She may argue that the intrusion by Jack and Kevin caused her fear of the commission of a trespass to the person (to herself and/or her children) such as an assault, battery or false imprisonment (see Chapter 4 for details of these torts). Certainly she may argue that she was acting to protect her property under s.18(1)(c) of the Act. Under s.18(5) the question whether the act against which force is used is of a kind mentioned in any of the paragraphs (a) to (e) of subsection (1) shall be determined according to the circumstances as the person using the force believes them to be. It is a subjective test.

Under s.1(2) of the Act:

> For the purposes of sections 17, 18 and 19 it is immaterial whether a belief is justified or not if it is honestly held but the

presence or absence of reasonable grounds for the belief is a matter to which the court or the jury is to have regard, in conjunction with any other relevant matters, in considering whether the person honestly held the belief.

The belief must be judged from Helen's perspective, and if she honestly held the belief that she was protecting herself, family or property and that her actions were reasonable in the context she believed she was in, this will provide a defence to any criminal assault charge brought against her.

9 Criminal Penalties

There are a number of theories underlying the principle of sentencing, which have fallen into and out of favour over the years.

Retribution looks for society to avenge the criminal conduct and for the criminal to receive his or her just desserts.

Incapacitation means preventing further criminal conduct by incapacitating the prisoner. The most extreme version of this was the death penalty, which was formally abolished in Ireland in 1990. Life imprisonment is now the most severe incapacitation penalty that can be imposed.

Rehabilitation aims to reintegrate the offender into society and to prevent re-offending in the future.

Restorative justice is a victim-based approach and aims to facilitate the offender in making restitution to the victim(s). For example, an individual who is guilty of criminal damage could repair the damage. This is a relatively new model in Ireland which has been piloted in Nenagh and Tallaght. It is being developed by the new National Commission on Restorative Justice.

Deterrence: this theory states that some criminals should be made an example of in order to deter others from committing similar offences.

Question: What do you think the maximum penalty for robbery should be and why?
Key Points: Robbery is defined in section 14 of the Criminal Justice (Theft and Fraud) Offences Act 2001.

The definition of the offence is set out below for information. It involves a theft and the use of force or the victim being put in fear of the use of immediate force.

14.—(1) A person is guilty of robbery if he or she steals, and immediately before or at the time of doing so, and in order to do so, uses force on any person or puts or seeks to put any person in fear of being then and there subjected to force.

The maximum penalty is life imprisonment.

Question: If you were a judge what factors would influence the sentences you might impose?
Key Points: You may have selected a number of factors such as the age of the defendant, the age and the vulnerability of the victim, the effect on the victim, the type of force used, the previous character and convictions of the defendant, whether the defendant pleaded guilty, whether the defendant had an addiction to support, etc. All these may be relevant factors.

9.1 Sentencing

The sentence will be set by the judge, often after having requested reports on the convicted person and after hearing the plea in mitigation. There may also be a victim impact statement. The maximum sentence will be outlined in the relevant statute which creates the offence.

Generally the sentence actually handed down will be far less than the maximum. Sentencing is at the discretion of the judge. Murder carries a mandatory life sentence. Capital murder, i.e. murder of members of the Gardaí, prison officers and others, carries a mandatory sentence with a minimum sentence of 40 years (s.4 Criminal Justice Act 1990)

There are minimum sentences for some offences. In the drug trafficking area there is a theoretical minimum sentence of ten years. However, judges may give a lesser sentence in exceptional circumstances.

Although sentencing is at the discretion of the judge he or she must follow any guidelines on sentencing laid down by the higher courts. If he or she fails to do this there may be a successful appeal made to the Court of Criminal Appeal.

For some offences a presumptive sentence has been set out by the Act under s.15A Misuse of Drugs Act 1977 (as amended) and under the Misuse of Drugs Regulations a minimum mandatory sentence of ten years should be applied unless there are exceptional and specific circumstances.

9.1.1 Plea in mitigation

Following a finding of guilt by the court or a plea of guilty by the defendant the judge may adjourn the case and the issue of sentencing until medical or probation reports are obtained. The defendant's advocate, solicitor (in the lower court) or barrister (in the higher court) will make a plea of mitigation. This will attempt to persuade the judge to give a lighter sentence than the offence may appear to justify. Matters that the advocate will address are:

- The offence itself and the circumstances in which the offence was committed, e.g. if it was a non-violent impulse crime.
- The personal circumstances of the offender and any mitigating features such as family circumstances and a previous good record.
- The vulnerability of the offender due to family or financial pressures.
- The impact of any sentence on family members.
- The offender's conduct in relation to the investigation and the trial, e.g. whether the defendant co-operated, gave an early guilty plea and showed genuine remorse.
- The effect of any possible sentence and the ability of the convicted to reform.

9.1.2 Victim impact statements

These are given by the victim (or by a member of the victim's family) after a guilty verdict has been reached by the jury. They have been the subject of much controversy in recent years in a number of high-profile trials. The material published by the Office of the DPP on Attending Court as a Witness includes details of the types of cases (sexual offences and violent crime) in which a victim impact statement may be made to the court.

The Court of Criminal Appeal (the judgment was given by Mr Justice Macken) made important general comments about the scope and limitations on the statements in an application brought by the DPP in *DPP v Wayne O'Donoghue [2006] IECCA 134*. The following is an extract from the comments.

> While the legislature has provided that a victim impact statement may be given by the living victim of a variety of crimes, no such legislative provision exists for the family or friends of a victim of an unlawful homicide. Nevertheless, a practice has developed by which a sentencing judge has a discretion to permit a victim impact statement to be made in such circumstances. In the view

of this court, that is as it should be for the reasons, firstly, that such a statement can be of assistance to the sentencing judge in determining the appropriate sentence to be imposed, and secondly, because it affords the family or friends of a deceased victim, such as in the present case, an opportunity to express the loss to them arising from the unlawful homicide.

It is the view of this court that in the event a sentencing judge, in his or her discretion, permits such a victim impact statement to be made, such a statement should only be permitted on strict conditions. In particular, a copy of the intended victim impact statement should be submitted both to the sentencing judge and to the legal representatives of the accused, it being assumed that it will already have been made available to the prosecution. This must be done in advance of the reading or making of the statement itself in court so that both the sentencing judge and the accused's legal representatives may have the opportunity of ensuring that it contains nothing untoward. Assuming that the content of the proposed statement meets this requirement, the person who proposes making the statement should be warned by the sentencing judge that if in the course of making the statement in court they should depart in any material away from the content of the statement as submitted, they may be liable to be found to have been in contempt of court. If it be the case that such departure occurs and involves unfounded or scurrilous allegations against an accused, that fact may be considered by the sentencing judge to be a matter to be taken into account in mitigation of the sentence to be imposed.

Question:
What, in your view, are the advantages and disadvantages of a victim impact statement?

9.2 *Types of sentence*

The outcomes of a criminal trial are varied. There may be an acquittal, if the accused is found not guilty or the judge directs an acquittal for legal reasons in the course of the trial.

Types of sentence include:
- imprisonment
- suspended sentences under the Criminal Justice Act 2006 with or without conditions. Breach of any of the conditions re-activates the sentence

- fines
- community service
- order to attend a drug treatment centre
- order to obtain psychiatric treatment
- order to attend an alcohol awareness programme
- compensation orders (under the Criminal Justice Act 1993)
- restriction on movement orders (under the Criminal Justice Act 2006).

10 Age of Criminal Responsibility

The age of criminal responsibility is the age at which a child can be charged with a criminal offence.

Before the Children Act 2001 was amended by the Criminal Justice Act 2006 the age of criminal responsibility in Ireland was 7. This position had been the subject of criticism by a number of international bodies.

Since the amendments to the Act came into effect in October 2006 the age of criminal responsibility has been raised to 12 years for most offences. However, for the most serious offences of murder, manslaughter, rape and others, children aged 10 and 11 can be charged.

The consent of the DPP is needed for proceedings against any child under 14 years.

There is provision for the Gardaí, when they have reasonable grounds for believing a child has committed an offence for which s/he cannot be charged due to their age, to take the child to a parent or guardian.

Summary

The commission of criminal offences generally involves the prosecution proving that the accused committed the *actus reus* of the offence with the required *mens rea*. The prosecution must prove all elements of the offence beyond reasonable doubt. Criminal offences are classified as summary offences or indictable offences, and this classification determines which court will hear the case.

The decision whether or not to bring a prosecution lies with the Director of Public Prosecutions. If a case comes to trial and there is a plea of not guilty there will be a full trial. The prosecution will open the case and call their witnesses to conduct an examination-in-chief. The defence will then have an opportunity to cross-examine the witnesses and to challenge the prosecution's version of events. The defence will then open its case and call the defence witnesses and evidence. This may or may not involve the defendant giving evidence on his or her own behalf. If there is a verdict of guilty the matter will proceed to sentencing.

REFERENCES

Healy, C. (2006). *An Introduction to Irish Criminal Law* (2nd edn). Dublin: Gill & Macmilllan.

Law Reform Commission (2006). *Prosecution Appeals and Pre-Trial Hearings* (LRC 81-2006).

7

CONSUMER LAW

At the end of this chapter you should be able to:
- Explain and apply the principal rights and remedies of a consumer under the Sale of Goods Acts.
- Explain the operation of the Small Claims Court to a consumer.
- Understand the importance of identifying the seller and be able to undertake a simple company name search.
- Appreciate the significance of European Union law in the protection of consumer rights.
- Understand some important issues and law concerning sales using e-commerce or online buying.
- Understand the key provisions under the Consumer Protection Act 2007 and the role of the National Consumer Agency.
- Locate statutory provisions and sources of consumer advice using the internet.

OVERVIEW
- The contract for the sale of goods and/or services.
- The definition of a consumer.
- The implied terms under the Sale of Goods Act 1893 and the Sale of Goods and Supply of Services Act 1980 in relation to provision of goods and services.
- Rights and remedies of a consumer and the Small Claims Court procedure.

1 Contract for the Sale of Goods or Services and the Consumer

In Chapter 5 the elements of a contract were considered. We saw that in order for there to be a valid and enforceable contract there must be the following elements:
- offer and acceptance leading to an agreement
- consideration
- intention to create legal relations
- capacity to contract
- lawful purpose

In the usual course of events, when a consumer buys an item or a service there will be no issue as to whether a contract has been formed. It will be the precise extent of the terms and whether there has been fulfilment or breach of the terms which will be the source of the dispute.

1.1 Express terms of the contract

These are the terms that are expressly agreed on, either orally or in writing, such as the price, specification, delivery date, etc. They can be further classified as either **conditions** of the contract or a **warranty**.

A condition of the contract is a fundamental term of the contract and if it is broken, the innocent party can repudiate the contract, reject the contract goods and recover the purchase price and also claim damages for any extra loss. Many written contracts will specify the term is a 'condition of the contract'.

A term which is classed as a **warranty** is a binding term of the contract but usually one of lesser importance. If a warranty term is broken it generally entitles the innocent party to sue for damages. The innocent party cannot reject the contract goods or claim a full refund of the purchase price for a breach of a term classified as a warranty.

Note on terminology: This is another example where terms have a specific legal meaning in contract law, which can be confusing. A **condition of the contract** is a type of fundamental term. You need to distinguish it from a contract which is made 'subject to terms and conditions' — a contract that depends on a factors such as stock availability or the credit-worthiness of the buyer. Similarly, a term classed as a warranty means a type of contractual term which is treated as of lesser importance than a condition of the contract and which entitles the innocent party to claim damages.

It should not be confused with a warranty attached to the purchase of a car, electrical goods etc. This warranty is a separate form of limited guarantee contract that is often entered into with the seller and has its own terms.

1.2 Implied terms

A term can be implied into the contract by the court if the court considers that a term has been mistakenly omitted from a written contract. An implied term might arise by virtue of custom and practice over a period of time.

Example: For the past two years D Ltd, a small farm-based

manufacturer, has delivered bottles of organic cider to S Ltd on a sale or return basis. There is no written contract. This means that if S does not manage to sell the bottles they can return them to D and they do not pay D for these returns. Last week D Ltd sent out written contracts to 'formalise the situation'. The written contract contained a provisions requiring payment in full on delivery and no sale or return facility. S Ltd does not sign the contract and argues there is an implied term for sale and return transactions. If the parties cannot settle the terms and litigation occurs the court may find that the sale and return term was an implied term of their business dealings and D Ltd may be in breach of contract if they withdraw this facility without reasonable notice.

1.2.1 Implied terms under statute —- the Sale of Goods Acts

This is the most important source of implied terms for consumers. There are two principal pieces of legislation, the Sale of Goods Act 1893 and the Sale of Goods and Supply of Services Act 1980. Due to the difficulty of reading the two acts together and the importance of the Acts to consumers and businesses a formal Restatement of the law consolidating the legislation was undertaken under the Statute Law (Restatement) Act 2002.

Restatement of the law in the Sale of Goods Acts

This process does not alter the substance of the law, but makes the legislation more accessible and puts it into a more readable form (as it is presented in **one authoritative document**). The Restatement can be relied upon in a court of law and has been certified by the Attorney General's office.

TASK

To access the Restatement of the Acts, as this contains the up-to-date and authoritative consolidated version of the Act.

Go to the website of the Attorney General and then click on 'Statute Law Revision'. There is an option for 'Restatement'. Click on this and read the overview of the Restatement process. Then access the Sale of Goods Act 1983 and Part II of 1980 Restatement. Read the Foreword and note that the layout is in chapters and that the sections of the relevant Act are given above each paragraph of the Restatement. You still refer to the sections of the relevant Acts, for example Section 13 SGA 1893. The relevant sections for our purposes are in Chapter 1 I (the Restatement, paras 12–15, 55); Chapter 2 paras 68–71; and the Schedule.

1.3 *The definition of a consumer for the purpose of the Sale of Goods Acts*

The Acts apply to business and consumer buyers. When the first 1893 Act was passed there were few 'consumers' as we understand the term now. The Act was originally designed to impose standards on traders or merchants in their dealings with each other, hence the term *merchantable* quality, something which was of saleable quality or acceptable to a merchant. As the number of transactions grew, consumer protection from unscrupulous traders became necessary and further provisions were enacted to give greater protection to the consumer buyer.

Question: Why does a consumer need protection in the law of contract?
Key Points: You may have identified some of these or thought of additional reasons. Consumers do not have equal bargaining or negotiating power with large business sellers; often goods are sold without the consumer having a chance to see or test the goods; the value of some consumer goods may be high; consumers do not generally have easy access to legal advice before or after they buy, and would have few resources to be able to enforce their contractual rights.

The definition of a consumer is important in relation to the implied terms of this Act. The key implied terms relating to the sale of goods cannot be excluded by the seller if the buyer is a consumer. The implied terms of description, merchantable quality and fitness for purpose are absolute rights for a consumer and cannot be taken away.

The definition of a consumer is found in Section 3 Sale of Goods Act 1980. You will find this set out in the Restatement of the Act in the Schedule to Chapter 2. Alternatively you can access it through the Irish Statute Book under the 1980 Act.

TASK

Read the section and identify the following:
1. Are any types of sale not to be considered consumer sales for the purpose of this Act?
2. What are the required elements for a consumer sale?
3. If there is an issue as to whether a person is dealing as a consumer, which party has the burden of proving that it was a consumer sale?

KEY POINTS

1. Sales by auctions of goods or sales by competitive tender are not covered by the Act. Section 3(2) SGA 1980.
2. There are three cumulative requirements: the buyer does not make the contract in the course of a business; and the seller does make the contract in the course of a business; and the goods are of a type ordinarily supplied for private use or consumption.
3. The burden of proving it was not a consumer sale is for the person claiming it was not a consumer sale under Section 5(3) SGA 1893. This rather long-winded point means that it is presumed to be a consumer sale unlesss a party can disprove that it was.

TASK

Apply this definition to the following scenarios and refer to the relevant subsection in your answer:

1. Marion buys a computer-aided design package for use in her freelance business as a property developer. She buys it from C Ltd. She pays for the software using her business account.
2. Nigel buys a second-hand car from his friend Tony.
3. Lesley buys a suite of furniture for her home at a local auction.

KEY POINTS

1. Marion buys from a seller acting in the course of a business. She makes the contract in the course of her business and it is not a consumer sale under s. 3(1)(a) SGA 1980.
2. Tony is not acting in the course of a business, so this will not be a consumer sale under s.3(1)(b)SGA 1893. If Tony regularly did up cars and sold them for a profit this might constitute a sale in the course of a business and would be a consumer sale.
3. An auction sale is not a consumer sale under s.3(2) SGA 1893.

2 Sale of Goods Acts 1893 and 1980

OVERVIEW

- Contracts for the sale of goods and services.
- The implied terms under the Sale of Goods Acts 1893 and 1980.
- Applying the implied terms to a set of facts.
- Remedies.

2.1 Scope of the Acts

A sale of goods contract is the most common type of commercial and consumer contract. Contracts were originally regulated by common law principles created by the judges. As the level of trade and commerce increased in the nineteenth century it became necessary for some level of protection for buyers to be introduced. The Sale of Goods Act 1893 was the result. The normal rule of *caveat emptor* (let the buyer beware) was displaced in certain circumstance by the inclusion of implied terms into contracts for the sale of goods.

In 1980 the Sale of Goods and Supply of Services Act made significant changes to the Act and included implied terms into services contracts. The Act gives commercial buyers and consumers important contractual rights. (We shall focus on the rights of consumers in this chapter.)

2.1.1 What is a contract for the sale of goods?

This is defined in Section 1 of the 1893 Act as a contract in which 'the seller transfers or agrees to transfer the property in goods to the buyer for a money consideration called the price'.

A sale of goods contract is not a hire contract (where the hirer does not acquire ownership or property in the goods). It also does not cover contracts to buy shares, cheques, exchange contracts or contracts in relation to the sale of land.

2.1.2 What is a contract for the supply of services?

Contracts for the supply of services cover contracts that involve labour costs or professional fees. Building contracts, consultations with an accountant, solicitor or doctor are all services contracts.

Often there will be a combination of services and goods in a contractual package in that you pay for ownership of goods and for services. These can be called 'work and material' contracts. A car service involves labour and generally new parts or products such as an oil filter or oil change. A double glazing contract involves installation and the new windows. The Sale of Goods and Supply of Services Act 1980 implies certain terms into service contracts.

2.2 The implied terms in a sale of goods contract

Task: Locate the relevant sections in the Restatement of the Acts (paras 12–15).

2.2.1 The seller must be able to pass ownership of the goods to the buyer

The seller must have the right to sell the goods or the buyer can sue the seller for the price that has been paid (Section 12 SGA 1893).

Example: Bert buys an antique fireplace from Sidney for €3,000. Unknown to both Sidney and Bert the fireplace was stolen from Oliver's house. Oliver, the owner, is entitled to the return of the fireplace. Sidney is in breach of the implied term under section 12 as he is unable to pass ownership of the goods to Bert. Bert can claim the €3,000 back from Sidney for breach of contract.

This implied term applies to all sellers and buyers irrespective of whether the buyer is a consumer or trade buyer.

2.2.2 Goods must comply with their description

This is an important implied term. The term is implied into all private and business sales.

A sale by description covers goods which are selected by the buyer. Descriptions of the goods by a label or other descriptive material (e.g. a brochure) may form part of the description.

Beale v. Taylor [1967] 1 WLR 1193
Facts: A buyer bought a car from a private seller, who sold the car as a Triumph Herald 1961 1200. The car had a disc with 1200. After the sale the buyer discovered that it was not a 1961 model, but two cars welded together, and it was not roadworthy. The court held there was a breach of the implied term that goods should be as described under Section 13 as it was not a 1961 model. The metal disc was part of the description. Even though the buyer had inspected the vehicle he was entitled to damages for breach of the implied term of Section 13.

2.2.3 Where goods are sold in the course of business they must be of merchantable quality

This is the most important implied term in practice. This implied term only applies where the **seller acts in the course of business**. Under Section 14(2) there is an implied condition that goods are of merchantable quality.

Acting in the course of business: the s.14 implied term will not apply where an individual who does not act in the course of business so in the case of *Beale v. Taylor* (above) the buyer could not claim for breach of merchantable quality and had to rely on breach of description because the seller was a private seller and not bound by Section 14 implied terms.

What is merchantable quality?

Goods are of merchantable quality when they are as fit for the purposes for which goods of that kind are commonly bought and as durable (lasting) as it is reasonable to expect having regard to the description, price and all other relevant circumstances. The standard of merchantability will differ according to the type of goods. So if you buy a brand new car the standard of merchantability will be higher than if you buy a second-hand, cheaper car. Another way of explaining merchantability is whether a reasonable buyer would consider the goods to be of satisfactory quality bearing in mind all the circumstances of the case.

Situations where the implied term may not apply

The implied term will not apply where the defects are specifically drawn to the buyer's attention before the contract is made or if the buyer examines the goods before contract with regard to those defects which that examination ought to have revealed.

Question: Fionnuala buys a table lamp from Homey Habitats Ltd. She sees it is labelled 'Discounted: Display model — damaged lampshade'. She later realises it is more badly damaged that she thought. Could she argue the lamp is not of merchantable quality and in breach of s.14(2) SGA 1893?

Key Points: Homey Habitats Ltd are acting in the course of a business. However, the implied term of merchantable quality under s.14(2) will not apply as the defect has been brought to her attention and she has examined the goods and the defects would have been obvious.

2.2.4 The goods must be fit for their purpose(s)

This applies when the purpose of the goods is implicit (e.g. food is to be eaten; a camera is to take pictures). If the goods have more than one purpose, they should be fit for all their ordinary purposes.

There is often an overlap between merchantability and fitness for purpose. If the goods are unmerchantable they are also unlikely to be unfit for their purpose. If you are anticipating using the goods for a specific purpose it is often advisable to make your purpose known to the seller to have the full benefit of this term and/or to make the purpose an express term of the contract.

Griffiths v. Peter Conway (1939) 1 ALL ER 685
This concerned a contract for sale of a tweed coat. The purchaser did
not inform the seller she had unusually sensitive skin. She contracted
dermatitis and sued for breach of the implied term of fitness for
purpose. She lost the case. The court ruled she had not made her
particular purpose known to the seller, i.e. the need for the coat not
to cause an allergic reaction. In this unusual case there was no breach
of the merchantability condition or the fitnesss for purpose
conditions.

2.2.5 Goods must conform to sample under section 15

Where goods are sold by sample the bulk must correspond with the
sample. The buyer should have a reasonable opportunity to compare
the sample and the bulk and the goods must be of merchantable
quality.

2.3 The rights of a buyer

If an implied term in relation to goods is broken the primary rights
are against the seller of the goods (not the manufacturer). The
contract is between the buyer and seller. If the breach of contract
becomes apparent after a short time the primary remedy is to reject
the goods and claim a refund of the purchase price. If you have had
the goods for some time the shop may offer you a repair or
replacement product.

*Can a seller restrict the rights of a buyer for breach of these implied
terms?*
Where the buyer is a consumer then the rights under the implied terms
cannot be excluded. This important provision is in s.55 SGA 1893.

Question: How might a seller seek to prevent the implied terms from
operating?
Key Points: If a seller includes a written term in the contract or a
notice such as 'No refunds' or 'Claims are limited to €500' this is an
attempt to exclude the full operation of the Act. These are known as
exclusion clauses or exemption clauses or notices. This means that a
notice saying 'No refunds after 14 days' or 'Credit notes only — no
refunds' or 'The seller can accept no liability for defective products'
will have no effect in a consumer sale if there is a breach of one or
more of the implied terms. These implied terms are known as your

statutory rights (they come from the Sale of Goods statutes). It may also be a criminal offence to post these types of off-putting notices (Section 11 Sale of Goods and Supply of Services Act 1980). This is the reason why it is important to identify what is a consumer sale.

2.3.1 Rejection of the goods

Breaches of Sections 12–15 are breaches of conditions, fundamental terms of the contract, and the buyer can reject the contract goods and claim back the purchase price. Alternatively, the buyer can retain the goods and claim damages.

The remedies that a buyer may claim are often said to be refund, repair or replacement of the contract goods. If a buyer does want to exercise their rights to reject the goods they must do this within a **reasonable time** of purchase.

What is a reasonable time? This is a question to which there is no precise answer. Generally it will be a matter of weeks, not months, and time runs from the date of purchase, not from the date of discovery of the defect. Section 35 SGA 1893 (as amended by the SGSSA 1980) provides that a buyer will be treated as having accepted the goods where:

> ... he does any act in relation to them which is inconsistent with the ownership of the seller or when, without good and sufficient reason, he retains the goods without intimating to the seller that he has rejected them.

If the buyer is deemed to have accepted the goods then s/he is limited to claiming damages for the difference between the value of the goods as bought and the value of the goods with the defect.

2.4 *The implied terms in a services contract*

Before the 1980 Act the court would imply terms of reasonable skill and care into these types of contract. The 1980 Act implied **statutory** terms into every contract to supply services where the supplier acts in the course of a business.

TASK

Using the Irish Statute Book locate the 1980 Act and Part IV Sections 39–41 of the Sale of Goods and Supply of Services Act 1980. Summarise the terms implied into contracts for services where the supplier acts in the course of business.

Key Points:
- The supplier has the necessary skill to supply the service.
- The service will be provided with due care and diligence.
- Where materials are used they will be sound and reasonably fit for their purpose.
- Where goods are supplied under the contract they will be of merchantable quality.

2.4.1 The exclusion of the implied terms

Under s.40 of the Act these implied terms may be varied or excluded by:
- an express term of the contract; or
- the course of dealing between the parties.

Additional protection for a consumer

Where the recipient of services is a consumer these implied terms can only be excluded or restricted to the extent it is **fair and reasonable** to do so and only where the express term is specifically brought to the consumer's attention (Section 40). There are guidelines to help assess what may be fair and reasonable.

Any attempt to restrict a consumer's rights further than is legitimate under the Act is an offence under Section 41 of the Act.

2.5 Making a consumer complaint

> Rory bought an expensive analogue watch for €2,000 from Jules Ltd. Three weeks after purchase he discovers the watch is not keeping time. Rory returns to the shop and the sales assistant is unwilling to refund his money but suggests he take a replacement product. The assistant tells him he is not authorised to refund items of over €500. He asks Rory to put the complaint in writing to the manufacturer and he will 'see what he can do'. Rory considers this is unsatisfactory and leaves with the watch. He asks you to write down some points he could use in his letter.

TASK

Identify three points of law that Rory could raise to support his claim to a refund.

Key Points

1. Rory's contract is with Jules Ltd, not with the manufacturer. His primary rights for breach of contract are against Jules. The shop cannot escape liability by telling him to write to the manufacturer.

2. The shop is acting in the course of a business. The watch is not keeping time and bearing in mind the price and the fact it is new this will mean it is unmerchantable under s.14(2) SGA 1893. It is also not fit for its purpose (of time-keeping) under s.14(3) SGA 1893.

3. The seller is in breach of the implied terms. They are conditions of the contract and Rory's primary remedy is to reject the goods and claim a refund. He has rejected the goods within a reasonable time of the purchase so he will not be taken to have accepted the goods. If he rejects the goods he is entitled to a refund of the purchase price.

TASK

Go to the website of the National Consumer Agency (consumerconnect.ie). Click on 'Quizzes' on the left-hand side and try the 'Clever Consumer' and 'How to be a Great Complainer' quizzes as revision of some of the key points about implied terms and remedies.

2.5.1 Information needed to support your complaint

Identify the company/organisation that sold you the product or the service. You have a contract with the company you paid.

Research your consumer rights before complaining and ensure you have proof of purchase. This can be the receipt, bank statement or credit card statement.

Make your complaint personally or by email, telephone or letter promptly after you discover the fault or problem.

Explain calmly what is wrong with the goods or services.

If the seller is unhelpful and you are concerned that your rights are not being recognised put your complaint in writing. Detail the date the goods were bought, the problem(s) with the goods and what you are seeking. Enclose a copy of the receipt.

Keep a copy of letters and documentation and the original receipt.

You may also write to the manufacturer/distributor as they should be concerned if their goods are faulty and may wish to make amends as a public relations issue. You do not have a contract with the manufacturer unless you have a contractual guarantee or warranty.

If the seller or service provider remains unhelpful you may consider a Small Claims Court action.

2.6 *Applying the law to a consumer problem*

TASK

Deirdre asks you to help with a legal problem. Three weeks ago she bought a new mountain bike from EasiRiders Ltd. The bike was new and cost €1,600. The salesman told her it was a limited edition model. Last week she went on a cycling holiday in the Pyrenees. While she was cycling on a track the gearing system broke. Another expert cyclist told her the bike was not a limited edition and was clearly of unsatisfactory quality. She had to ship the bike home and rent another bike at the cost of €350.

Assuming Deirdre used the bike correctly at all times, what advice would you give her?

Key Points

Here is a suggested approach to contract issues.

1. *Identify the type of contract at issue*

   Here it is a sale of goods contract covered by the Sale of Goods Acts 1893 and 1980.

2. *Identify the terms of the contract*

   Express terms; the terms expresssly stated by the sales person — that it was a limited edition model.

   Implied terms — the goods must comply with description (Section 13 SGA). That is was a limited edition model is part of the description of the goods.

   The sale is in the course of a business so the bike must be of merchantable quality and fit for its purpose (Sections 14(2) and (3)).

3. *Identify whether there has been a breach of contract*

   The bike gearing broke. The goods are clearly not merchantable, given that it was a new mountain bike. It is also not fit for its purpose. There have been breaches of the implied terms.

   The goods do not comply with their description so there is a breach of an express term and also s.13 SGA.

   (Note: If there is more than one breach of contract you should state this.)

4. *Consider any remedies the consumer may have*

   Deirdre may reject the goods and claim a refund or a new

replacement bike. She may also wish to claim damages for the cost of hiring a replacement bike while on holiday as this cost ʾvas directly caused by the breach. She should keep receipts, photographic evidence of the damage to the bike, etc. She may have expert witnesses (members of the cycling tour party) who can back up her claim in writing and she should get a letter detailing the damage to the bike and the fact that it is not a limited edition model, in case she needs to pursue the claim in the Small Claims Court.

3 The Small Claims Court

3.1 Introduction

The aim of the Small Claims Court procedure is to provide an inexpensive, fast and easy method for consumers to resolve disputes of up to €2,000, without needing a solicitor. The procedure can be used for complaints about goods purchased, service contracts and package holidays. The cost of applying to the Small Claims Court is currently €9. A claim can be lodged online. The claim is made to the District Court where the contract was made.

If the claim is for more than €2,000 the District Court will deal with the matter. The small claims procedure cannot be used for debt, personal injury, rent deposit or breach of leasing agreements claims.

3.2 Preparatory steps

Before lodging a claim you should check the following information.
- Ensure that you have made a complaint in writing to the supplier detailing the problem with the goods or services and setting out how you want the matter resolved.
- Collect your evidence together, copies of receipts, photographs, etc.
- Make sure you know the correct identity and address of the person or business you are claiming against. Many businesses operate as a limited company and trade under a different name. For example, a shoe shop may be registered as a company but trade with a more distinctive name such as NB Ltd trading as Nooshoos. When taking action against a company you should send any correspondence to the registered office of the company.

3.3 *A company search*

You will need to do a company search or business name search in the Companies Registration Office (CRO). This is the office that regulates companies and it maintains electronic records of important company information and addresses of those trading under business names. You can telephone the Companies Registration Office or look up the information online.

In the 'Online Services' option of the CRO website you will see a search facility for company names and business names.

Type in the name of a local store or supermarket to test the system. It is often better to type in one or two words than the whole name.

If your search is unsuccessful you can contact the European Consumer Centre for help.

3.4 *Applying to the Small Claims Court*

TASK

Go to the Courts Service website and download or print off the application form. (Alternatively you can follow the link on the consumerconnect page.)

Consider these facts and complete the application form.

> James Oliver (of 12 Cherry Walk, Dundonald) bought a combined washer-dryer machine from ElectroStores Ltd, of registered office at Unit 5, Dundonald, Co. Leath, for €1,200 on 11 March 2008. It was fitted by a qualified plumber. (You can assume it was plumbed and used properly.) A week after it was fitted the tumble dryer stopped working. James phoned ElectroStores Ltd a number of times but only ever got through to an answer machine. He called into the shop and was told to contact the manufacturer. The manager was always out. He has written to ElectroStores Ltd setting out his complaint and wants to take the matter to the Small Claims Court. It is now 2 April 2008.

Note: In the Respondent section you need to accurately complete the registered office of the company. If you just complete the name of the shop on the form it will be returned to you by the Small Claims Court.

3.4.1 Detailing the claim

You do not need to be a lawyer to do this. The aim of the Small Claims Court is to be a layperson's forum to settle disputes.

You need to set out the facts of the case clearly.

Checklist
1. When were the goods or services purchased?
2. What went wrong with the goods/service and when? Identify the breach of the relevant implied terms (s.14 SGA 1893).
3. What steps have already been taken? Refer to letters of complaint already sent to the respondent.
4. The reason for court action. In the scenario above, the consumer has received no satisfactory response at all from the respondent.
5. The amount that is being claimed. If the claim is not disputed, you may get judgement without having to go to court. In this case James will be seeking a refund of the purchase price, for ElectroStores to collect the machine from him and possibly an amount for reasonable launderette costs (for which James should have a receipt).
6. The application form should be signed and dated and sent to the relevant District Court with the fee of €9. (The relevant court is where the contract is made so in this case it would be Dundonald, Co. Leath.)

3.5 *The next stage*

A copy of the claim and a Notice of Claim is sent by the Court to the respondent. ElectroStores (the respondent) may do one of a number of things:
1. Admit the claim in whole and pay immediately through the Registrar of the Court.
2. Admit the claim in part (they may dispute certain expenses, etc.) or make the payment conditional on the return or collection of goods.
3. Dispute the claim.
4. Counterclaim (this means making a claim against the claimant, e.g. that the claimant has not fully paid for the goods and the respondent is seeking the balance). This will not be relevant in James's situation.
5. Do nothing.

If ElectroStores admits the claim it has fifteen calendar days to reply and complete a Notice of Acceptance of Liability, and return it to the Registrar. ElectroStores sends a cheque, payable to the claimant, to the Registrar.

On the other hand, if ElectroStores disputes the claim and returns a Notice of Dispute within fifteen days the Registrar will send James a copy of the Notice of Dispute and try to settle the dispute. If no settlement can be reached, the matter is then set down for court hearing.

The court hearing is informal and held in private rooms and the Registrar will hear both sides put forward their issues.

If the matter cannot be resolved by the Registrar a date and time will be set for the claim to be heard before a judge of the District Court.

4 Consumer Law and the European Union

Consumer protection measures are part of the drive towards a single market and the harmonisation of safety and product standards throughout the EU. In Chapter 4 we considered an early consumer protection measure, the Product Liability Directive. The EC Treaty sets out consumer protection as a principal aim (Article 92). Consumers need to feel confident when buying goods in their own member states and in cross-border transactions. Travelling and buying goods and services within Europe is now part of ordinary consumer behaviour. Internet shopping is a growing market. The strengthening of consumer confidence and the remedies of consumers are major themes of European Union involvement. In this section the Europa and European Consumer Centre websites will be used to explore this area.

The majority of consumer protection rights provided by European Union law have been set out in Directives. Directives have to be implemented by member states by a certain date. Member states must make sure their implementing legislation is effective and must interpret national legislation in line with the European Directive as far as possible.

TASK

Locate an overview of EU law and policy on a specific area.

Go to the Europa website, click on 'Gateway to European Union', then on the 'Activities' list, and then on 'Consumer'. Under the 'In Brief' section, click on 'Find out More': this gives an overview of consumer legislation. Read through this material and note the breadth of European involvement on this area. This is a brief summary of some of the main areas:

Product safety: The Product Liability Directive 85/374 (as amended) imposes financial liability on the producers for damage caused by unsafe products (see Chapter 4).

Specific products: There is a mass of European legislation setting out standards for specific products. These are known as sector directives on, for example, safety of toys, electrical equipment (e.g. the Directive on Electrical Equipment Designed for use within Certain Voltage Limits (LVD) Motor Vehicles Directive (MVD)). The newer Directives have a system for the award of the familiar CE mark on products.

Safety of products generally: The General Product Safety Directive (GPSD) 2001/95 extends and updates an earlier Directive. There is a general obligation to place only safe products on the market and a procedure for the adoption of standards covering risks and categories of risks. There are obligations placed on producers, distributors and authorities of member states. Member states must inform the Commission of measures taken to ensure safety of the product which restrict the marketing of products or require the withdrawal or recall of products. In an emergency situation involving dangerous products there is a system of rapid alerts to other member states (the RAPEX system). There are provisions requiring consumers to be informed of risks of products.

Unfair terms in consumer contracts: Directive 93/13 EC protects consumers from unfair contract terms. Unfair contract terms may be clauses in the contract which are unreadable, or which are incomprehensible or which deprive a consumer of their legal rights. Ireland implemented the Directive by the European Communities (Unfair Contracts) Regulations 1995. Under these regulations contractual terms which have not been individually negotiated are to be regarded as unfair if they are contrary to the requirement of good faith and cause a significant imbalance in the parties' rights and obligations under the contract to the detriment of the consumer. Whether or not a term is unfair will depend upon an assessment of the nature of the goods and services and all the circumstances surrounding the contract.

Distance marketing of consumer financial services: The EU regulated this area by Directive 2002/65 EC concerning the distance marketing of consumer financial services (which amended earlier Directives). The Directive was implemented in Ireland by Regulations passed in 2004. There are different provisions in relation to cooling-off periods and information in respect of financial services from those relating to goods and other types of service. (We will not consider the regulation of this area further.)

4.1 The Distance Selling Directive and online shopping

Shopping on the internet is increasing. Statistics for Ireland indicate that US$592 million was spent on online shopping in 2007 (Euromonitor International figures). Directive 1997/7/EC on the Protection of Consumers in respect of Distance Contracts (Distance Selling Directive) aims at ensuring that consumers who buy goods or services via distance selling means (without any face-to-face contact with the supplier), which include online sales, have similar rights to those who buy in face-to-face contracts. The Directive covers both goods and services.

Certain types of contract, such as financial services (which are covered by a separate Directive), are excluded. The Distance Selling Directive contains various regulatory options which are open to the member states in implementing the Distance Selling Directive. Article 14 (known as the 'minimal clause') allowed member states to introduce or maintain more stringent provisions to ensure higher levels of consumer protection, which has created variation between the national laws implementing the Distance Selling Directive.

The European Communities (Protection of Consumers in Respect of Contracts made by Means of Distance Communication) Regulations 2001 and later amendments which took effect in 2005 implement the Distance Selling Directive in Ireland.

4.2 Scope of the Regulations

The Regulations cover the distance selling of goods and services by internet, telephone, fax, email or mail order.

Excluded from the Regulations are internet auctions, contracts for the provision of services which are tied to a specific date such as airline flights, concert or hotel bookings. The aim is to ensure the same base level of protection wherever a supplier is based in the EU by setting out information requirements and giving a cooling-off period for consumers.

4.2.1 Before placing an order

Before the contract is entered into, clear and comprehensible information must be given about a number of matters. These should be included in the distance contract. These include: the name and address of the supplier, the main characteristics of the goods/service, the price (including taxes and delivery costs), method of payment and delivery, the existence of a right to cancel, the minimum duration of the contract and other matters. (Regulation 4 and Schedule 3 of the Regulations.)

4.2.2 Written confirmation
The supplier must give written confirmation to the consumer before or at the time the goods or service is delivered. This should detail how the contract can be cancelled, and the address for complaints. Information on guarantees and after-sales service that apply must also be given (these matters are detailed in the Sale of Goods and Supply of Services Act 1980).

4.2.3 Delivery or performance of the contract
Generally the supplier must deliver the goods or service within thirty days of the placing of an order, unless otherwise agreed between the supplier and consumer.

4.2.4 The cooling-off period
The 'cooling-off' period of seven days begins on receipt of the goods or purchase of the service and when written confirmation of the purchase was received. It gives the consumer time to withdraw from the contract without giving any reason and without incurring any costs (except the cost of returning the goods). If the correct information has not been given, the cooling-off period is extended to three months following delivery of the goods or, in the case of services, from the date of the contract or when the required information was given. There are limited exceptions where cancellation will not operate (e.g. if computer software seals/DVD seals have already been broken by the consumer).

4.2.5 Reimbursement
The seller must reimburse the consumer within thirty days.

Annette decides to do her Christmas shopping online during November. She chooses a site which has been recommended. Annette purchases six books and ten DVDs. Six weeks after she ordered the items her credit card has been debited but she has not received the goods. She received an email confirmation of her order when she placed it, but has heard nothing from the Customer Service department of the website.

Question: What steps could Annette take?
Key Points: Under the European Communities Protection of Consumers in Respect of Contracts made by Means of Distance Selling Regulations 2001 (as amended) generally the goods should arrive within thirty days (unless otherwise agreed by the parties). She should check the terms of the written contract. She should email the company, terminate the contract and request an immediate refund.
(The European Consumer Centre can give advice to Annette or she can contact the National Consumer Agency.)

5 The Consumer Protection Act 2007

This is a major piece of consumer protection legislation. Case law will be created concerning the definition of terms within the Act. Where the Act is implementing EU law, the definitions outlined in the Directives and interpretations given by the ECJ will be followed by the Irish courts. As the Act is so recent there is little case law on the area.

Use the National Consumer Agency website to check on action taken by the Agency and on any interesting court cases enforcing the Act.

OVERVIEW
- The National Consumer Agency (NCA) is established on a statutory basis. This replaces the former Office of the Director of Consumer Affairs.
- The EU Directive on Unfair Commercial Practices (UCPD) Dir 2005/29 EC is transposed into Irish law.
- Certain old consumer laws are repealed (such as the Consumer Information Act 1978).
- There is a general prohibition on misleading consumer practices and criminal offences created for breach of certain provisions of the CPA 2007.

5.1 The National Consumer Agency (NCA)

The functions of the NCA are to promote and protect the interests and welfare of consumers by enforcing consumer legislation, advocacy, research, education and awareness. The functions of the previous Office of Director of Consumer Affairs were transferred to this new statutory body. The NCA has authority to issue Codes of Practice to promote higher standards in sectors of trade. It has a range of enforcement powers such as issuing compliance notices, seeking undertakings from organisations and prosecuting organisations. It may apply to the Circuit Court for a Prohibition Notice against an undertaking. In relation to price display breaches the NCA can issue on-the-spot fines as an alternative to prosecution.

5.1.1 Consumer Protection List and power to publish

The NCA must maintain a Consumer Protection List (s.86, CPA) in which details of enforcement actions are recorded. The NCA may publish details of this list in any manner it considers appropriate.

5.2 Unfair Commercial Practices Directive (Dir 2005/29 EC)

The Directive aims to harmonise unfair trading laws in all EU member states and contains a general prohibition on traders treating consumers unfairly. The Directive is intended to provide a base level of protection. National laws which give a consumer more protection are unaffected.

The Directive prevents businesses misleading consumers through acts or omissions or engaging in aggressive commercial practices such as high-pressure selling techniques. The UCPD Directive and the Consumer Protection Act 2007 only applies to business-to-consumer transactions. It does not apply to business-to-business transactions.

5.3 Pricing regulations

The Act replaces some of the old legislation on the display of prices. Section 60 makes it an offence for a trader to prevent, without reasonable cause, a person reading prices of products on display. The NCA may impose fixed penalty notices in respect of these types of offences.

5.4 Prohibited practices

There is a 'blacklist' of outlawed practices which are unfair in all cases (Section 55). These include:

- Claiming to be part of a Code of Conduct when the trader is not part of a code.
- Displaying a quality mark, etc. without authorisation.
- Claiming without authorisation that the trader, product or practices have been approved or endorsed by a public or private body.
- False claims that the trader is about to move premises or cease trading. Signs such as 'All stock must go — moving premises' when the trader is not moving is a prohibited practice (s. 55(1)(c)). Until this Act, this was a typical form of cheap window marketing.
- Failure to leave the consumer's residence when requested.

Task

Go to the NCA website and access the Guide to the Consumer Protection Act 2007. (At the time of writing this was most readily accessed through the 'Press Releases' section.) You can download the summary of the Act. Go to the material on s.55 and identify more prohibited practices.

Question: Have you come across any prohibited practices under the Act?

5.5 Unfair commercial practices

According to the Directive and the Act a commercial practice is unfair if:

a) it is contrary to the requirements of professional diligence, and

b) it materially distorts or is likely to distort the economic behaviour with regard to the product of the 'average consumer' whom it reaches or to whom it is addressed, or of the average member of that group when a commercial practice is directed at that group.

If a breach of good faith occurs and the 'average consumer' is denied the reasonable standard of skill and care to which he or she is entitled this will constitute an unfair consumer practice.

5.6 Misleading practices

A commercial practice is misleading if it contains false or untruthful information or in any way deceives or is likely to deceive an 'average consumer', and cause or be likely to cause him/her to take a transactional decision that s/he would not otherwise have taken and lead to a breach of the trader's standard of professional diligence. Misleading information can concern the existence of a product, the price and its characteristics.

5.6.1 An average consumer

This phrase has been defined by the European Court of Justice as 'reasonably well informed and reasonably observant and circumspect, taking into account social, cultural and linguistic factors'.

5.7 Aggressive trade practices

Under Section 53 these are defined as the use of harassment, coercion or undue influence where it would be likely to:

1. cause significant impairment of the 'average consumer's' freedom of choice or conduct; and
2. cause the 'average consumer' to make a transactional decision that he/she would not otherwise make.

Examples are provided in the NCA Guide that include: the use of threatening or abusive language or behaviour; the exploitation of a consumer's misfortune or circumstance when the trader is aware that the consumer's judgement is impaired; the imposition of onerous or disproportionate non-contractual barriers by the trader when the consumer wishes to terminate a contract or switch to another trader.

5.8 Defences for traders

There is a due diligence defence for traders: if the offence was due to a mistake or reliance on information supplied to the defendant, or to an act or default of another person, an accident or some other cause beyond the defendant's control, and the defendant exercised due diligence and took all reasonable precautions, the defendant may escape criminal liability. (This does not apply to pyramid selling offences.)

5.9 Remedies for consumers

A consumer who has been affected by the actions of a trader can apply to the District, Circuit or High Court for damages. The NCA may, with the consent of the consumer, apply to the court for a compensation order under Section 81, requiring a trader who has been convicted of an offence to pay compensation in respect of any loss or damage to the consumer resulting from that offence. The compensation order may be instead of, or in addition to, any fine or penalty the court may impose.

5.10 Pyramid selling schemes

Under the new Act there is a prohibition on organising, promoting or participating in pyramid schemes and the Act replaces the former Pyramid Selling Act 1980. The new provisions apply to business-to-consumer schemes and consumer-to-consumer schemes.

5.10.1 What is a pyramid scheme?

A pyramid promotional scheme is based on the receipt of a gift in money or money's worth for an opportunity to receive financial compensation, which is derived primarily from the **introduction of other persons into the scheme** rather than from the supply of a product. These schemes often focus on the ordinary consumer and persons are introduced into the scheme by fellow consumers. The Act covers these types of consumer-to-consumer introductions. It makes these agreements void. (This is an example of a contract being unenforceable due to public policy grounds — refer to Chapter 5 on contract law.)

The Gardaí and the NCA can take action and prosecute individuals. The limits for fines are up to €150,000 and/or up to five years' imprisonment. A consumer cannot seek redress through the Act for pyramid selling schemes as they are treated as void agreements.

Eazistairs are a company that fit chair lifts for the elderly or those with mobility problems. The brochure advertising their product states:

Fitted within one day this product will change your life forever. It gives guaranteed safe mobility up and down stairs. No more wear and tear on aching joints or dangers from falling, anxiety will be a thing of the past. As members of the Professional Guild of Mobility Facilitators we are an accredited organisation. Guaranteed quick

> *and tidy installation. Product costs according to type of staircase but range from €4,000 to €10,000. Complete money back guarantee if not satisfied within two weeks.*
>
> Homer is aged 82 and in frail health. He decides to have a staircase fitted. The sales director calls to his house at his request and measures and inspects the staircase. He is quoted a price of €8,000 plus VAT. On three occasions he is telephoned and told that the fitters are 'in his area' and the next time they would be able to fit Homer in would be six months later, by which time labour costs could be higher. Homer is anxious about his impaired mobility and the risk of paying a higher price and agrees to the contract. One week later the Eazistairs fitters arrive. They install the product, but ruin the stair carpet by spilling plaster and grouting materials on it. Although the lift works well for the first two days it is extremely noisy and his next-door neighbour complains. When he tries to contact the company to seek a refund, the company tell him that there was a misprint on the brochure and it should read 'within two days', so he is out of time. He also discovers there is no Professional Guild of Mobility Facilitators.

Questions:
1. Identify any possible breaches of the Consumer Protection Act 2007. (Homer will also have contractual remedies under the Sale of Goods and Supply of Services Act 1980.)
2. Could you suggest to Homer any sources of help with his problem?

Key Points:
1. This may be a misleading commercial practice as it contains false or untruthful information (the complete money back guarantee). It may deceive or is likely to deceive the 'average consumer', and cause or be likely to cause him/her to take a transactional decision that he/she would not otherwise have taken. The package of promises in the brochure may well, given the nature of the product, play on the average consumer's hopes and could constitute a deception.

The high-pressured sales technique, using the fact that unless the work was booked quickly there would be a considerable delay and possible cost increase, could be judged to be an aggressive commercial practice. The age and infirmity of Homer and his anxiety given the circumstances would all be factors a court would consider. If it is not judged an 'aggressive practice' it could certainly be a misleading practice.

A trader is prohibited from claiming that they are members of a self-regulatory body when they are not. The assertion regarding the Professional Guild is untrue. This is a prohibited practice (s.55(1)(b)) and the NCA may take action against the company.

Given the number and manner of breaches it is unlikely that Eazistairs would be able to use due diligence as a defence under the Act.

2. Homer could phone his solicitor, if he has one and is prepared to pay for advice on the issue. He could contact the National Consumer Agency and hope that they take action against the company. He may be awarded a compensation order on foot of a successful prosecution. He could contact another agency such as a Citizens Information Centre or the European Consumer Centre to explain his rights and possibly contact the agency on his behalf.

6 *An Approach to Contract Issues and Problem Questions*

This chapter ends with a suggested approach to dealing with possible contract problems in an assessment or in your life as a consumer.

1. Are the elements of a binding contract present? This will generally be obvious in the scenarios with which you will be presented. Briefly outline the elements, unless there is a real issue of whether there is an intention to create legal relations, consideration, capacity, etc., in which case deal with the particular issue in more detail.

2. Identify or classify the type of contract if possible, e.g. is it a contract for sale of goods (covered by the Sale of Goods Acts 1893 and 1980) or a contract for work and materials (covered by the Sale of Goods and Supply of Services Act 1980)? Is it a particular type of contract, which may have additional protection, such as a consumer contract with unfair terms or a distance-selling contract?

3. Identify the relevant terms of the contract:
- express terms (written or oral)
- implied terms, which may be:
- implied by a relevant statute e.g. Sale of Goods Act 1893; and/or
- implied by other means, for example by a course of dealing between the parties.

Explain the scope and meaning of the terms (e.g. what is covered by the goods must match their description under s.13). What does merchantability mean?

4. Identify any breach(es) of the contract. Remember: there may be

multiple breaches of the contract.

5. Check whether there is a valid exclusion clause incorporated into the contract protecting the seller from liability. There is national legislation and EU legislation governing the validity and/or fairness of many exclusion clauses.

6. If there is no exclusion clause or if the exclusion clause may be ineffective or void there is an actionable breach of contract. What are the available remedies?

7. If a written complaint explaining the breach(es) and remedy requested does not work consider a Small Claims Court action for a consumer claiming under €2000.

7 Sources of Help for Consumers

An effective way of enforcing consumer legislation is empowering and informing consumers on the scope of their rights and how to enforce them. Sources of information and assistance are:

- Citizens Information Centres
- European Consumer Centre
- Small Claims Court Office, which will give information about filling in forms.

Summary

The original consumer protection legislation is contained in the Sale of Goods Act 1893, important legislation which is still in force and implies terms into contracts concerning the description and quality of goods. These implied terms cannot be excluded in consumer sales. The protection was supplemented by the 1980 Act, which covers contracts for services. Membership of the EU, and the need to protect consumers and to give consumers confidence when buying products or services from home or abroad, has generated a mass of legislation, especially in the last fifteen years. European Directives have been used to harmonise consumer protection measures on product safety, package holidays, safety of certain products such as toys and electrical items, online and other forms of distance selling.

The Small Claims Court is the primary forum for resolving small consumer claims in an informal setting. There are now a variety of sources of information and advocacy help for consumers to enforce their rights. The new Consumer Protection Act 2007 created the statutory National Consumer Agency.

QUESTIONS

1. Evan buys a ring displayed as 'Sapphire' for his girlfriend Fiona for €1,800. When Fiona shows it to Gill, a gemologist, she tells her it is an aquamarine stone and worth about €250.
   Advise Fiona on whether there could be a claim for breach of contract.
2. Harry sees a car advertised in Wotmota as a '1985 FordXR3 Collector's Dream' by Mark Mechanic. Mark is a hobby car enthusiast who regularly does up and sells car from his garden shed. After seeing it Harry buys it for €4,500. He shows it to a colleague who tells him it is actually a cut-and-shut car.
   Advise Harry on any remedies he may seek.
3. Your brother Ciaran has just returned from a tattoo artist, Daire Inks. He was rather angry. He had arranged to have the name of his girlfriend, Niamh, tattooed on his left shoulder. He had written the spelling down and the price was agreed at €300. When the tattoo was complete it said 'Meave'. When he became angry Daire had shrugged and said that he had got distracted and that Ciaran had signed a form that excused him from any mistakes. Ciaran had signed a form that the tattooist had said was a 'consent form'. He shows you a copy and it contains the phrase 'tattoos undertaken at client's own risk' at the bottom of the consent form in very small lettering.
   Ciaran now wants to go to another tattoo artist to have the name erased. This will cost about €400.
   Advise him generally:
   a) Whether he might have a claim and under what piece(s) of legislation.
   b) What further information you might need to make a claim.
   c) Any evidence that may be useful to support his claim.
   d) The amount of damages he would be claiming.

REFERENCES

Euromonitor International statistics, www.euromonitor.com/factfile.
Guide to the Consumer Protection Act.
www.consumerconnect.ie/eng/Get_Your_Rights/Consumer_
Protection_Act.pdf

8

ASPECTS OF EUROPEAN UNION LAW

At the end of this chapter you should be able to:

- Demonstrate an understanding of the concept of the internal market and of key Treaty Articles.
- Outline relevant EU law relating to free movement of goods and services.
- Locate and navigate EU law sources and be able to undertake independent research and problem-solving tasks.
- Explain the role of the European Court of Justice (ECJ) in developing the principles of EU law such as supremacy of EC law, direct effect, indirect effect and state liability.
- Explain methods of enforcing EU law.
- Understand some basic concepts of competition law.

1 Introduction

Historical background and development of Europe

When the European Economic Community was established its primary aims were political and economic. The stabilisation of Europe and the enhancement of living and social conditions were fundamental aims. Economic co-operation was the vehicle to achieve these and the creation of a common market. The time-line of the development of the EU was given in Chapter 3.

This chapter will use the Eur-Lex and Europa websites to look at EU legislation and case law.

TASK

The membership and development of the EU and the Europa website.

This task introduces you to the main authoritative source of information on the EU, the Europa website. This is the official portal to the European Union. It is updated regularly and contains proposed legislation, law, news and reports on the work of the EU. You will be using the website frequently, so you should become familiar with the layout and content of the site, and the areas of activity within the EU. (We shall look at specific aspects of EU law later in the chapter.) This task should take no longer than 40 minutes.

Go to the Europa website — http://europa.eu — and click on 'Gateway to the European Union'. Go to 'Europe at a Glance' in the left-hand margin and then 'Panorama of the EU'.

Read the first two topics listed in the margin ('Home' and 'What does the EU Do?') and make brief notes on the major headings. Then answer the following questions. (You do not need to follow the links within the topic — just extract the main points.)

1. How many people are subject to European Union rules?
2. Identify an action that the EU is taking to address the issue of greenhouse gases.
3. Identify three economies where the euro is not yet used.
4. In which decade was the rule of the equal pay for equal work between men and women first set down in the EU Treaty?
5. Identify two areas in which the European Union rules impact on justice and security issues.
6. Which are the two most recent members of the European Union?

2 The Three Pillars of the European Union

This structure was introduced by the Maastrict Treaty and explains the relationship between the European Union and European Community.

The European Community operates under the EC Treaty. Maastrict introduced new areas of co-operation and action between the member states to be undertaken outside the existing framework of the EC. This explains why the terms EU and EC are both used. We focus on law arising under the EC pillar and the EC Treaty. The pillars of the European Union comprise:

- The European Communities (the EC and EURATOM).
- Common Foreign and Security Policy.
- Judicial Co-operation on Justice and Home Affairs (now called the Area of Freedom, Security and Justice (AFSJ). (The European Arrest Warrant is an example of co- operation in this pillar.)

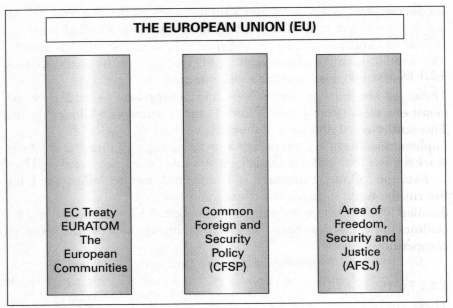

The Three Pillars of the European Union

3 A Reminder of the Main Sources of EC Law

3.1 Primary legislation

3.1.1 Treaty Articles

Examples:

Article 13 EC — 'Without prejudice to the other provisions of the Treaty ... the Council, acting unanimously on a proposal from the Commission and after consulting the European Parliament, may take appropriate action to combat discrimination based on sex, racial or ethnic origin, religion or belief, disability, age or sexual orientation.'

Article 25 — 'Customs duties on imports and exports and charges having equivalent effect shall be prohibited between member States. This prohibition shall also apply to customs duties of a fiscal nature.'

Treaty Articles are short, framework provisions setting out key principles. They often require further filling out by EU secondary legislation. For example, the anti-discrimination Article 13 was the basis for Directive 2000/79, which established a general framework for equal treatment in employment and occupation and combating discrimination on the grounds of religion or belief, disability, age or sexual orientation as regards employment and occupation.

3.2 Secondary legislation (Article 249 EC)

The types of legislation are specified in Article 249 EC.

3.2.1 EC Regulations

These are binding in their entirety and are directly applicable in all member states. They do not require a national act to implement them. Thousands of Regulations are made by the EU each year. They implement Treaty policies and are used to regulate the internal market.

Example: Council Regulation 1/2003 on the implementation of the rules on competition laid down in Articles 81 and 82 EC. This detailed Regulation explains key concepts of EU competition law and outlines powers of the European Commission in the field of competition law.

3.2.2 EC Directives

These are binding, as to the result to be achieved, upon each member state. However, the national authorities are left the choice of form and methods to achieve their objectives. Since the member states are bound only by the objectives laid down in directives, they have some discretion, when framing them into national law, to take account of specific national circumstances. Transposition must be effected within the time limit laid down in a directive.

Example: Directive 2004/38 EC on Citizens' Free Movement sets down the freedoms of EU citizens and their families to move throughout the EU.

3.2.3 EC Decisions

These are binding measures addressed to a specific member state or individual.

Example: A European Commission Decision of 27 June 2007 prohibited Ryanair's proposed acquisition of Aer Lingus on competition grounds. Ryanair appealed to the Court of First Instance arguing that the EU Decision was invalid.

3.3 Judgments of the ECJ and Court of First Instance

This institution interprets and enforces EU law. It gives binding rulings on cases brought before it. Although it does not have a rule of precedent, so is not formally bound by previous rulings, it does have a consistent case law base and has had a significant role in developing Community law principles.

3.3.1 The importance of the preliminary ruling procedure (Article 234)

National courts which are faced with an issue of EU law may refer a case to the European Court of Justice for clarification on the scope or meaning of EU law under the preliminary ruling procedure. This procedure has clarified the scope and applicability of EU law and has allowed the ECJ to develop principles of direct effect, supremacy and state liability.

4 Introduction to the Internal Market

One of the principal aims of the original European Economic Community was to establish a common market. Although we now take this for granted it important to understand what this concept entails. Before the common market, goods that crossed a border would generally be subject to a customs duty or tariff. Beef exported from Ireland to France would be subject to a duty/tax on importation. This meant that the goods would be more expensive and transit could be delayed for administrative reasons. Duties often operated to protect domestically produced goods, and allowed states to operate protectionist policies. The Common Market established a customs union which abolished customs duties and quotas (numerical limits) on trade between member states.

4.1 Meaning of a common market

This comprises:
- a customs union; and
- a common tariff with third states; and
- freedom in the factors of production.

It is made up of a customs union with a **common customs tariff** which is applied to trade with third states (outside the EU). This is a list of categories of goods and the rates of customs duties payable in trade with third countries. Once customs duties have been paid on the relevant goods imported from a third country these goods are then said to be in **free circulation** within the customs union. In addition, freedom in other 'factors of production' — labour mobility, enterprise mobility and capital mobility — is secured. These are often referred to as the fundamental freedoms of the EC.

The concept is that supply for goods or services of a certain kind from all over the Common Market should meet demand for those goods or services from all over the Common Market without being interrupted by natural boundaries.

For an overview of the internal market concept access the Europa site. Having entered the Gateway, select the 'Internal Market' heading under 'What Europe does by Subject'. Read the 'In Brief' introduction and the 'Find out More' overview.

Questions:
1. Identify two areas where the single market has significantly cut costs for consumers.
2. Which agreement signed in Luxembourg removes most border controls on the movement of persons?

4.2 The four fundamental freedoms

The four freedoms are:
1. Free movement of workers throughout the EU (Article 39 EC).
2. Free movement of goods within the EU (Articles 23–30, 90 EC).
3. Freedom of establishment of a business and the provision of services throughout the EU (Articles 43–55 EC).
4. Free movement of capital (Articles 56–60 EC).

TASKS: THE FREE MOVEMENT OF WORKERS (ARTICLE 39)

This task has two parts. For an excellent overview of key issues start with the Citizens Signposting Service and watch a short video.

Part 1: Knowing your EU rights. Go to the Europa website and having entered the 'Gateway' click on the 'Internal Market' heading under 'What Europe does by Subject'. Then under the 'Commission' heading look at the 'Internal Market' page and then the 'Citizens Signpost Service'. Watch the short five-minute video, first selecting the appropriate language.

Note the range of issues that a person who wishes to move to another member state might face and the means of accessing information on this.

Part 2: The aim of this task is to explore the structure of Treaty Articles (primary legislation of the EU) and the need for secondary legislation by focusing on the free movement of workers. This is a key right of EU citizens. If you have worked abroad on a placement or holiday job, or anticipate doing so in the future, you will be relying on these rights. The full Article is set out below. The Article gives workers who have EU nationality a right to move freely throughout the Community to take up job offers on the same terms as nationals. There are some limitations to the right.

Article 39
1. Freedom of movement of workers shall be secured within the Community.
2. Such freedom of movement shall entail the abolition of any discrimination based on nationality between workers of the member states as regards employment, remuneration and other conditions of work and employment.
3. It shall entail the right, subject to limitations justified on grounds of public policy, public security or public health:
   (a) to accept offers of employment actually made;
   (b) to move freely within the territory of member states for this purpose;
   (c) to stay in a Member state for the purpose of employment in accordance with the provisions governing the employment of nationals of that state laid down by law, regulation or administrative action;
   (d) to remain in the territory of a member state after having been employed in that State, subject to conditions which shall be embodied in implementing regulations to be drawn up by the Commission.
4. The provisions of this Article shall not apply to employment in the public service.

1. Freedom of movement is defined in Article 39(1). There is no 'definition' or 'interpretation' section in the EC Treaty. The key phrases are either to be developed in secondary legislation and/or interpreted by the European Court of Justice in case law. The freedom under Article 39(1) only applies to nationals of the European Union.

Question: How would you define a 'worker'? Do you think that somebody who is employed for two hours a week and nearly completely reliant on social assistance is a 'worker' whose status gives the person a number of 'gateway' rights?
Key Points: The definition of a 'worker' has been left to the European Court of Justice to define. One of the functions of the court is to give

authoritative judgments on interpretation of the Treaty in the preliminary ruling procedure. Generally, fundamental Treaty rights are interpreted widely by the ECJ.

C-139/85 Kempf v. Staatssecretaris von Justitie [1986] ECR 1741

The ECJ was asked to give a preliminary ruling on whether the part-time job of Mr Kempf, which paid him less than a subsistence wage, categorised his as a 'worker' under EU law. The ECJ ruled that provided the job was 'effective and genuine' and not 'marginal and ancillary' he would be classed as a 'worker' under EU law. The ECJ has also ruled that somebody who is a genuine jobseeker with genuine chances of finding work is classed as a worker. This liberal interpretation of the concept of worker was given in case *C-292/89 R v. IAT ex parte Antonissen [1991] ECR I–745.*

2. The right under Article 39 prohibits discrimination on the grounds of nationality in areas of pay and other conditions. This provision is found in Article 39(2)EC.

Question: Olga is a Polish national. She works for D Ltd, a company based in Dublin. She finds out that Irish workers receive one week's Christmas bonus, whereas she does not. She thinks this is due to her nationality. Advise Olga.

Key Point: If the discrimination is based on nationality grounds then as a worker she can rely on Article 39(2) in a national (Irish) court or tribunal. This right is termed **directly effective** as Article 39(2) is clear, precise and unconditional. The concept of direct effect is looked at in detail below.

3. The Article 39 rights allow workers who are citizens of the EU to accept offers, move freely within the EU, to stay in a member state and to remain in a member state having been employed (subject to secondary legislation).

Question: Is this an absolute right or are there limits on the exercise of the right?

Key Point: Under Article 39(3) a member state may be able to justify restrictions placed on workers on the grounds of public security, public policy or public health. A member state may wish to prevent a worker entering its territory. For example, a person who has been convicted of gun crime or drug trafficking may pose a threat to society and a member state may wish to block his or her entry to the country. In order to set down guidelines for the exercise of this restriction by the member states a Directive was passed and updated in Directive 2004/38. These restrictions or derogations from the Treaty are interpreted narrowly by the ECJ and a member state must be able to justify any restriction or limitation and act proportionately.

4. The final paragraph of Article 39 states that the freedom of workers does not apply to the 'public service'.

Question: Would you consider nurses, teachers and railway drivers part of the 'public service'? If they fall within this category the Article 39 rights would not apply to these categories of worker.
Key Point: This is another example of a general phrase with a specific legal meaning. Generally, we use the phrase 'public service' to mean a civil servant or someone who is paid by the State. If all these types of employees were excluded from the free movement regime, the right would be hollow. The ECJ has interpreted this restrictive phrase very narrowly. In the case of *C-149/79 Commission v. Belgium [1980] ECR 3881* the ECJ ruled that this applied only to narrow categories of public servants where there is a 'special relationship of allegiance to the State' and the job involves 'safeguarding the general interests of the State'. Positions such as very senior civil servants, diplomats, senior officers of the security forces and members of the judiciary may fall into this category.

PROBLEM QUESTIONS

1. Brendan is an Irish citizen. He recently started work in Italy as a fashion designer on a part-time basis and after starting work he discovered he is paid considerably less than existing Italian employees. He considers this is due to his Irish nationality. Is this contrary to EU law?

2. Deirdre is a police officer in Ireland. She wishes to move to Germany to live with her boyfriend and continue her career. She has been told that she will not be able to work as a police officer in Germany. Does she have a right under European Community law to do this?

Key Points
1. Brendan is an EU national and will be classed as a worker provided his part-time work is classed as 'effective and genuine' as established by *C-139/85 Kempf v. Staatssecretaris von Justitie*. Article 39(2) gives

him a right not to be discriminated against on the ground of nationality in respect of his terms and conditions. This right will be directly effective as it is clear and precise and unconditional and he will be able to bring a case against his employer in Italy if he can prove the discrimination is based on nationality grounds.

2. Deirdre is a national of the EU and also a worker. Generally workers have a right to move within Europe and can seek and change jobs without discrimination. However, this is not an absolute right and under Article 39(4), as her job is part of the public service and linked with safeguarding the State, as defined in the case of *C-149/79 Commission v. Belgium* Germany may be able to restrict her rights if the State can prove the restriction is justifiable and proportionate.

In addition to the primary Articles of the Treaty which give workers rights there is secondary legislation which gives further detail to the core rights under Article 39.

Regulation 1612/68 EC on the Free Movement of Workers adds detail to the non-discrimination provision. There are a number of Directives that provide for the qualifications of certain professions to be recognised in other member states. To facilitate academic qualifications being recognised throughout Europe a Mutual Recognition of Diplomas was enacted in Directive 92/51.

Finally, and most recently, the EC reviewed and updated Directive 2004/38, which explains the rights of citizens and members of their family to move freely and reside within the EU. Members of a worker's family may accompany and live with him/her. The types of relationship that fall within the definition of 'family member' are outlined in the Directive.

5 The Concept of Direct Effect

OVERVIEW

- Meaning of direct effect.
- Distinction from the direct applicability concept.
- Case law that created the concept.
- Significance of direct effect in enabling EU citizens and business enterprises to enforce EU law in national courts.

5.1 Introduction and definition

In the section on free movement of workers the concept of direct effect was mentioned. This fundamental concept of EU law is now looked at in more detail.

5.1.1 Definition

Direct effect allows an EU provision to be used in a national court to bring an action or as a defence to civil or criminal proceedings.
Article 39 EC is a **directly effective** provision.

The principle of direct effect is not defined in the EC Treaties. It is a concept which was created by the ECJ. Direct applicability and direct effect are frequently referred to, often interchangeably, by both courts and commentators. They are different concepts. **Directly applicable** laws are provisions which take effect in the legal system of a member state without further implementation by the member state. Treaty Articles and EC Regulations are directly applicable provisions.

If a provision of EU law has **direct effect** it can be relied on in proceedings in the national court (District Court, Circuit Court, etc). It can be used to base a claim or as defence to a civil or criminal action. The ECJ has also stated that a national court faced with directly effective rights must provide adequate legal remedies to enforce EU law rights.

5.2 Criteria of direct effect and the Van Gend en Loos case

The ECJ has set down certain criteria for a provision to be capable of direct effect. The legal provision must:
- be clear and precise; *and*
- be unconditional; *and*
- give a member state no discretion regarding implementation.

These criteria were established by one of the most famous cases of the ECJ.

C-26/62 Van Gend en Loos v. Nederlandse Administratie der Belastigen [1963] ECR 1

Facts: The case concerned the imposition of customs duties by authorities in the Netherlands in breach of an EC Article (the prohibition is now covered by Article 25 EC). The importer, who had suffered financial loss, brought a case in the Dutch courts claiming that the action taken by the customs authorities was contrary to EC law.

The Dutch authorities argued that the only action that could be taken against them was by the European Commission, who could bring an action before the European Court of Justice for breach of EC law. The Dutch courts referred a question to the ECJ for a preliminary ruling. The European Court of Justice ruled that as long as certain criteria were met the EC law provision could be used in **national courts** to claim a remedy for breach of EC law.

The criteria listed are known as the *Van Gend en Loos* criteria.

5.3 *The purpose of the direct effect principle*

The European Court of Justice recognised that in order to make EU law become part of the legal systems of each member state and to be part of a citizen's rights it had to make EU law readily enforceable. Individuals and businesses do not have direct access to the ECJ to complain about the actions of a particular member state, authority or employer who may be flouting EU law. A court action against a defaulting state can be taken by the European Commission and by another member state. To make member states comply with European law the most effective mechanism was to allow EU law to be used in national courts and tribunals, to make EU law enforceable at 'grass roots' level. In this way, it was thought that EU law would become pervasive throughout all the legal systems of the member states. If there were uncertainties about the scope of meaning of an EU provision the national court of tribunal could request a preliminary ruling for clarification before enforcing the directly effective provision.

The *Van Gend en Loos* case had enormous impact.

There is no provision in the EC Treaty allowing individuals or business enterprises to take a **direct action** before the European Court of Justice in Luxembourg against other individuals, business enterprises or authorities of member states for breach of EU law.

National courts are the place in which individuals can bring legal proceedings to assert their EU law rights. A consequence of the creation of the direct effect principle was that individuals bringing cases throughout the community were to become the principal enforcers of community law within Europe.

An early case, which established equal pay for men and women for equal work or work of equal value, is a good example of the impact of direct effect.

TASK: CASE STUDY

Access the EC Treaty using the Eur-Lex site. Select the 'Treaties' option and then call up the most up-to-date Consolidated version of the Treaty on European Union and the Treaty establishing the European Community.

Go to Article 141 EC, which outlines the right to equal pay without discrimination on grounds of sex. This begins, 'Each member state ...'

Member states were slow to implement the principle of equal pay into their legal systems: indeed there is still a gender-based pay gap throughout Europe today. As a result of national governments failing to adequately legislate to ensure equal pay, a number of cases were brought in national courts relying on the direct effect principle.

C-43/75 Defrenne v. SABENA [1976] ECR 455

Facts: A female member of cabin crew brought a legal action against her employer (SABENA) in the Belgian courts. She argued that male cabin crew were paid more than female workers. She relied on the Equal Pay Article 119 (which is now Art. 141). A preliminary issue before the national court was whether she could rely on EC law in the national court against her employer, i.e. whether the Article had **direct effect**. Questions were referred to the ECJ who made a preliminary ruling.

The ECJ ruled that as the equal pay obligation was to pay men and women the same rate for the same work was direct, precise and unconditional, the provision had direct effect.

The ECJ also ruled that the EC law could be used against private employers as well as against state employers.

The ECJ ruled:

> ... the principle of equal pay contained in Article 119 may be relied upon before national courts and these courts have a duty to ensure the protection of the rights which this provision vests in individuals ... carried out in the same establishment or service, whether public or private.

5.4 Limits on the scope of direct effect

The Van Gend en Loos criteria must be satisfied for the EU provision to be capable of being used and enforced within the national courts.

If the EU provision is vague, conditional or dependent on the member state exercising discretion, it will not be directly effective. An example of a Treaty Article which does not fulfil the directly effective criteria is Article 10 EC:

> Member States shall take all appropriate measures whether general or particular, to ensure fulfilment of the obligations arising out of the Treaty or resulting from action taken by the institutions of the Community. They shall facilitate the achievement of the Community's tasks.
> They shall abstain from any measure which could jeopardise the attainment of the objectives of this Treaty.

Article 10 is too general to have direct effect. It lacks the clarity of Article 39 (the free movement of workers provision discussed above). The Articles dealing with the establishment of the single market, equal pay and competition law have all been ruled to fulfil the criteria and to have direct effect. This means that they have real impact in each member state.

5.4.1 Vertical and horizontal direct effect

The ECJ have drawn a distinction between the types of direct effect and this is most relevant when discussing whether a provision of a **Directive** can be relied upon in a national court. The use of an EU provision against a private concern or individual within the national court is known as a **horizontal direct effect** as the provision is used against an entity of the same type of status.

The use of an EU provision against the state or a public body or agency of the state is known as **vertical direct effect** as the provision is used against the state, to describe the elevated status of the state compared to individuals or businesses.

5.4.2 Direct effect of Directives

Directives are directed to member states and compel them to achieve a certain goal by a certain deadline. Directives require member states to implement them by passing primary or secondary legislation. In comparison with Treaty Articles and EC Regulations, which are directly applicable and binding in their entirety on individuals and businesses alike as soon as they are passed, Directives are 'softer' types of measure and for this reason the ECJ has limited their direct effect.

In addition to the criteria laid out in *Van Gend en Loos* the ECJ have set down additional criteria for a Directive to have direct effect:

1. The implementation date must have passed (*C-148/78 Pubblico Ministero v. Ratti [1979] ECR 1629*). Directives give member states a time span to implement the Directive. Directives cannot have direct effect before the expiry of the time limit; *and*
2. Directives can only have **vertical direct effect** in a national court.

This vertical direct effect principle means that Directives can only be used against a state or an emanation of the state (a public body). The authority for this principle is the famous case of *C-152/84 Marshall v. Southampton and Southwest Hampshire AHA [1986]ECR 723*

Facts: Marshall worked for the health authority in the UK. She was compulsorily retired (dismissed) at the age of 62. A man in the same job would not have been compulsorily retired until the age of 65. She sought to rely on the Directive 76/207 (the Equal Treatment Directive) against her employer in the national court. Her argument was that the national legislation (the Sex Discrimination Act 1975) was inadequate and did not properly implement EC law.

The Court of Appeal in England referred questions to the ECJ about the scope of the Directive and the direct effect of the directive.

The ECJ ruled that the prohibition on discrimination with regard to working conditions contained in the directive was clear, precise and unconditional (it fulfilled the Van Gend en Loos criteria), the deadline for implementation of the Directive had passed and it could be relied upon against a state or public authority.

As the Area Health Authority, her employer, was a public body she could use the Directive to challenge her discriminatory treatment. The case was then sent back to the Industrial Tribunal in the UK, which found her employer to be in breach of EC law.

A second preliminary ruling was then requested in relation to the award of compensation she should receive for her discriminatory treatment and unfair dismissal. The UK had placed a 'cap' on compensation for unfair dismissal and the ECJ ruled that any such ceiling should not operate to deprive a claimant of an effective remedy. The UK had to alter its provisions on unfair dismissal compensation as a result of this ruling.

TASK: CASE STUDY

Look up the case *C-91/92 Paolo Faccini Dori v. Recreb Srl* on the Eur-Lex website. In the left-hand margin you will see a 'Simple Search' option. Search by the File Category of Case-law. Make sure that the 'judgments' option is checked, then in the search terms type 'Faccini Recreb'.

Read the case and write a short summary using the following questions to focus on the important aspects.

Note on the Case: This important preliminary ruling was given before the Treaty provisions were renumbered. Article 189, now Article 249, describes the different types of legislation the EU may pass.

1. Which Directive was being relied upon by the consumer in this case?
2. How did the case arise?
3. Why did the ECJ state that individuals should be able to rely on the direct effect of Directives, if clear, precise and unconditional, against the state (i.e. that Directives could have vertical direct effect)?
4. Did the ECJ rule that a Directive could be used against an individual (i.e. have *horizontal* direct effect)?
5. Can you identify any other ways in which the ECJ identify that the consumer could seek to enforce the EU law?

Key Points

1. Directive 85/577 EC on door-to-door sales. This gives consumers rights in relation to the provision of information and a cooling-off period to terminate the contract.
2. The consumer was approached at the railway station and entered into a contract for an English course there. The contract was not made on the business premises of the seller, but in the station. She then tried to cancel the agreement, relying on her right to do so under the EC Directive. The cancellation right was not recognised by the company or the court. Italy had not implemented the provisions of the Directive. A judgment for the amount and interest was entered against her. She sought to rely on the EC Directive as a defence and questions were referred to the ECJ as to whether, even though the Directive had not been transposed, it could be relied on in the national court.
3. If Directives could not be used against the state this would allow the state to take advantage of its own breach of EU law. Member states are under an obligation to implement Directives by the due date (see paras 21 and 23 of the judgment).
4. The ECJ repeated its early ruling in *Marshall* that a directive could not create obligations between individuals (para. 20) and therefore did not have horizontal direct effect.

5. This is a difficult question. The other possible avenues of seeking redress are looked at later in the chapter, but by way of introduction to these topics, in para. 26 the ECJ states, relying on earlier case law, that a national court must try to interpret any existing national legislation to comply with EU law and the consistent line of case law since the case of *C-14/83 Von Colson and Kamann v. Land Nordrhein-Westfalen [1984] ECR 1891*.

The other important remedy that the ECJ refers to is the obligation for member states to compensate individuals who have suffered damage or financial loss due to the failure of the state to comply with its EU obligations. The EU obligation in this case is the requirement to implement the Directive by the due date.

5.5 What is a public body or emanation of the state?

The ECJ has repeatedly stated that a Directive can only be used against a state or an emanation of the state/public body. It has set out some definitions for a public body or emanation of the state.

C-188/89 Foster v. British Gas [1990] ECR I-3313

This case arose from employees wishing to use the Equal Treatment Directive 76/207 to challenge differential retirement ages which operated in a privatised industry. Questions were referred to the ECJ as to whether such a company could constitute an 'emanation of the state', in which case the Directive would have vertical direct effect.

The ECJ stated that the exact form of the undertaking (i.e. whether it was a public or nationalised industry or a privatised industry) was irrelevant. To be classed as an emanation of the state it had to:

- be made responsible by a statutory measure for the provision of a public service which is under the control of the state; and
- have special powers over and above those normally given to undertakings or individuals.

Question: Which of the following do you consider would definitely be considered an emanation of the state?

- a local authority
- the ESB
- a national school
- the Gardaí
- a cosmetic surgery clinic
- a public hospital
- a computer software company.

Key Points: All of the bodies except the computer software company and the cosmetic surgery clinic are bodies which are required by the State to provide public services and which have special powers over and above those given to individuals. Under the *Foster* case principles they are capable of being classed as 'public bodies' and individuals and companies can use Directives against these bodies.

5.6 Application of the direct effect principles

Consider these situations:

> Suzanne is employed by the local authority as Manager of Horticultural Policy. Therese is the manager of a large garden centre provider called Greener plc. By an EU Directive 2004/2000 (fictitious) every employee is entitled to two days' paid leave for computer training. The directive was due to be implemented by 1 April 2008. Ireland has not transposed the Directive. Suzanne and Therese take two days off to undertake a course. They do not receive any pay and seek your advice as to whether they could use the Directive in support of their claims.

Key Points: If the Directive is clear, precise and unconditional it will fulfil the Van Gend en Loos criteria and may be capable of direct effect. The deadline for implementation has passed as required by the case of *C-148/78 Pubblico Ministero v. Ratti*. However, directives only have vertical direct effect and can only be invoked against the State or public bodies.

Suzanne is employed by a local authority and will be able to use the direct effect of the directive. Therese is employed by a private concern with no special powers and she will be unable to rely on the direct effect of the directive.

6 The Indirect Effect Principle in EU Law

This is another principle created by the ECJ as a way of enforcing EU law. It can be defined as an obligation placed on national courts to interpret national legislation in conformity with European Union law. It is also known as the Von Colson principle, from the case that defined it. The principle ensures that any existing national legislation should be interpreted so far as possible to comply with EU obligations. In Chapter 2 the purposive approach to construction was considered. This principle obliges national courts to construe purposively in EU matters.

Partly as a response to the fact that directives could not be directly enforced by individuals/undertakings against private individuals or entities (as Directives only have vertical direct effect (see above)), the ECJ ruled that national courts are obliged to 'interpret their national law in the light of the working and the purpose of a directive'.

C-14/83 *Von Colson and Kamann v. Land Nordrhein Westfalen* [1984] ECR 1891

Facts: Proceedings were brought by two female workers who had been refused jobs in an all-male prison. Remedies for this discrimination were prescribed in German law as being limited to 'Vertrauensschaden', or disappointment damages. This compensation provision purported to implement the Equal Treatment Directive 76/207. The German Labour Court interpreted the German law as only allowing the reimbursement of travel expenses, which was a nominal amount.

Von Colson argued, relying on Article 6 of the Directive, that the remedy was inadequate to enforce the prohibition on discrimination under EC law and was therefore a breach of EC law under Article 5 of the Treaty.

This particular provision of the Directive was not clear and precise enough to have direct effect under the Van Gend en Loos criteria.

The ECJ on a preliminary ruling noted that although full implementation did not require any specific sanction for unlawful discrimination, it must be such as to ensure **real and effective** judicial protection. If compensation was the chosen mechanism, the compensation had to be adequate in relation to the damage sustained. In this situation it clearly was not sufficient to enforce the rights.

Under Article 5 EC (now Article 10 EC) the obligation placed on member states to take all appropriate measures to ensure fulfilment of Treaty obligations is binding on the national courts. In applying national law, 'and in particular the provisions of a national law specifically introduced in order to implement ... National courts are required to interpret their national law in the light of the wording and purpose of the Directive' in order to achieve the result required by the Directive.

This method of using EU law is termed **indirect effect** and it allows any EU law provision, whether an EC Article, Regulation or Directive, to be used in a national court in order to interpret any contrary national provision to conform with the EC Directive.

An example from the UK illustrates the operation of the doctrine of indirect effect.

Litster v. Forth Dry Dock and Engineering Co Ltd [1989] 2 WLR 634

Facts: An EC Directive 77/187 obliged member states to enact legislative protection for employees when the employer they worked for was transferred to another employer. This frequently happens following a take-over or merger. Prior to the Directive many employees were simply sacked by the new employer when the old company was taken over. The Directive stated that employees would retain their jobs on the takeover as a going concern unless there were economic, technical or organisational reasons which justified termination of employment and that both the previous and new employer would be financially liable for unjustifiable dismissals.

The UK had implemented the Directive by secondary legislation (the Protection of Employment Regulations). However, there was a flaw in the secondary legislation, which allowed employers to escape from the provisions if they sacked employees before the transfer took place. This was clearly contrary to the spirit of the Directive. The House of Lords construed the national legislation purposively, i.e. in line with the EC Directive and read words into the defective UK regulations to cure the defect.

The effect of this interpretation was that employees dismissed due to the transfer could claim they had been unfairly dismissed and claim compensation from the new owners of the company. The Court used a purposive method of statutory interpretation as required by the ECJ in the Von Colson case.

7 The Supremacy of EU Law

The EC Treaty and secondary legislation made by the Community institutions regulate a huge range of activities. Inevitably discrepancies arise between EC legislation and a member state's legislation. Early in the development of the EC the issue of which law took priority caused constitutional questions. Many member states regarded their own law as superior to European Community law. (We looked at the constitutional provision in Ireland in Chapter 2.)

The Treaty does not specifically deal with the issue of which law takes precedence: there is no Article that states 'EU law has a higher authority than national law'. Conflicts between national provisions and the then EEC law provisions were highlighted by the concept of direct effect operating in the national system which was being developed by the European Court of Justice.

In a number of cases the European Court of Justice felt its way to an unequivocal assertion of the supremacy of European Community law over any form of conflicting national legislation.

The case of *C-6/64 Costa v. ENEL [1964] ECR 585* was one of the first occasions when the ECJ had to deal with the issue.

Facts: The Italian courts referred a number of questions to the ECJ for clarification concerning the status of EC law. The Italian court questioned whether it should apply and enforce an Italian legislation provision which was passed after the EEC Treaty was signed and questioned whether the Preliminary Ruling Procedure was applicable at all, and was of the opinion that national provisions overrode EC law. The ECJ did not agree with the assertions of the Italian government and stated:

> ... the terms and the spirit of the Treaty, make it impossible for the States ... to accord precedence to a unilateral and subsequent measure over a legal system accepted by them on a basis of reciprocity.

It ruled that the Italian court must apply and enforce EC law rather than any incompatible Italian provision. It made a number of significant and much-quoted statements:

> By contrast with ordinary international treaties, the EEC Treaty has created its own legal system which, on the entry into force of the Treaty, became an integral part of the Legal Systems of the Member States and which their courts are bound to apply.
>
> By creating a community of unlimited duration, having its own institutions, its own personality, its own legal capacity ... and real powers stemming from a limitation of sovereignty or a transfer of powers from the states to the Community, the member states have limited their sovereign rights and have thus created a body of law which binds both their nationals and themselves.

Question: Consider why the ECJ felt it necessary to create and emphasise this principle.

Key Points: It was necessary to assert the supremacy of EC law to ensure that EC law was uniformly applied throughout the then Community and now Union. The ECJ stressed that it could not be open to member states to select which provisions of EC law they would apply in full; the Treaty and secondary legislation were a complete code.

Task: Case Study

Access the Eur-Lex website and click on 'Case-law'. This will bring up the most recent cases from 2007.At the end of this list is a search facility. Use the 'Numerical access to the case-law', which requires you to know the year of the judgment and the case name. Search for C-11/70 (the eleventh Judgment of 1970 made by the ECJ). This will enable you to access *C-11/70 Internationale Handelsgesellschaft mbH v. Einfuhr und Vorratsstelle für Getreide und Futtermittel*.

A note on the case: Do not be put off by the font or the detail (many of the older cases were put on the database in upper case). What we are interested in is the format and key principle of this very important judgment. The preliminary ruling procedure at the time of this case was Article 177.

Facts of the case: A German businessman challenged the validity of an EC Regulation that controlled the grant of export permits for grain under the Common Agricultural Policy. The system established a procedure for a deposit to be paid by the trader for the grant of the licence. The deposit was lost in whole or part if the grain was not exported by a set time. The claimant argued that the EC Regulation was contrary to the principle of proportionality which was enshrined in the German constitution. Proportionality is a principle which states that any measure should be legitimately justified and should go no further than is necessary to achieve a legitimate object. The trader argued that forfeiture of the deposit was disproportionate. He brought a case in the German courts arguing that the German constitutional provision was superior to EC law and that he was entitled to a refund. A preliminary ruling was sought by the German Administrative Court from the ECJ.

You will see the Judgment is organised into headings (Summary, Parties, Subject of the Case, etc.). It is the summary that encapsulates the important principles.

Read through paragraph 1. What is the ECJ stating?

Key Points: The validity of Community law cannot be challenged by reference to national legal provisions in national courts. National laws, of whatever status, constitutional provisions or legislation, cannot limit the validity of EC law. The ECJ is asserting the **supremacy** of EC law here.

In paragraph 2 the ECJ recognises that there are inherent principles in member states' legal systems (at the time of the judgment there were only six member states) which are recognised by the

Community. Although the ECJ is not more explicit here, the principle of proportionality is one of these common, general principles of community law.

On the preliminary ruling before it, the ECJ ruled that the EC Regulation was valid as it was a valid regulatory measure which fulfilled the requirements of proportionality.

8 Free Movement of Goods in the European Union

The first part of this chapter focused on the development and principles created by the ECJ. We shall now consider some substantive provisions of the EU Treaty.

When the European Economic Community was first established there was a legacy of protectionism in most European states. To create an internal market the economic barriers to the free movement of goods had to be dismantled. Articles 25–30 and Article 90 are now the main provisions covering this area. Early in the Community's development customs duties and restrictions on importers could often be easily identified and challenged. Nowadays, many member states and agencies still have restrictive policies, but they are more subtle and difficult to identify. Although 1992 marked the supposed completion of the internal market following the Single European Act, there are still restrictions that impede the free movement of goods and service. These include tariff barriers, non-tariff barriers, anti-competitive agreements, state aids, regulatory restrictions and discriminatory taxation.

Task: Access the relevant Treaty Articles from the Europa website. Under 'Activities' go to the 'Internal market' section and then to 'Legal texts'. Click on Article 23. The Articles on customs duties will appear and you can scroll down to see all the other relevant Articles too. Reading and applying the primary source of law is always the starting point.

8.1 Prohibition on customs duties

Customs duties are prohibited under Article 25. A customs duty is any financial charge, however small, which is imposed by virtue of the crossing of a national boundary. The *Van Gend en Loos* case (above) was an early and important case on this area.

Measures that have an equivalent effect to customs duties are also prohibited. These might include charges for inspections of plants or animals that are not required or sanctioned under EU law, or other administrative fees or hurdles that are imposed on crossing a national boundary.

8.2 Prohibition on discriminatory taxation

A tax is a fiscal charge which is applied based on objective criteria. However, if the operation of the tax operates to discriminate against a sector (or product of a country) this runs counter to the free movement provisions. The aim of Article 90 is to prevent a heavier burden being placed on imported goods than domestic goods (thus favouring domestic production). Article 90 aims to prohibit fiscal barriers to free movement.

C-112/84 Humblot v. Directeur des Services Fiscaux [1985] ECR 1367

Facts: The case concerned the French registration system for cars. The French road tax operated on a sliding scale on cars below 16CV (16hp) and the maximum tax was 1,100 francs. On cars over 16CV there was a lump sum tax payable of 5,000 francs. It was found that French manufacturers of cars produced nothing more powerful than 16CV. Humblot brought a Mercedes in France (36hp) and was obliged to pay the levy of FF5,000. Humblot brought an action before the French courts seeking repayment of the excess of the tax over FF1,100, arguing that it contravened Article 95 (since the Amsterdam Treaty the provision has been renumbered Article 90). Humblot relied on the direct effect of the provision to challenge the French law in the French court. The French court referred the issue to the ECJ for a preliminary ruling.

The ECJ ruled that although the tax system contained no formal discrimination based on the origin of products it:

> ... manifestly exhibits discriminatory or protective features contrary to Article 95, since the power rating determining liability to the special tax has been fixed at a level such that only imported cars, particularly from other Member States, are subject to the special tax, whereas all cars of domestic manufacture are liable to the distinctly more advantageous differential tax.

It was an indirectly discriminatory and protectionist measure preferring French-produced cars. There was no objective justification for the differential treatment.

8.3 Prohibition on quantitative restrictions and measures of equivalent effect

Quantitative restrictions and measures of equivalent effect (QRMEE is a useful shorthand) are prohibited on imports under Article 28. Article 29 prohibits QRMEE on exports, but this is rarely used as most states do not wish to inhibit exports. This area of EU law has been the subject of so much litigation and comment that a textbook could be written on it alone. We shall focus on the main elements. Under Article 30 EC there are grounds permitted under the Treaty for member states to impose restrictions on public health or public policy grounds.

Question: Consider any situations in which member states may legitimately wish to restrict or prevent importation of certain goods which may be marketed elsewhere in the EU and which are not governed by EU rules.

Key Points: You may have identified food scares such as risks associated with contaminated foodstuffs or the possibility of contamination, such as BSE in British beef in the 1990s, and more recent food scares concerning foot and mouth, bluetongue disease and bird flu, which had necessitated limits on exports and import bans. You may also have identified categories of films or videos which may have different certifications or age ratings in other member states on public protection grounds. Pornographic materials have been the subject of legitimate restrictions. Certain kinds of knives or weaponry could also be the subject of restrictions. Drugs would be an example where member states have different policies in relation to importation and use.

8.3.1 Definition of QRMEE

Quantitative restrictions are 'classic' protectionist measures which limit the free movement of goods, typically imports, by reference to value, amount, etc. (i.e. quantitative criteria or quotas). An outright ban is a quota of zero. For example, *C-7/61 Commission v. Italy [1961] ECR 317* (ban on pork imports). Sometimes bans on the export and importation of products are necessary and the EU will issue a Decision formally regulating the area, such as in the case of safety or health scares, for example the BSE risks in British beef in the early 1990s and outbreaks of bird flu.

The measures we focus on are those imposed by member states for various reasons, which have the effect of restricting the free flow of goods.

Measures having equivalent effect is a significant phrase in Article 28. It is designed to prohibit barriers to free trade which are not quotas, but which nevertheless make it more difficult to import or export, i.e. a measure that has the ability to deflect normal trade patterns.

C-8/74 Rewe-Zentral AG v. Bundesmonopolverwaltung für Branntwein Dassonville [1974] ECR 834 (referred to as Dassonville)
Facts: The case arose out of criminal proceedings that had been taken against Belgian importers of Scotch whisky. They had imported whisky in contravention of a Belgian requirement that Scotch whisky should possess a British Certificate of Authentication. This rule clearly favoured direct importers from Scotland importing whisky into Belgium over importers from other member states as it was extremely difficult to obtain such a certificate.

The ECJ defined a measure having equivalent effect to a quantitative restriction. 'All trading rules enacted by member states which are capable of hindering, directly or indirectly, actually *or* potentially, intra-Community trade are to be considered as measures having an effect equivalent to quantitative restrictions.'

Articles 28–30 are directly effective and restrictive requirements can be challenged by traders in their national courts. A complaint can also be made to the European Commission, which may take infringement proceedings against a member state.

A fundamental principle of the free movement of goods is that of **mutual recognition**. Goods that have been lawfully produced and marketed in one member state should generally be able to be marketed (without undue and disproportionate restrictions) in any of the other member states.

TASK: CASE STUDY ON THE CASSIS DE DIJON CASE

Locate the case with a case number reference of C-120/78 (the 120th case lodged in 1978). You can do this in a number of ways. To practise on the Europa website go to the 'Gateway to the European Union'. Above the subjects listed there are tabs. Click on 'Institutions', then on 'European Court of Justice'. There are various search options. Because this is an older case and we have the case number, look in the 'Numerical Access' section and 'Cases lodged before 1988'. Type in the 120/78 reference and the full case should appear as *Rewe-Zentral AG v. Bundesmonopolverwaltung für Branntwein*. The subject matter of the case was the blackcurrant liqueur cassis, so the case is commonly called Cassis de Dijon.

Note on the case: The case was decided when the relevant Treaty Articles were Article 30 and 34 EC. They have since been renumbered to Article 28 and 30. The fundamental points of law remain the same. Similarly, you will see reference to Article 177 (which is now the preliminary ruling procedure under Article 234). Ignore the references to Article 37. We are concerned with the **main principles** which were created by the ECJ to regulate the free movement of goods and to set guidelines for the common situation in which member states refused to allow access to their domestic market of various foreign goods on a number of pretexts. This case is short and complex but had a huge impact. What we are interested in is an outline of the facts that gave rise to the case and the main principles spelt out by the ECJ relating to measures equivalent to QRMEE. Read the case and answer the questions below.

Facts: A German law laid down that the drink could be imported but not marketed as a liqueur as it had an alcoholic content of 15–20 per cent. The German law stipulated that a drink must have an alcoholic content of at least 25 per cent to be marketed as a liqueur. This effectively meant that French cassis was excluded from the profitable German liqueur market and it could not compete with nationally produced products such as schnapps, etc.

Questions
1. Did the ECJ rule that this type of measure was a measure equivalent to a quantitative restriction?
2. What did the ECJ rule in relation to possible restrictions on the marketing of goods where there are no relevant Community rules?
3. How did the German government attempt to justify the restriction?
4. What steps to protect the European consumer did the ECJ suggest?

Key Points
1. Yes, the fixing of a minimum alcohol content for a classification of goods, when the same product was lawfully produced and marketed in another member state, fell within the prohibition of Article 30 (now Article 28) as it created a hurdle to importation and fell within the Dassonville definition.
2. The ECJ ruled that in situations where there were no Community rules (such as Regulations and Directives governing certain products) a member state could impose restrictions on the

marketing of products *if* they could prove there were **mandatory reasons** for doing so. These included reasons of fiscal supervision, public health, fairness of transactions and consumer protection.

3. The claim was that they wished to stop too many low-alcohol products entering the market and inducing alcohol tolerance, while protecting the consumer. The ECJ was unconvinced by these arguments, noting that any alcoholic product could be diluted. The German ban was clearly a disproportionate measure.

4. The ECJ stated that supplying information to consumers by requiring labelling the products as to alcohol content could be justifiable.

This case introduced the possibility of member states being able to justify restrictions on free movement of goods on narrow and proportionate grounds, provided the restrictions applied to imported and domestically produced goods alike. Any measure which only applied to imported products would be discriminatory and be caught by Article 28 unless the derogations under Article 30 applied. The German government's arguments in this case were not accepted. However, the case set out the key principles for future cases.

Another early example of a member state attempting to impose restrictions on the marketing of products which inhibited imports was the case of *113/80 Commission v. Ireland (Irish Souvenirs) [1981] ECR 1625*. Irish legislation required imported souvenir-type goods to bear an indication of 'foreign' on jewellery, motifs or character of souvenirs. The Commission brought infringement proceedings against Ireland and argued that the restriction, which lowered the value of an imported product or increased production or distribution costs, must be regarded as being a QRMEE. The Irish government pleaded consumer fairness. This argument failed as it was a discriminatory measure. It was unnecessary for the consumer to know the origin unless such origin implied a certain quality, basic material or process of manufacture. As the products in this case were 'cheap' pictorial reminders with little commercial value the measure was disproportionate and contrary to EU law.

The ECJ has ruled in a number of important cases that trading rules of member states that apply to the marketing of a product and service (termed a 'selling arrangement' by the ECJ) are not generally caught by the Article 28 ban. Therefore member states can have different shop opening hours and different rules as to what types of goods may be stocked or advertised.

In *C-292/92 Hünemund* the ECJ gave a preliminary ruling that a rule prohibiting the advertisement of pharmaceutical products other than in pharmaceutical premises fell outside the prohibition in Article 28 and was a legitimate restriction.

However, if the national rules operate to discriminate a product or service from getting access to the market this may operate as a measure equivalent to a quantitative restriction and be contrary to EU law.

TASK: CASE STUDY ON AN ADVERTISING BAN

Using the Europa or Eur-Lex website access Articles 28–30 EC and make notes on the key elements. Then use the case-law search facility to access the Swedish case of *C-405/98 Konsumentombudsmannen v. Gourmet International Products*.

Note: The Articles referred to in this case are Articles 30 and 36 (now Articles 28 and 30). The provisions in relation to the freedom to provide services are also considered. We focus on the freedom to provide goods. Alcoholic beverages are again at issue.

There are many reasons why drink generates so much EU case law. Most countries have their own 'national drink' and many states try to protect their national product. Also tax excise on drink is an important source of revenue for many governments and classifications are important in this regard. Health and social concerns are also generating restrictions on the promotion and marketing of alcohol.

Read the case using the questions to identify the main issues. The relevant paragraphs of the judgment are indicated in the question.

Questions
1. What was the nature of the Swedish prohibition on the marketing of alcohol? (Paras 4–6.)
2. What questions did the Swedish national court, the Stockholms Tingsrätt, refer to the ECJ? (Para. 11.)
3. In the judgment the ECJ refers to a major ruling of *C-267/91* and *C-268/91 Keck and Mithouard [1993] ECR I 6097*, which permits differences in national selling arrangement requirements (as long as they do not relate to the goods, composition or packaging, etc.) provided they do not operate to hinder goods from other member states. For example, if a German pharmacy closes every Saturday at noon this is a restriction which prevents sales, but which affects domestic and imported pharmaceuticals in

exactly the same way, as neither can be purchased during closing hours.

How does the defendant (GIP) in these proceedings say that the advertising ban impacts more on imported goods than on domestic goods? (Para. 16.)

4. Does the ECJ rule that this type of blanket ban on advertising adversely impacts on imported products? (Paras 20, 21, 24, 25.)

5. How did the ECJ deal with the argument that Sweden put forward justifying the restriction relying on public health grounds for the advertising ban? (Paras 28–30.)

9 The Right of Establishment and the Freedom to Provide Services

The right to set up a business enterprise or undertaking on a long-term basis in the EU by an EU national or an undertaking which is incorporated or based in an EU state is termed the **freedom of establishment**. This right covers a huge range of activities. It covers large multinationals establishing bases in other EU states and also a single consultant working on a freelance basis elsewhere in the EU. The Treaty provisions relating to freedom of establishment are found in Articles 43–48 EC. The key provisions have direct effect, and so can be relied upon in a national court.

The freedom to provide **services** is governed by Articles 49–55. These provisions can often overlap. Generally they cover a less permanent stay in another member state for the purpose of providing (or receiving) commercial services. The provisions will cover the temporary stay of a self-employed builder in France to provide building services, and the ability to provide and receive medical and dental services elsewhere in the EU. The aim of both sets of rights is to facilitate free movement of persons as individual providers and recipients of services and of business enterprises. The ECJ has given detailed guidance in preliminary rulings on the extensive scope of these rights. Once again, the scale of the subject matter warrants a complete book, but we shall focus on the right to receive medical treatment/services within the EU as an example of how the rights have been interpreted and applied by the EU.

9.1 The right to provide and receive services

Articles 49 and 50 of the EC Treaty prohibit restrictions on the freedom to provide services within the EU in respect of nationals of member states or nationals of a third country who are established within the Community.

The right applies to individuals and to business entities (an individual who is self-employed, independent contractors, companies, partnerships).

The Article aims to allow cross-border services, for example a postal service company based in Germany wishing to provide a service in Ireland and the UK.

The provisions are backed up by an important general provision against discrimination on nationality grounds on any Treaty matter (contained in Article 12 of the Treaty). This means that in any area covered by the principle that an individual who is a German national and seeking to exercise his EU rights in France, for example, must not be treated differently from a French national in the same circumstances.

> Jean is a French professional squash coach who wishes to set up a set of intensive squash summer camps for adults in Ireland for three months during the summer.
>
> Jean will be providing professional services and will be covered by Article 49. If there are no public policy or public security issues concerning Jean, he would have a directly enforceable right to provide squash services in Ireland on the same basis as an Irish national.

Question: What sort of 'public policy' or 'public security' grounds might allow Ireland to prevent Jean from exercising this Article 49 right?

Key Points: The ECJ has interpreted these restrictions strictly. A public policy ground would have to be proven and it would have to be shown that Jean was a threat to the fundamental interests of society. A pattern of serious criminal conduct which could be repeated (e.g. serious drugs or gun offences) would be an example.

9.1.1 The definition of services — Article 50

Article 50 gives a definition of services which includes industrial, commercial, professional and craft work. Services should normally be provided for 'remuneration'. The ECJ has considerably extended the scope of this Article and in a number of important rulings has ruled that not only is there a right to deliver services, but there is also a corollary right to **receive** services.

C-186/87 Cowan v. Le Trèsor Public [1986] ECR 195
Facts: An English tourist was mugged on the Paris Metro. He was unable to claim French criminal compensation due to his nationality.

The ECJ ruled that the individual was availing of tourist services in France and was entitled to be treated in the same way as a French national who had been mugged. Cowan successfully relied on the directly effective right to 'provide services' to cover his right to receive services without discriminatory treatment on the grounds of nationality.

In Ireland the freedom to receive information services on the availability of abortion elsewhere in the EU was the subject of a preliminary ruling. In the case of *C-159/90 SPUC Ireland Ltd v. Grogan [1991] ECR-I 4685* the ECJ ruled that information services were capable of being classed as a service. Fertility services have also been ruled to be a service under EU law in *R v. Human Fertilisation and Embryology Authority ex parte Blood [1997] 2 All ER 687*, in which a British woman successfully invoked her directly effective EU law rights to ensure that sperm taken from her critically ill husband, contrary to strict UK guidelines, was not destroyed and could be exported to facilitate her fertility treatment elsewhere in the EU.

9.1.2 The right to be provided with medical services/treatment elsewhere in the EU

This is an interesting area for a number of reasons. Medical treatment is a personal and emotive issue. It is an expensive service and member states have different ways of providing for treatment and financing their health services. It is also a political subject. The pressures and priorities of a member state were summarised by the ECJ in the *Watts* case (see below).

> Where the demand for hospital treatment is constantly rising, primarily as a consequence of medical progress and increased life expectancy, and the supply is necessarily limited by budgetary constraints, it cannot be denied that the national authorities responsible for managing the supply of such treatment are entitled, if they consider it necessary, to institute a system of waiting lists in order to manage the supply of that treatment and to set priorities on the basis of the available resources and capacities.

The preamble of the EC Treaty refers to the 'constant improvements of the living ... conditions of their peoples'. Article 2(p) of the Treaty refers to activities to secure attainment of a high level of health **protection**. Health treatment or the provision of medical services is not explicitly mentioned in the Treaty. Although certain social security aspects are harmonised by EU regulation, member states had been anxious to control their obligations towards nationals of their own member states and other EU nationals with regard to medical treatment due to the financial implications of providing health treatment and care. The European Court of Justice in a series of rulings made it clear that the right to receive medical services elsewhere in the EU is an important and directly effective right.

Recent health care cases have dealt with cross-border health care and whether national administrative requirements that the patient obtain prior authorisation for treatment abroad were contrary to the EU Treaty provisions on the free movement of services.

The current EU social security regulation is Regulation (EC) No. 883/2004 on the co-ordination of social security systems. This replaced earlier provisions and laid down a duty to grant an authorisation in question in particular where the treatment cannot be given in the member state of residence 'within a time-limit which is medically justifiable, taking into account his/her current state of health and the probable course of his/her illness'.

Joined cases C157/99 BSM Gereats-Smits v. Stichting; Ziekenfonds VGZ and HTM Peerboom v. Stichting CZ Groep — Zorgverzekeringen European Court Reports 2001 Page I-05473
This landmark case raised difficult issues concerning the most effective treatment and the appropriate time frame for treatment and the possibility of 'clinic shopping' within the EU. It concerned the reimbursement of hospital treatment costs incurred in Germany and Austria. The first claimant had sought multi-disciplinary treatment in Germany, which was unavailable in the Netherlands. The second claimant had fallen into a coma after a road traffic accident and had been transferred to Innsbruck for experimental treatment not available in the Netherlands. The cases raised similar issues and were therefore 'joined' in order that the ECJ could reply to certain key issues.

The ECJ made a number of important rulings.

The fact that medical service fell within arrangements of social security did not exclude it from the scope of protection under Article 50 (ex 60).

Article 49 permits member states to require prior authorisation in order to cover treatment abroad and to impose criteria that the treatment is regarded as 'normal' in professional circles and that the treatment is necessary. The ECJ set out how these types of criteria should be interpreted.

First, that the concept of 'normal' treatment covered treatment that was sufficiently tried and tested by international medical science.

Second, that authorisation can be refused on the lack of medical necessity **only** if the same or equally effective treatment can be obtained without undue delay at an establishment having a contractual arrangement with the insured person's sickness insurance fund.

C-372/04 R (Watts) v. Bedford Primary Care Trust and Another

Facts: Mrs Watts was on an NHS list (for free treatment) to have a hip replacement in the UK. Mrs Watts decided she could not wait any longer and her request for prior authorisation under the relevant Regulation to have a hip replacement surgery in France paid for by her health authority was refused. The Primary Care Trust (PCT) argued that there was a waiting list for treatment. She went ahead and had the operation in France and brought judicial review proceedings afterwards, claiming the refusal of the authorisation was unlawful under EU law and reclaiming the cost of the operation she had undergone as a private patient. The PCT argued that the refusal was justified due to the requirements of priorities and waiting lists.

Her argument was that she was entitled to the free treatment under the EU Regulation and Article 49 and she relied on her directly effective EU rights before the British courts.

The ECJ ruled that a refusal to grant the authorisation on the ground that there was a waiting list for hospital treatment could be made if the social security institution could establish that the waiting time did not exceed an acceptable period on the basis of an objective medical assessment of the clinical needs of the patient in all the circumstances.

9.1.3 Impact of the judgments and rights in Ireland

When travelling abroad within Europe a European Health Insurance Card should be obtained in order to secure your right to emergency and other types of treatment. There are limitations on the other types of treatment that you can obtain.

TASK

You are consulted by Helen, a sixty-year-old who requires treatment for a serious arthritic condition. She has been on the public health waiting list for over a year and is suffering a lot of pain and anxiety. She lives on her own and is worried that she may lose her independence. She has heard from her daughter, who lives in France, that there is excellent treatment available there. Neither Helen nor her daughter can afford to pay for the operation to be done privately.

Using the Citizens Information website and your notes from the earlier part of this section, briefly outline whether you consider she may have a right under European Union law to travel to France.

The National Treatment Purchase Fund was set up in 2002 after the key judgments of the ECJ and in the face of rising public health waiting lists.

TASK

Access the site of the National Treatment Purchase Fund and read the introductory material about the operation and scope of the fund. In which European countries will the fund consider paying for treatment?

9.1.4 The Services Directive

A new Services Directive 2006/123/EC was passed in December 2006 and is to be transposed by all member states by 28 December 2009. There was much debate amongst member states about this Directive and some sectors excluded from its ambit as a result of negotiations between the states prior to its enactment. This secondary legislation supports Articles 43 and 49 and covers freedom of establishment and services. It establishes a general framework for any service provided for an economic return with the exception of banking and financial services, transport services, health services, private security services, gambling and services connected with official authority. The Directive requires member states to assess and, if necessary, to simplify procedures and formalities applicable to accessing a service activity. The Directive requires the identification of a point of single contact to be able to complete all administrative formalities and also to be able to achieve this online.

10 The ECJ and the Enforcement of EU Law

10.1 The preliminary ruling procedure

The majority of cases considered in Chapters 2, 3 and 8 on EU law have been the results of requests for preliminary rulings made by national courts.

TASK

Locate Article 234 using the Europa website. Note that this Article gives the ECJ jurisdiction to give preliminary rulings on the interpretation of the EC Treaty and 'the validity and interpretation of the acts of the institutions'. This means the ECJ can rule on the interpretation to be given to EC Regulations, Directives and Decisions.

A question must be referred from a court or tribunal of a member state where an issue of EU law has been raised. The national court must consider it necessary for a preliminary ruling to be given. The national court frames questions about the issues requiring clarification. The ECJ does not decide the case for the national court; it gives general, not specific, **guidance** on the interpretation of EU law. While the preliminary ruling is being considered by the ECJ, the national court case is suspended pending the outcome of the ruling.

This short Treaty Article (previously Article 177) has immense significance in the development of EU law. It allows courts of member states to seek an authoritative ruling on matters of law including the status of the provision over national law, interpretation of terms and methods of application. From use of this procedure fundamental principles of EU law have emerged, such as: direct effect, supremacy of EU law, state liability for breach of EU law, etc.

10.2 The enforcement of EU law

Every effective legal system needs methods of enforcement and sanctions. The EC Treaty has set down procedures for enforcement actions to be brought before the ECJ. In addition, the ECJ has developed a principle of state liability for a serious breach of EU law.

10.2.1 Proceedings before the ECJ

If the Commission considers that a member state has failed to fulfil a Treaty obligation it shall deliver a reasoned opinion on the matter to the state and allow the state a chance to submit observations. If the member state fails to comply the Commission can bring proceedings in the ECJ (Article 226).

A member state may bring proceedings in the ECJ against another member state for breach of EU law (Art 227 EC). If the ECJ finds that there has been non-compliance with a judgment of the ECJ it may impose a fine (Art 228). This has rarely been invoked by the ECJ.

An individual has no direct access to the ECJ to bring an action to challenge an infringement of EU law by an individual, undertaking or state of the EU. Challenges can be made using a directly effective EU provision within a national court. An individual or undertaking can bring actions in the Court of First Instance and the ECJ challenging the legality of an EU provision or action of an institution of the EU. There are strict procedural limits on these judicial review actions.

10.2.2 Action in the national courts

1. Direct effect. An individual or undertaking can rely on the direct effect of EU law to override conflicting national law. We have seen that this is an effective way of enforcing EU law, but that there are limits in enforcing Directives as they can only be used against the State or an emanation of the State.

2. Indirect effect. An individual may rely on the requirement placed on national courts by the case of *Von Colson* to interpret national legislation in conformity with overriding EU obligations, the principle of EU law having indirect effect and being used as a method of interpreting national legislation which does not comply with relevant EU law.

10.3 The principle of state liability

In addition to the methods above, the ECJ extended the possibility of individuals suing the state for failure to comply with EU law in the national court. It established the principle that member states should be financially liable for losses or damage caused by their failure to comply with a Treaty Article, Regulation or obligations under a Directive. The first case that established this was *C-6/90 and C-9/90 Francovich v. Italian Republic [1991] ECR I-5357.*

Facts: An EC Directive set out employment rights (of payment of a portion of salary) for employees if an employer became insolvent. The Italian state failed to implement the Directive and there was therefore no national legislation for employees to rely upon when the employer was insolvent. The Directive lacked direct effect as it left an area of discretion (and did not therefore comply with the third criterion of *Van Gend en Loos*).

The employee sued the state for failure to comply with EU law and a preliminary ruling was sought from the ECJ as to whether Italy could be financially liable.

The ECJ set down conditions for state liability:

- the Directive must grant rights to individuals
- those rights should be identifiable from the Directive
- there must be a causal link between the breach of the state's obligation and the loss suffered.

10.3.1 The development of the principle

The ECJ clarified the scope of the principle of state liability for breach of EU law in a number of cases. The principle was not confined to the breach involving failure to implement a Directive (as in Francovich). The court limited the scope of the action by stating that the breach of EU law by the member state must be 'sufficiently serious'.

The relevant criteria for state liability which must be proved by the claimant before the national court are:

- the rule of law must create rights for individuals
- the breach must be 'sufficiently serious'
- there must be a direct causal link between the breach of obligation by the state and the damage sustained by the injured parties.

The 'sufficiently serious' aspect has been clarified by the ECJ. The claimant must prove the State 'manifestly and gravely disregarded the limits on its discretion' in EU law.

The ECJ outlined a series of factors that the national court may consider. These include:

- The clarity and precision of the EU rule that has been broken.
- The level of discretion a member state has to exercise (in the implementation of Directive there may be considerable discretion, in the compliance with an absolute Treaty Article, such as Articles 12 and 25, there will be no discretion).
- Whether the infringement was voluntary or involuntary nature. (Were there extenuating circumstances explaining the breach?)
- Whether an EU institution may have contributed to the omission (such as incorrect guidance having been given by the European Commission).

These criteria were applied in:
C–5/94 R v. MAFF ex parte Hedley Loams (Ireland) Ltd [1996] All ER (EC) 493.
Where there was no or very little discretion in granting the licence that could in itself be a sufficiently serious breach and entitle the claimant to compensation for state liability.

C-178, 179, 189 and 190/94 Dillenkofer v. Germany [1996] All ER (EC) 917
Facts: This concerned the failure of Germany to implement Directive 90/314, the Package Holidays Directive, which grants rights to individuals for a number of aspects, including being financially affected by the insolvency of the tour operator. Article 7 of the Directive aimed to protect consumers and the content of the rights was identifiable.

The ECJ gave a preliminary ruling stated that a failure to implement a Directive where little or no legislative choice was involved could be a sufficiently serious breach, as if a member state failed to take any of the steps to implement a Directive within the time limit that member state had 'manifestly and gravely disregarded' the limits on its discretion.

C-283/94 Denkavit International BV v. Bundesamt für Finanzen [1996] ECR I-5063
Where other member states, after discussion with the Council, had adopted the same interpretation of the Directive as Germany and there was no relevant case law of the Court it was ruled the breach was not sufficiently serious.

11 Competition Law

OVERVIEW
- The need for competition law in the marketplace.
- Key competition law concepts.
- The significance of EU competition law.
- Types of anti-competitive agreements.
- Abuse of a dominant position in the marketplace — examples.

11.1 What is competition law?

Competition law aims to regulate and control the way in which businesses behave when they are seeking to gain customers, establish market share and enter into business deals. It aims to promote open and fair competition in the interests of economic efficiency by encouraging innovation and technical progress. Competition law also aims to protect the interests of consumers by allowing them to acquire goods and services at the best possible value.

Competition law policy aims to ensure that any anti-competitive practices by companies or national authorities do not hinder healthy competition. From a European perspective it can be seen as a vital element of the creation of a single internal market.

Many of the competition law principles upon which the law is based are founded on economic principles. Competition law and policy can be economically and politically controversial. It seeks to protect the end user/consumer against unfair market behaviour by a business and it can be viewed as interfering with commercial freedom. The competition law provisions of the EU could be said to be the most important provisions of the Treaty from the perspective of businesses.

The EU has a highly developed body of competition law. EU rules apply to undertakings based within the EU and outside the EU.

From a business point of view it is important to note that EU law is always treated as having a higher status than domestic law, so if there is any contradiction between them EU law will take precedence. In Ireland the Competition Acts 2002–2006 follows the framework of the EU approach and establishes the Competition Authority as the enforcement agency in Ireland.

11.2 Competition law and the EU

11.2.1 Sources of EU competition law

Treaty Articles:

- Article 81 — anti-competitive agreements (this is the focus in this chapter).
- Article 82 — abuse of a dominant position in the market.

Regulation 1/2003 EC — gives the European Commission extensive powers to investigate alleged infringements, decide whether there has been a breach of EU competition rules, and gives extensive powers to fine undertakings in breach of the rules.

Other Regulations — allow certain types of agreement to be made between undertakings (e.g. research and development, etc.) without contravening the competition rules.

Case law of the European Court of Justice and the Court of First Instance.

11.3 Competition and the single internal market

The key aim of the EEC when it was established was to create a common market with factor mobility. From the outset competition law was part of the strategy of the EEC to encourage a competitive, open marketplace. Firms that agree to carve up the market along national lines face severe penalties under Community competition law.

An early case in Europe in this area stated the aim of the competition law principles:

Metro-SB Grossmarkte GmbH v. Commission

> The requirement contained in the Treaty (Articles 3, 81) that competition shall not be distorted implies the existence on the market of workable competition, that is to say the degree of competition necessary to ensure ... the creation of a single market achieving conditions similar to a domestic market.

Example: a potentially anti-competitive agreement
Infant, Jouer, Kinder and Leanbh (I, J, K, L) are all large companies which manufacture children's toys. Their product ranges are basically the same and principally consist of high-quality wooden toys. The companies are based respectively in the UK, France, Germany and Ireland. There is a meeting of the managing directors where it is agreed that:
- each manufacturer will focus on customers within its own member state and will not seek to sell to customers in other member states, so I will not export its toys to France, Ireland or Germany; J will not export to the UK, Ireland or Germany, etc.; *and*
- they will ensure that they charge the same prices for the products they all manufacture.

Question: From a competitive point of view, what does this type of arrangement achieve?
Key Point: The manufacturers are co-operating with each other to minimise risks from competitors.

Generally in an ordinary competitive marketplace producers of a product will be competing against each other to build up a market share. In this situation the potential competitors have got together and made sure that each one does not face competition in its home market (this is a **cartel** arrangement) and also, due to the price-fixing agreement, that the customers cannot buy the product from its competitors at a cheaper price.

If there are plenty of other sources of such toys then customers can obtain the goods from elsewhere, from a producer that is not within this cartel. However, this type of agreement is open to abuse, particularly if the manufacturers are very large or the dominant suppliers in the market. The manufacturers could use this sort of agreement to stifle price competition in the market.

This type of agreement also goes against the idea of a single market, as the participants have effectively divided the market up into separate (territorial) blocks.

TASK

Access Articles 81 and 82 EC, the primary legislation governing EU competition law.

11.4 Article 81 EC

This is a general ban on anti-competitive agreements and collusion between competitors. It is the most used provision in the competition area and it is aimed at preventing a range of business activities which could interfere with trade and competition in the EU.

The Article has three core elements:

1. A general prohibition on all agreements, decisions and concerted practices between undertakings, which may affect trade between Member States and which have as their object or effect the prevention, restriction or distortion of competition. (Examples of types of anti-competitive agreement are given in the Article.)
2. It makes such agreements automatically void. This means they cannot be enforced under contract law.
3. It allows for certain types of beneficial agreements to exist. There are stringent conditions for these, and there must be a consumer benefit involved.

11.4.1 Types of prohibited agreement under Article 81 EC

Some initial concepts should be clarified.

It catches agreements both on the *horizontal plane* (i.e. agreements between operators at the same level on the distribution chain) and *vertical agreements* (i.e. agreements between operators at different levels, e.g. manufacturer and distributor).

Undertakings: This is a broad concept. Article 81 covers all forms of commercial enterprise, e.g. companies, partnerships, co-operatives and individuals, and state-owned corporations are covered by Articles 81 and 82.

Agreements/decisions/concerted practices: No formal or written agreement is required. This term covers agreements binding legally and also those binding in honour only (*ACF Chemiefarma v. Commission [1970] ECR 661*, a so-called 'gentlemen's agreement').

The Polypropylene Cartel was investigated in the 1980s. The participants tried to defend themselves on the basis that it was a rolling operation with fluid membership, and the parties did not in any event stick to the price agreements. The ECJ ruled that the structure of agreement was a cartel.

Decisions by associations of undertakings: Decisions by trade associations may well amount to a concerted practice. Recommended prices may fall foul of the provision. If two trade associations reach an agreement the terms of which will affect their members then all members may be liable for a fine.

Concerted practices: This definition is a catchall. It covers informal co-operation between undertakings where there is no formal agreement or decision. Where there are only a few operators in the market i.e. an **oligopoly** exists, there may be a high level of stability or stagnation and market shares may remain constant. When one operator moves on the market by, for example, cutting prices the other may tend to react in a similar fashion. This is known as the concept of **parallel behaviour**.

Provided undertakings act **independently** and react to such moves by an operator then their behaviour will not infringe Article 81.

Woodpulp [1992] 4 CMLR 407
Article 81(1) does not prohibit undertakings from adapting their behaviour intelligently to existing or anticipated behaviour of a few competitors on the market.

However, parallel behaviour may be a *strong indication of concerted practices*. This will be the case if there is no plausible explanation for their behaviour.

Clear examples of this will include operators seeking to partition or divide up territories in order to market their goods.

Article 81(1) outlines facets of agreement which prima facie have a restrictive effect on competition.

Directly/indirectly fixed purchase or selling prices or other trading conditions. Price fixing is prohibited. Generally price fixing will attract large fines due to the overt nature of the restriction.

Distribution agreements:
Export bans. A number of cases have confirmed that the prohibition under Article 81 automatically applies to export bans in distribution agreements.
T 43/92 Dunlop Slazenger International Ltd v. Commission
The Court has not been impressed by arguments that export bans that were part of distribution agreements were not actually enforced and has found such clauses to be illegal. 'A clause prohibiting exports constitutes a restriction on competition ... since the agreed purpose is to isolate a part of the market.'

Share markets or sources of supply. Typically these will be horizontal agreements which have a highly restrictive effect on trade.

Applying dissimilar conditions to equivalent transactions. Agreements to charge dissimilar prices to different customers are permissible if they reflect different costs such as storage, insurance, transport costs. Operators may offer discounts for bulk purchases if this reflects cost savings.

11.5 Agreements that escape the prohibition under Article 81(1)

Article 81(3) exempts certain categories of agreement which contribute towards the improvement of production or distribution of goods or promoting technical or economic progress while allowing consumers a fair share of the resulting benefit *and must not* impose unnecessary and disproportionate restrictions or allow undertakings the possibility of eliminating competition in respect of a substantial part of the products in question.

The *Yves St Laurent Perfumes* case concerned the distribution of luxury perfumes. The agreement was granted exemption even though the system ensured that prices were kept higher than would otherwise have been the case. The justification was that the agreement promoted the distribution and image of the goods and was of benefit to consumers.

Block exemptions. There are some types of agreement which enhance competition and are common among commercial enterprises. It was clear that for certainty and administrative purposes a framework for legitimate agreements had to be created by the Commission. Accordingly, the Commission issued various block exemptions which provide that certain agreements which have beneficial features are not to be regarded as anti-competitive. Examples of these include:

- Reg. (EC) No. 2658/2000 Specialisation Agreements
- Reg. (EC) No. 2659/2000 Research and Development Agreements.

Agreements which have little competitive effect will not contravene EU competition rules. Agreements which do not appreciably restrict trade between member states or competition will generally not be caught by the prohibition in Article 81. The main criterion for exemption is the market-share threshold and the Commission Notice on Minor Agreements governs this area.

Agreements not covered by the exemption. The exemption does not apply to agreements between competitors which are aimed at:

- limiting production or sales
- fixing selling prices
- restricting product supplies to customers.

The exemption does not apply to agreements between non-competitors relating to:

- the sale price of products (however, maximum or recommended prices are generally authorised)
- restriction of territory or of customers
- restriction of sales in a selective distribution system
- restriction on own suppliers of spare parts as regards the sale of such parts to end users or to independent repairers.

11.6 Consequences of contravening Article 81(1)

Article 85(2) provides that such an agreement is **void**. It cannot be enforced by any of the parties.

The Commission has wide powers to investigate and punish offending undertakings.

Under Regulation 1/2003 the Commission may impose fines of up to €1 million or ten per cent of global turnover in the preceding business year of each of the undertakings participating, either intentionally or negligently, in the infringement.

The level of fine will depend upon factors such as the type of breach, the economic status of the undertaking and the relevant market share. The duration of the infringement, whether or not the infringement was deliberate or hidden and whether or not the undertaking has already been found to be in breach of EU law will also be relevant.

The Commission also has power to fine for failure to supply information to the Commission and periodical payments for failure to end a prohibited practice. There is provision for interest on fines.

11.6.1 Examples of fines

The European Commission imposed fines exceeding €855 million on a number of European and Japanese companies that participated in an international vitamin cartel in breach of European competition law. They related to an international cartel that raised the price of a range of vitamins for periods of four to ten years. The cartel was led by Hoffman La Roche AG of Switzerland, BASF of Germany, and supported by at least six other smaller producers. Roche was fined €462m, BASF €296m, with the other participants fined a total of €97 million. The cartel came to light as a result of an immunity programme.

Since 2002 there has been a new leniency policy for companies which supply information on cartels between two or more firms prohibited by Article 81 of the Treaty. It provides for immunity as well as a reduction in the amount of a fine and is designed to encourage firms to 'whistle blow' on serious violations of the competition rules.

11.7 The role of the European Commission in competition law

The Commission has wide investigative powers. It can carry out inspections of business premises without giving prior notice and can demand to see the necessary documents.

Before taking a decision, it gives the firms and member states concerned the opportunity to explain their position at organised hearings.

Firms or member states which are the subject of a Commission decision may challenge the decision before the Court of First Instance and the Court of Justice in Luxembourg.

Note: It is possible for individuals or firms who believe they are the victims of anti-competitive behaviour to complain to the national Competition Authority and/or to take their case before the national courts, as Articles 81 and 82 are directly effective.

CASE STUDY: PLASTERBOARD

In November 2002 the European Commission imposed fines totalling €478 million on four companies which operated a long-running cartel on the market for plasterboard, a product widely used in the building industry and by DIYers. Two of the companies involved were committing their second infringement of EU law on restrictive agreements. The then Commissioner states:

> The building industry is the pulse of the economy. The substantial amount of the fine reflects the size of the market, the impact of the illicit agreement on the consumer and the repeated infringement of the competition rules by two of the companies. The Commission is focusing its drive to stamp out cartels on the key sectors of the European economy, where its action can directly improve the well-being of consumers.

Nature of the market. The plasterboard market had a turnover of more than €1.2 billion in 1997. The cartel affected 80 per cent of consumers in the European Union, namely in France, the United Kingdom, Germany and the Benelux countries. Plasterboard is a manufactured product used as a prefabricated construction material or by DIY practitioners. It consists of a sheet of gypsum plaster sandwiched between two sheets of paper or some other material.

The companies produced virtually all the plasterboard manufactured in the countries concerned, in some of which the name of the relevant company's product is commonly used to designate the product itself (e.g. 'Gyproc' in Belgium), with the names of the companies being very clearly identified as a brand name by consumers.

Commission investigation. There was an in-depth investigation, including surprise inspections, in 1998. The Commission concluded that several undertakings participated in a plasterboard cartel.

The nature of the agreement between the parties. The cartel started at a meeting held in London in early 1992 at which the representatives of BPB and Knauf decided to end what they called the 'price war' that was then taking place and expressed the common desire to reduce competition to a level that suited their interests on the German, French, United Kingdom and Benelux markets. After the London meeting, a secret information-exchange system was set up to monitor market trends and avoid over-aggressive competition. Others later joined the arrangement. Through high-level contacts the parties exchanged information on their sales volumes so as to provide reassurance that the price war had ended and they repeatedly gave each other advance warning of price increases.

Summary

The European Economic Community began as a political movement seeking stability and economic recovery and co-operation after the ravages of World War II. Originally comprising six member states its membership has grown to 27 states. It has developed to encompass a wide range of activities — economic, social and environmental — and is now commonly referred to as the European Union.

The Treaty establishing the Economic Community sets out the framework of policies and laws and gives authority to the institutions to enact secondary legislation, which consists of Regulations, Directives and Decisions. The scope and interpretation of primary and secondary legislation is the chief function of the European Court of Justice, which clarifies and develops EU law by delivering preliminary rulings on questions referred to it by national courts.

In particular the ECJ has developed the principles of direct effect, the supremacy of EU law, the indirect effect principle and the principle of state liability for serious breach of EU law.

QUESTIONS

(You may find it useful to look back to Chapter 2 when considering these questions.)

1. Briefly summarise the development of the European Union from its origins as a European Economic Community established in post-war Europe by six states.
2. What is meant by the expression 'the pillars of the European Union'?
3. Why is it still correct to refer to European Community (EC) law ?
4. Outline the four fundamental freedoms that are the basis of the concept of a common market. Give an example of each freedom in operation.
5. List the types of secondary legislation that the EU institutions may pass.

6. Which Article provides for the free movement of European Union nationals who are classed as workers? What rights does a worker have if they are working elsewhere in the European Union?
7. Define the principle of direct effect and give the case law authority that created the principle.
8. An EU Directive is said to have 'vertical direct effect'. Explain the type of bodies that a Directive can be relied upon to challenge practices or laws that are contrary to EU law.
9. Identify the leading case of the ECJ that defines the concept of 'public body or emanation of the state'.
10. The ECJ have created a principle of EU law which ensures that national courts of the EU must recognise and apply EU law and interpret national law to comply with EU law. What is this principle called?
11. Closely related to the principle of indirect effect is the issue of supremacy of EU law. Give a brief explanation of two key cases that outline the principle.
12. What do you understand by the term 'single market'? When, in theory, was the single market supposed to have been fully achieved?
13. List three types of measures which are outlawed by the EU Treaty to ensure the existence and functioning of a single market.
14. Give an example of a measure equivalent to a quantitative restriction (QREE).
15. What type of restriction was at issue in the Cassis de Dijon case? What type of restrictions did the ECJ suggest may be imposed by a member state?
16. What do you understand by the terms 'freedom of establishment' and 'freedom to provide services'? Give an example of each type of right.
17. Are medical services covered by the European Union Treaty as a 'freedom to receive services'? What advantages and disadvantages do you think this right might present for member states?
18. An effective legal system must have an effective system of enforcement or sanctions. Outline three methods by which EU law is enforced.
19. A member state of the EU may now be sued by an individual or undertaking which has suffered loss due to a breach of EU law by the state. In what circumstances may a state be financially liable? Use case law authority to support your answer.
20. Why is it essential that the EU has an effective competition law policy? Briefly explain the concept of an 'anti-competitive agreement' prohibited by Article 81 EC.

ASPECTS OF HUMAN RIGHTS LAW

At the end of this chapter you should be able to:
- Summarise the background to and the significance of the European Convention on Human Rights and Fundamental Freedoms (ECHR).
- Understand the scope of some key rights protected by the Convention.
- Explain the impact of the European Convention of Human Rights Act 2003 on Irish law.
- Navigate the Council of Europe website and locate and research significant cases of the European Court of Human Rights.
- Have an appreciation of topical issues concerning human rights and the concept of conflicting rights and balancing of human rights.

OVERVIEW
- The human rights background.
- Constitutional rights and internationally protected human rights.
- Key features of the European Convention on Human Rights (ECHR).
- Summary of rights.
- Impact on the Irish legal system.

1 Background to Modern Law on Human Rights

The concept of the protection of human rights has been a topic of political discussion for centuries. The modern law on this area can be said to be largely a post-war phenomenon. There were notable human rights documents which long pre-dated the world wars. The American Declaration of Independence of 1776, for example, asserted:

> We hold these truths to be self-evident, that all men are created equal, that they are endowed by their Creator with certain unalienable Rights, that among these are Life, Liberty and the

pursuit of Happiness. — That to secure these rights, Governments are instituted among Men, deriving their just powers from the consent of the governed.

Note the reference to 'inalienable' human rights, that is rights that exist by virtue of our human condition which cannot be taken away. The Irish Constitution also uses this phrase in Articles 1, 41 and 42 (see Chapter 2).

It was the reaction against the horrors of the genocide and brutality of World War II that led to the foundation of the modern law on human rights.

The United Nations was established under the Charter signed in San Francisco in 1945. The Preamble to the Charter sets out the aims of the UN as being:

> To save succeeding generations from the scourge of war, which twice in our lifetime has brought untold sorrow to mankind, and To reaffirm faith in fundamental human rights, in the dignity and worth of the human person, in the equal rights of men and women and of nations large and small, and To establish conditions under which justice and respect for the obligations arising from treaties and other sources of international law can be maintained ...

1.1 The Universal Declaration of Human Rights (UNDHR) 1948

The Universal Declaration was adopted by the General Assembly of the United Nations in 1948. It sets out fundamental human rights as 'a common standard for achievement for all peoples and nations'.

Question: If you were drafting a document to contain only ten fundamental human rights, which rights would you incorporate?

Key Points: Recalling key rights in the Irish Constitution and/or drawing from your general knowledge on this area, you may have included the following: the right to life, the right to a criminal trial, the right of equality, the right to freedom of expression, the right to a democratically elected government in free and fair elections, freedom to associate with others, freedom of religion, the right for a child to be educated, freedom from slavery and forced labour, freedom from torture and inhuman treatment, the right to own property, the right to seek asylum in another country, the right to privacy.

You may consider that these rights have different priorities and if you had to limit the list to ten you would have to omit some from the list above. You may believe that some of these rights are **absolute** and there could be no limitations or qualifications on their existence (for example the right to freedom from torture). You may also consider that some of the rights could be limited or **qualified** in certain cases. For example, you may consider the right to freedom of expression could be limited in certain cases.

You may consider that some of these rights could be more properly described as social, economic or political rights rather than basic human rights. This is a distinction the United Nations developed after the Charter. Social and economic rights depend on the level of economic development in each nation. Accordingly the United Nations adopted the Covenant on Economic, Social and Cultural Rights in 1966 and also a Covenant on Civil and Political Rights which expands on the statements in the Declarations.

TASK

Go to the United Nations website and locate and read the Universal Declaration of Human Rights. Identify the fundamental rights outlined.

Questions: Are these rights absolute?

Key Points: One specific limitation is spelt out in Article 14(2). However, there is a general power to qualify the rights under Article 29. The reference is to limitations 'determined by law'. This means that states cannot impose arbitrary restrictions and that any restriction must be justified on the grounds listed in the article.

Article 29

(2) In the exercise of his rights and freedoms, everyone shall be subject only to such limitations as are determined by law solely for the purpose of securing due recognition and respect for the rights and freedoms of others and of meeting the just requirements of morality, public order and the general welfare in a democratic society.

(3) These rights and freedoms may in no case be exercised contrary to the purposes and principles of the United Nations.

You may consider the wording of the Declaration as mainly stating aspirations, since it has clearly not prevented genocide and brutality from re-emerging in the world. However, it has undoubtedly led to individual and national awareness of human rights issues and protection on a global level and has resulted in action being taken, for example to prosecute war criminals.

Other important Conventions include:
- the International Convention on the Suppression and Punishment of the Crime of Apartheid 1973
- the United Nations Convention on the Rights of the Child 1989.

2 The Origins of the European Convention on Human Rights and Fundamental Freedoms 1950

The Council of Europe was established in 1949, after the UN Declaration. Due to circumstances in post-war Europe, particularly the legacy of destruction and occupation, displaced populations and the beginning of the division of Europe by the Iron Curtain, it was felt necessary to have a European institution to promote unity, democracy and the rule of law and the protection of human rights.

The aim of the Council set out in the founding document was 'to achieve a greater unity between its members for the purposes of safeguarding and realising the ideals and principles which are their common heritage and facilitating their economic and social progress'. It can be seen as a 'concrete expression' of the UNDHR and it also set in place an enforcement structure for contracting states which were in breach of their obligations.

The European Convention on Human Rights (EHCR) was signed in 1950 and came into force in 1953. Since that date a number of Protocols (additional agreements) have extended the Convention to cover issues such as the abolition of the death penalty and the protection of property rights. It has two key enforcement mechanisms: the European Court of Human Rights and the Committee of Ministers.

Based in Strasbourg, the European Court of Human Rights (ECtHR) delivers binding judgments and can award just satisfaction to a successful applicant. The Court can sit in Grand Chamber (where 17 judges sit) to hear the most difficult cases. The majority of cases are dealt with in sections, which are courts consisting of chambers of judges. In 2006 the European Court of Human Rights gave more than 1,500 judgments (Annual Report of 2006, European Court of Human Rights).

The Committee of Ministers has the responsibility of monitoring the enforcement of the judgments of the European Court of Human Rights. It issues Reports on state measures taken to comply with judgments.

Member states must comply with the judgments of the ECtHR (Article 46). The Court may order the state to provide just satisfaction, which may consist of a declaration of a violation and/or compensation for a breach of the convention. The judgment may require action by the member state. After the decision in *Airey v. Ireland* (see below) Ireland introduced a limited scheme of legal aid for civil matters.

Other remedial measures could include the destruction of information gleaned in breach of privacy rights, the prevention of extradition to a country where the death penalty or serious mistreatment is likely, a review and reform of legislation which is in breach of the Convention.

Task: Signatories to the European Convention on Human Rights

Identify the 47 members of the Council of Europe and signatories to the ECHR using the Council of Europe website. Note the extent of the territory covered by the ECHR and that it is a much larger territorial area than the EU.

The human rights record of a state is one of the factors that the EU considers when assessing whether an applicant country can join the EU.

3 Key Features of the ECHR

There are features of the Convention which mark it out from earlier conventions and which have contributed to its influence and effectiveness.

1. The Convention is enforceable through a judicial system created by the Council of Europe. It has its own court, the European Court of Human Rights (ECtHR) in Strasbourg.
2. The rights are given to persons who are in the territory of a member state irrespective of nationality or citizenship status and who can be classed as 'victims' of breaches of the Convention.
3. An individual who claims his or her rights have been violated may bring proceedings before the European Court of Human Rights in Strasbourg, provided the member state has accepted the right of individual petition and all domestic remedies have been exhausted. Ireland accepted the right of individual petition at the

time of ratification of the Treaty in 1953.

4. Under the Convention one member state may lodge a complaint against another member state (an inter-state application). This type of application is rare.

5. The Convention can be described as a 'living instrument'. It is subject to changes (agreed under Protocols) and the interpretation of phrases by the ECtHR in the Convention can change over time.

6. Due to the diversity of the cultural, democratic and religious traditions of the signatories to the Convention the Court has accepted that member states may have different approaches or a 'margin of appreciation' in relation to some issues under the Convention.

7. Under Article 41, if the Court finds there has been a violation of the Convention then 'just satisfaction' may be ordered by the Court to be paid by the defaulting State.

4 The Main Provisions of the Convention and the Protocols

You should read through the full text of the Convention (Articles 1–15) and Protocols. You can do this by accessing the European Convention on Human Rights Act 2003 on the Irish Statute Book website. At the end of the Act the Schedule gives the text of the Convention. Alternatively, go to the Council of Europe site and access it through the 'Human Rights' tab.

Articles:

Article 1 —   obligation to respect human rights
Article 2 —   right to life
Article 3 —   prohibition of torture and inhumane and degrading punishment and treatment
Article 4 —   prohibition of slavery and forced labour
Article 5 —   right to liberty and security
Article 6 —   right to a fair trial within a reasonable time
Article 7 —   right to freedom from retrospective criminal law
Article 8 —   right to respect for family and private life, the home and correspondence
Article 9 —   freedom of thought, conscience and religion
Article 10 —   right of freedom of expression
Article 11 —   right of freedom of assembly and association
Article 12 —   right to marry and found a family
Article 13 —   right to an effective remedy for a violation of the Convention

Article 14 — prohibition on discrimination in the application of Convention rights

Article 15 — provides for a derogation possibility in times of emergency

Protocols:

Protocol 1 — protection of property, right to education and right to free elections

Protocol 4 — prohibition of imprisonment for debt, freedom of movement and prohibition on collective expulsions

Protocol 6 — abolishes the death penalty in peacetime (the Russian Federation has signed but not yet ratified this)

Protocol 7 — procedural safeguards in relation to expulsion, appeal in criminal matters, compensation for wrongful conviction and others

Protocol 11 — made important organisational changes to the institutions and fused the role of the Commission on Human Rights with the European Court of Human Rights.

4.1 Limitations on rights

The majority of the Convention rights are not absolute. An example of an absolute Article is Article 3, the prohibition on torture and inhumane and degrading treatment.

There is a limited possibility to derogate from certain rights during emergencies, which means that a state may restrict the rights on certain grounds.

In Article 8, on respect for private and family life, the terms of the limitations provide a good illustration of the form of the limitations:

Article 8 Right to respect for private and family life

1 Everyone has the right to respect for his private and family life, his home and his correspondence.

2 There shall be no interference by a public authority with the exercise of this right except such as is in accordance with the law and is necessary in a democratic society in the interests of national security, public safety or the economic well-being of the country, for the prevention of disorder or crime, for the protection of health or morals, or for the protection of the rights and freedoms of others.

Restrictions may be justified in a 'democratic society' for a number of reasons. However, any restriction must be justified by the state. The state must prove it is a legitimate and proportionate restriction. This is part of the balancing of interests and rights.

Proportionality is a fundamental principle in European Union law and human rights law under the ECHR. It means that a measure should pursue a legitimate aim and go no further than is necessary to achieve that aim.

Article 8(2) of the Convention protects the right of privacy and family life. However, it permits restrictions imposed by a public authority which are in accordance with the law and which are necessary in a democratic society in the interests of national security, public safety or the economic well-being of the country, for the prevention of disorder or crime, for the protection of health or morals, or for the protection of the rights and freedoms of others.

Question: What types of legitimate restriction on family and privacy rights might a state try to impose?
Key Points: A state may seek to impose surveillance on a person suspected of crime, or monitor telephone and computer usage to prevent terrorism on national security grounds. It may impose restrictions on prisoners.

4.2 Case law of the European Convention on Human Rights

The European Court of Human Rights gave judgments in over 1,500 cases in 2006. Below is a snapshot of case law that indicates the breadth of issues covered by the Convention in certain Articles. The European Court of Human Rights website is an excellent resource with easily accessible judgments, press releases which summarise the judgments and webcasts of judgments. You should take time to look at the website and follow up one of the Articles to practise searching for information.

Note that the applicant must be classed as a 'victim' of the breach to bring an application against the state and that often more than one violation of the Convention will be alleged.

4.2.1 Article 2: the right to life

The right to life is the most fundamental human right. The Article prevents the state from engaging in practices which result in unjustified killing. If there is a death due to state action or a death occurs while a person is in the custody of the state (for example in police custody or in prison) then the state must investigate and provide an explanation, otherwise there will be a breach of Article 2. The Court has also ruled that states must take appropriate positive steps to safeguard the lives of those within its jurisdiction.

The death penalty was abolished by Protocol 6 to the Convention. The Article 2 right also protects those who face extradition or deportation by a contracting party to a state where they would or could have a serious risk of facing judicial execution. The Court has ruled that this could be a breach of Article 2 and the state should secure an undertaking from the recipient state that the death penalty will not be used.

In *McCann and Others v. UK* (1995) the ECtHR considered the scope of Article 2 for the first time. The case arose from the killing of three Republicans, Daniel McCann, Mairead Farrell and Sean Savage, in Gibraltar by British security services. The ECtHR sitting in Grand Chamber considered in detail the phrase under Article 2(2) which qualifies the right to life as the UK government argued that the killings were justified in view of an impending bombing campaign.

> Article 2(2) Deprivation of life shall not be regarded as inflicted in contravention of this article when it results from the use of force which is no more than absolutely necessary:
> a in defence of any person from unlawful violence;
> b in order to effect a lawful arrest or to prevent the escape of a person lawfully detained;
> c in action lawfully taken for the purpose of quelling a riot or insurrection.

Although the court ruled that the soldiers who had shot and killed the terrorists could not be directly blamed, the organisation of the operation was a breach of Article 2 as a number of serious errors had been made, including:

> ... the decision not to prevent the suspects from travelling into Gibraltar, to the failure of the authorities to make sufficient allowances for the possibility that their intelligence assessments might ... be erroneous and to the automatic recourse to lethal force when the soldiers opened fire.

The force used was more than was absolutely necessary and there was a breach of Article 2.

Ten years later the Court considered a case from Turkey, *Simsek and Others v. Turkey* (Application nos. 35072/97 and 37194/97). The police had reacted to two violent demonstrations arising out of an incident in 1995 in a neighbourhood of Istanbul where most residents belonged to the Alevi sect. The police opened fire on the demonstrators, killing seventeen people. While observing that the use of force may be legitimate for the purpose of quelling a riot, the Court noted that the Turkish police had shot directly at the demonstrators, 'without first having recourse to less life-threatening methods, such as tear gas, water cannons or plastic bullets'. The lack of equipment to disperse the crowd safely (such as water cannon or tear gas), the lack of training and of a clear and centralised command structure in these circumstances constituted a breach of Article 2.

The failure of the authorities to hold a prompt and effective investigation into the use of lethal force and the procedural failings including the 'dilatory and half-hearted' conduct of the investigation meant that Turkey was also found in breach of Article 2 in this regard.

A controversial issue, which has caused litigation in the Irish and UK courts as well as the ECtHR, is the question of when life begins for the purposes of Article 2.

In the recent case of *Natalie Evans v. UK [2005]* the Grand Chamber of the ECtHR (comprising seventeen judges) had to determine whether frozen embryos were entitled to protection under Article 2.

Facts: The applicant Evans and her partner, Johnston, commenced IVF treatment. Both parties were informed that it would be possible for either of them to withdraw their consent to the IVF treatment at any time before the embryos were implanted in Evans. They signed separate consent forms. Six embryos were successfully frozen and stored. The applicant then had to undergo treatment for cancer and her ovaries were removed. After the breakdown of the relationship Johnston told the clinic to destroy the embryos. Evans sought an injunction to compel Evans to restore his consent. Under the Human Fertilisation and Embryology Act 1990 (which governs the position in the UK), the requirement of consent of both parties was seen as fundamental to the regulation of the field.

The Grand Chamber relied on its earlier case law and said that as there was no European consensus on the legal and scientific definition of the beginning of life, it was up to each state to decide on this issue. The states have a 'margin of appreciation' in this area. The Court ruled that the embryo did not have independent rights or interest and could not claim a right under Article 2.

At the opposite end of the life spectrum cases have come before the court arguing for a right to die (or euthanasia) as part of the principle of human dignity. In the case of *Diane Pretty v. UK [2002] (Application no. 2346/02)* the applicant was suffering from motor neurone disease, a progressive debilitating illness. She sought a legal assurance from the DPP in England that if her husband assisted her suicide he would not be prosecuted. She was physically unable to commit suicide herself. The DPP refused to grant her husband immunity. She argued that the UK was in breach of Articles 2, 3 and 8 (and others). The European Court ruled that Article 2 did not imply that there was a right to die or a right to choose when to die. There was no breach of Article 2 (or of the other Articles in this case).

Suggestion: This is an interesting and instructive case to read in full. You can access it on the ECtHR website.

4.2.2 Article 3: prohibition of torture

No one shall be subjected to torture or to inhuman or degrading treatment or punishment. This is an absolute Article. There are no possible qualifications or restrictions, irrespective of the conduct of the victim. Inhuman treatment was defined to mean treatment that 'deliberately causes severe suffering, mental or physical, which, in the particular situation is unjustifiable'.

The European Convention is a framework Convention and does not define terms used such as 'torture', 'criminal proceedings', 'privacy', etc. It has been a key role of the European Court of Human Rights to define these terms. The definitions are not static; they can change with time. This is one reason why the Convention is said to be a 'living instrument'.

An early example of consideration of the scope and application of Article 3 came in an inter-state application, where one state alleges another is in breach of the Convention, in the context of the situation in Northern Ireland in the early 1970s.

Ireland v. UK 1978 2 ECHRR 25 was an inter-state application brought by Ireland against the UK concerning Operation Demetrius in Northern Ireland in the 1970s, a dragnet of dawn raids, arrests and interrogations using special powers of arrest and detention without trial (internment). Notices of derogation under Article 15 were lodged by the UK. Ireland argued that conditions in custody and interrogation techniques amounted to torture and inhuman treatment. Although the practices were discontinued, and the respondent did not contest this aspect of the case, Ireland asked for a formal court order declaring the breach of the Convention. The interrogation practices consisted of five techniques which had been applied with premeditation, in combination, for hours at a time. The techniques consisted of wall standing, hooding, noise, sleep deprivation and restricted food and drink. The techniques caused physical and mental suffering to such a degree that they amounted to inhuman and degrading treatment. The Court was not of the opinion that they could be classed as torture. The UK was found to be in breach of Article 3 ECHR.

Soering v. UK [1989]11EHRR439

Facts: Soering, a German national, was awaiting extradition to Virginia, USA where he faced charges of murder which carried the death penalty. He argued that extradition from the UK to the USA would breach Article 3 as he would be subjected to the so-called 'death row phenomenon'.

The European Court of Human Rights, sitting in Grand Chamber, said that in the circumstances:

> Having regard to the very long period of time spent on death row in such extreme conditions, with the ever present and mounting anguish of awaiting execution of the death penalty, and to the personal circumstances of the applicant, especially his age and mental state at the time of the offence, the applicant's extradition to the United States would expose him to a real risk of treatment going beyond the threshold set by Article 3.

In this case there was a more proportionate response available in sending him to Germany to face trial for murder.

Breaches of Article 3 have been found in relation to the force feeding and searching of prisoners, and extradition to a state where ill-treatment was a real possibility.

In *Nevmerzhitsky v. Ukraine*, the specific issue of how to react to a hunger strike, and in particular the use of force-feeding, arose. The Court concluded that the methods used (handcuffs, a mouth-widener and a special rubber tube), given the detainee's resistance and the absence of any medical necessity, amounted to torture. The Court also found that the failure to provide adequate medical assistance to the applicant amounted to degrading treatment and the conditions in which he was held also constituted degrading treatment.

The Court noted (in its survey of cases in 2005) that over 20 judgments concerned ill treatment in detention in Turkey and that this was a 'persistent problem'.

Task: The ECtHR Website

The Court has its own search facility and portal called HUDOC. You need to enter information precisely, otherwise the response will be 'no documents found'. Note the date range at the bottom of the form and make sure you make it fit the possible range of cases you are searching for. If you do not find the result first time, alter your search. If you want to look at all the cases against Ireland on the database just enter 'Ireland' in the box labelled 'Respondent state'. Each case has an application number and if you just have the number you can access the case.

Locate the case of *Tuncer and Durmufl v. Turkey Application no. 30494/96*, which concerns breaches of Articles 3 and 5 of the Convention. The application was lodged in 1996 and the final judgment was delivered in 2005. The delay was due to a number of factors, including the fact that the highest Turkish court did not deal with the appeal until 2001. Read through the case. (Ignore the first paragraphs on procedure as the procedures have since been changed to make the process quicker.)

The facts of the case concern police mistreatment and arrest. The Court established the facts and then went on to apply the law relating to Articles 3 and 5 to the facts. There was a lack of a plausible explanation by the Turkish authorities in this case and the Court summarised a state's obligations to persons within its custody.

Article 3 has also been used to challenge corporal punishment, the failure of states to investigate 'disappearances', failure to give adequate medical care while in police custody and use of excessive force in arrest.

The European Convention for the Prevention of Torture

This Convention came into force in 1989 and it established a European Committee for the Prevention of Torture and Inhuman or Degrading Treatment or Punishment, which can make visits to any establishment in the contracting states: prisons, psychiatric hospitals, police stations, etc. It visits countries periodically and prepares a report, inviting replies from the state. On the European Committee website you may be interested to read the recent publication of the Report on the visit to Irish prisons in 2006.

4.2.3 Article 4: prohibition of slavery and servitude

There are few cases on this area. One case against France in 2005, *Siliadin v. France*, made important points about the reality of servitude in Europe and the need for states to take positive steps to eradicate it.

Facts: The applicant was a 15-year-old girl from Togo who was taken to work in France until she had paid for her plane ticket. Her passport was confiscated and she worked as an unpaid housemaid. She was not provided with any education or training and worked long hours, seven days a week. A prosecution had been brought against her employers but it was unsuccessful. The Court stated that governments have 'positive obligations ... to adopt criminal-law provisions which penalise the practices referred to in Article 4 and to apply them in practice'. As far as the applicant's actual situation was concerned, the Court considered that it did not constitute slavery in the strict sense but that it could be classified as 'servitude', that French law did not criminalise slavery and servitude as such and that French law at the material time had not provided effective protection against the actions of which the applicant had been a victim. There had been a breach of Article 4.

4.2.4 Article 5: right to liberty and security

This protects the liberty and security of the person, particularly from arbitrary arrest and detention. Any arrest should have lawful authority. It specifies that the reasons for the arrest are to be given in a language understood by the detained. The individual should be brought promptly before a judge. A trial should occur within a reasonable time.

This Article gives six permitted exceptions to the right of liberty.

Question: In what circumstances do you consider that a person could be justifiably detained?
Key Points: You may have listed being detained for questioning after an arrest, being remanded in custody pending a trial to prevent a person from not answering bail (absconding), to being arrested and brought to the court pursuant to a court order (sometimes called a bench warrant), being committed to a psychiatric hospital for treatment, etc.

The reasons that may be used by a state to justify detention set out in the ECHR are:

1. The lawful detention after conviction by a competent court.
2. The lawful arrest of a person for non-compliance with a court order.
3. The lawful arrest of a person on reasonable suspicion of committing an offence for the purpose of bringing him before the court or to prevent him absconding.
4. The detention of a minor by lawful order for the purpose of educational supervision or lawful detention for the purpose of bringing him before a legal authority (this was at issue in the case of *D.G v. Ireland*, below).
5. The detention on grounds to prevent the spread of disease, persons of unsound mind, addicts or vagrants.
6. A lawful arrest to prevent unauthorised immigration or to effect a deportation or extradition.

D.G. v. Ireland (Application no. 39474/98)

Facts: the applicant was a minor with a criminal history who was considered to have a personality disorder and to be a danger to himself and others. In March 1997 it was decided that he should be placed in a high-support therapeutic unit for 16–18-year-olds. However, as there were no secure educational facilities available in Ireland, the High Court decided in 1997 that he should be detained for three weeks in St Patrick's Institution as the 'least offensive' of the various inappropriate options available. Efforts were made to find another suitable placement. The High Court renewed the order and after being moved to other accommodation DG absconded. The Court ordered his further detention in St Patrick's.

The applicant complained that his detention in St Patrick's in June and July was contrary to Article 5.1 as it was not 'in accordance with a procedure prescribed by law' or for the purposes of 'educational supervision' or of 'bringing him before any competent legal authority' within the meaning of Article 5.1(d). In addition, he was a minor in need of special care but was detained in a penal institution where his unique status (uncharged and not convicted) caused other detainees to believe that he was a serious sexual offender, as a result of which he was insulted, humiliated, threatened and abused. (He also claimed breaches of Articles 3, 8 and 14.)

The Court ruled that St Patrick's Institution could not be considered an educational facility (the Irish Government did not argue that it was) and neither was the detention an interim custody measure preliminary to a regime of supervised education. The detention was unlawful under the Convention.

The right to be promptly brought before a judge (Article 5(3))
Everyone who is arrested must be brought before a judge or other judicial office promptly. The purpose is to prevent people being held incommunicado without anybody else knowing. The state may try to justify incommunicado detention on the grounds of prevention of terrorism, destruction of evidence and protection of law officers and witnesses surrounding the case.

Question: How would you define 'promptly' in this context?
Key Point: This word has generated much case law, often concerning sustained periods of detention imposed on the grounds of prevention and detection of terrorism.

Brogan and Others v. UK (Application nos. 11209/84; 11234/84; 11266/84; 11386/85)
This case concerned the extended detention periods under the Prevention of Terrorism (Temporary Provisions) Act 1984. The four applicants had been arrested and detained for questioning. On the day after the arrests, each applicant was informed by police officers that the Secretary of State for Northern Ireland had agreed to extend his detention by a further five days under Section 12(4) of the Act. None of the applicants was brought before a judge or other officer authorised by law to exercise judicial power, nor were any of them charged after their release. The Grand Chamber of the Court decided on a majority verdict that even taking account of the circumstances in Northern Ireland at the time of the arrests the applicants had not been brought before a judge promptly and there was a breach of Article 5(3).

The right to access to a court review of reasons for detention
Under Article 5(4) anyone who is deprived of their liberty is entitled to take proceedings before a court to challenge the lawfulness of his or her detention and a release should be ordered if the detention is unlawful. There is an enforceable right to compensation if an arrest or detention is unlawful under Article 5(5).

4.2.5 Article 6: right to a fair trial

This is a wide-ranging Article which guarantees a fair trial in civil and criminal cases. It is the Article that is most often relied upon by applicants. The European Court will examine the procedure to ensure it complies with the standards of fairness under the Article, but it will not substitute or replace the national court's finding of fact or of law with its own. Applicants must have access to an independent and impartial court or tribunal for resolution of civil and criminal disputes.

The rights in this Article have been interpreted widely. It is set out in full below.

Article 6 Right to a fair trial

1 In the determination of his civil rights and obligations or of any criminal charge against him, everyone is entitled to a fair and public hearing within a reasonable time by an independent and impartial tribunal established by law. Judgment shall be pronounced publicly but the press and public may be excluded from all or part of the trial in the interests of morals, public order or national security in a democratic society, where the interests of juveniles or the protection of the private life of the parties so require, or to the extent strictly necessary in the opinion of the court in special circumstances where publicity would prejudice the interests of justice.

2 Everyone charged with a criminal offence shall be presumed innocent until proved guilty according to law.

3 Everyone charged with a criminal offence has the following minimum rights:

   a to be informed promptly, in a language which he understands and in detail, of the nature and cause of the accusation against him;

   b to have adequate time and facilities for the preparation of his defence;

   c to defend himself in person or through legal assistance of his own choosing or, if he has not sufficient means to pay for legal assistance, to be given it free when the interests of justice so require;

   d to examine or have examined witnesses against him and to obtain the attendance and examination of witnesses on his behalf under the same conditions as witnesses against him;

   e to have the free assistance of an interpreter if he cannot understand or speak the language used in court.

Thousands of cases have been decided on this area. One issue that falls under Article 6(1)(c) is the availability of legal aid.

In *Steel and Morris v. the United Kingdom A 68416/01 2005* (also known as the McLibel trial) the applicants challenged the lack of civil legal aid in the UK for defamation cases. They claimed the UK was in breach of the Convention. Steel and Morris had been sued by McDonald's for defamation after making statements concerning their products in pamphlets distributed to the public. They were unable to get legal aid to defend themselves against defamation proceedings. The Court noted that 'the disparity between the respective levels of legal assistance enjoyed by the applicants and McDonald's ... was of such a degree that it could not have failed, in this exceptionally demanding case, to have given rise to unfairness' and ruled there was a breach of Article 6. It also ruled there was a breach of the right to freedom of expression under Article 10.

Airey v. Ireland (1979) Series A 2 EHRR 305

Facts: A wished to seek a decree of judicial separation from her husband on various grounds. She had a low income. Mrs A sought to protect her position in the matrimonial home. She was unable to find a lawyer due to the lack of legal aid and she could not afford to be a private client.

The Court found that the failure of the Irish legal system to provide for legal aid for the purpose of seeking a judicial separation (or any civil matter) was a breach of Article 6.

The Irish Government argued there was nothing to prevent her being a litigant in person (and representing herself). The Court decided that any remedy available must be 'practical and effective' and not 'theoretical and illusory' and it was not realistic to expect Mrs A to conduct the case herself in an effective manner. There was also a breach of Article 8 in that her family rights were not adequately protected. As a result of this decision a scheme of civil legal aid was established in Ireland.

In *McMullen v. Ireland (2004) (Application no. 42297/98)* the Court found that delays in High Court and Supreme Court procedures which were not explained by the state meant that proceedings were not dealt with within a 'reasonable time', as required by Article 6 (1).

There have been a number of important cases on the extent of the right to remain silent in the face of police questioning. Under some national legislations a failure to answer questions may allow the prosecution to request that adverse inferences be drawn about the defendant at trial. The ECtHR has ruled that silence and the right not to incriminate oneself guaranteed by Article 6(1) are not absolute rights.

John Murray v. UK (Application no. 18731/91) concerned the legal provision operating in Northern Ireland that allowed a trial judge to draw an adverse inference (an inference of guilt) due to the fact the applicant had remained silent under police questioning and also at his trial. He had been cautioned at the time of the arrest that he did not have to say anything, but that his failure to mention facts which he relied on his defence could be treated as supporting the case against him. The applicant argued that the operation of this provision was in breach of Article 6(1) and (2) by depriving him of a right to silence and a right not to incriminate himself and also operated to reverse the presumption of innocence. The Court found there had not been a breach of these provisions by the drawing of adverse inferences in these circumstances. The Court relied on the fact that a caution had been given and that there had been no jury and the experienced judge had drawn adverse inferences from his silence when questioned in the context of the 'formidable' weight of evidence that had already been presented.

However, the Court found the denial of access to a solicitor for 48 hours and being interviewed twelve times without a solicitor (who could not explain the caution to him) did constitute a breach of Article 6(1) and 6(3)(c).

4.2.6 Article 8: protection of private and family life

This Article has developed in a way which the framers of the Convention might never have envisaged as it has had to evolve with advancing European concepts of privacy, family life, home and surrounding environment and sexuality rights. It is an Article which is expressly limited (as are Articles 9–11). It is set out in full below.

Article 8. Right to respect for private and family life

1   Everyone has the right to respect for his private and family life, his home and his correspondence.
2   There shall be no interference by a public authority with the exercise of this right except such as is in accordance with the law and is necessary in a democratic society in the interests of national security, public safety or the economic well-being of the country, for the prevention of disorder or crime, for the protection of health or morals, or for the protection of the rights and freedoms of others.

The right to family life was also used as a basis of argument in the Natalie Evans case (see Article 2 above). The ECtHR was of the opinion that the consent provisions in the national legislation were justifiable and that Evans had known that Johnston would be entitled to withdraw his consent to the use of the embryos in implantation at any stage prior to that process. The Court ruled there was no breach of Article 8 in this case.

Roche v. UK (Application no. 32555/96) concerned the issue of whether the state's failure to meet its obligation to provide information concerning participation in tests of nerve and mustard gas while in the army had failed to protect his right to respect for his private and family life. The Court found that the issue of access to information which could have allayed the applicant's fear about possible health risks to which he was exposed fell within Article 8 and that a positive obligation arose to provide an effective and accessible procedure enabling access to all relevant and appropriate information without having to initiate litigation to obtain it. The Grand Chamber found unanimously that there had been a breach of Article 8.

In *Christine Goodwin v. UK (Application no. 28957/95)* the European Court of Human Rights held unanimously that the UK was in breach of Article 8 by failing to legally recognise Christine Goodwin's identity by granting her a birth certificate following gender-reassignment surgery. This impacted on her rights regarding pensions and also impacted on her life generally, causing her humiliation and anxiety. The Court ruled that the balance was in favour of the applicant and there had been a failure by the UK to respect her right to a private life. The UK later passed legislation to provide for gender reassignment issues).This is also the issue that the Irish High Court ruled on in the *Foy* judgment (below).

In the famous case of *Norris v. Ireland [1988] (Application no. 10581/83)* Senator David Norris challenged the Irish criminal law, which at that time criminalised certain homosexual acts between consenting adults conducted in private. The Court found that there was an interference with Norris's right to respect for his private life and that the state had not justified the existence of the restriction. Accordingly there was a breach of Article 8. The judgment resulted in Ireland passing amending legislation decriminalising the acts between consenting adults.

In *Keegan v. Ireland [1994] 18 EHRR* Keegan challenged the Irish law of adoption. Keegan was the father of a child from a non-marital relationship which had broken down before the birth of the child. The mother placed the child for adoption without Keegan's knowledge or consent and the child was placed with the prospective adopters. Keegan applied through the Irish courts for guardianship and custody and was awarded custody by the Circuit Court. However, there was a reference to the Supreme Court, which ruled that the wishes of the natural father did not give an automatic entitlement to guardianship and the welfare of the child was the paramount consideration. The High Court reconsidered the case in the light of this ruling and ruled in February 1990 that the applicant's request for guardianship and custody should be dismissed, because with the additional passage of time the child's attachment to the prospective adopters had grown stronger and the traumatic effect on the child of any move would be greater. An adoption order was subsequently made in respect of the child.

The European Court of Human Rights ruled that the fact that the law allowed for the secret placement of the child without the applicant's knowledge or consent, which had led to the bonding of the child with the potential adopters, and a later adoption order, was an interference with the applicant's right to respect for family life. The failure to provide that the father of a child from an unmarried partnership had a right to be consulted on the adoption process of his child was a breach. The concept of 'family' under Article 8 was not limited to marriage unions. The concept was wider and can cover other partnerships where the partners are living together. Children born out of such relationships are clearly part of that family group. (Compare this with the restrictive definition of family under Article 41 of the Constitution of Ireland.)

As a result of this judgment the Adoption Act 1998 provides a statutory procedure for consultation. This consultation requirement facilitates the father making an application to the court to be appointed a guardian of the child.

(The applicant's rights under Article 6(1) had also been broken as he had no rights under Irish law to challenge the decision to place the child for adoption and his rights to bring guardianship and custody proceedings were not an effective alternative as by the time these proceedings had ended the child had already been in the care of the potential adopters for some time and this had prejudiced his position.)

In the *Lydia Foy* case the High Court ruled that Ireland was in breach of its obligations under the ECHR due to its failure to recognise a gender realignment surgery. The state had refused to grant Lydia Foy a new birth certificate that reflected her female gender and this was a failure to protect her right to privacy. New legislation to remedy the situation is expected to be introduced.

4.2.7 Article 9: right to freedom to religion

A controversial area of litigation under this Article concerns the wearing of the Islamic headscarf by Muslim women.

Leyla Şahin v. Turkey concerned a circular issued by Istanbul University prohibiting wearing the headscarf at lectures, exams and tutorials. The applicant, a student, was refused access to lectures and examinations and was then suspended for participating in a demonstration against the instruction. Her attempts to challenge the rules in the administrative courts failed. She argued that the Turkish action was in breach of her freedom to practise her religion.

The Grand Chamber ruled that there was no breach of Article 9. It considered the wording on the limitations to the right under Article 9. It focused on the importance of secularism in the Turkish constitutional system and concluded that the regulation met a pressing social need by seeking the legitimate aims of protecting the rights and freedoms of others and the maintenance of public order and was, therefore, necessary in a democratic society. The Grand Chamber also stressed the importance of gender equality, as well as the political significance the headscarf had taken on in Turkey and the existence of extremist political movements there. The very specific Turkish context was an important factor in the Court's consideration of the case. The court considered the proportionality of the measure and took into account the fact that practising Muslim students were free to practise their religion. It found that the interference was justified and proportionate.

5 The Irish Human Rights Commission

This was established by the Human Rights Commission Acts 2000 and 2001 as a result of the Belfast Agreement.

Its role is to promote and protect human rights in the jurisdiction. (The Human Rights Commission in Northern Ireland was also established under the Agreement.)

Its role covers human rights secured by the Irish Constitution and by international agreements such as the ECHR. It has wide-ranging powers and functions. The Commission can make recommendations to government, enforce human rights law by taking legal proceedings, advise the court on human rights issues by being appointed an *amicus curiae* by the court.

If you are interested in this area you should look at the website of the Commission.

6 The European Convention on Human Rights Act 2003

The European Convention on Human Rights Act 2003 makes the provisions of the European Convention on the Protection of Human Rights and Fundamental Freedoms part of Irish law. The courts are required to interpret and apply national law in line with the Convention so far as possible. Before the Act came into force the Convention could not be directly relied on in the courts in Ireland. It could be referred to in argument and could be used as an aid to interpretation in cases but there was no right to directly enforce Convention rights in the national legal system.

6.1 The impact of the Convention in Ireland under the Act

The major change is that under the Act human rights issues covered by the Convention can be raised in the High Court and Supreme Court and remedies can be sought for breach of these rights.

The Act incorporated the Convention into Irish law from the end of December 2003. Until this date the Irish courts could have regard to the provisions of the Convention and the case law of the European Court of Human Rights, but public authorities, including the courts, were not formally bound by the Convention. People who had a 'human rights issue' under the Convention had to take the long route of bringing a case before Strasbourg.

Section 2 imposes an interpretative obligation on the courts. When interpreting and applying any statutory provision or any rule of law a court must, in so far as is possible, do so in a manner compatible with the State's obligations under the Convention provisions. This means that where Convention rights are relevant the courts should use a **purposive** approach and interpret provisions in order to comply with the ECHR.

Section 3 provides that every organ of the State shall perform its functions in a manner compatible with the State's obligations under the Convention provisions. It also provides that if an injury or loss is suffered as a result of a breach of the Convention damages may be claimed. Claims must be made against the relevant public body within one year of the alleged breach of the Convention.

Section 4 provides that the judges must consider any relevant declaration, decision, advisory opinion or judgment of the European Court of Human Rights (and other relevant institutions of the Council of Europe). This means that the judgments of the European Court of Human Rights are now part of the body of case law that can be relied upon by lawyers and judges in deciding cases in Ireland.

6.2 Declaration of incompatibility

Under Section 5 of the Act the High Court and Supreme Court can declare that a provision of Irish law is incompatible with the Convention.

A recent example of litigation relying on the provisions of the Convention is the case brought by Dr Foy against the Registrar of Births. Dr Foy had argued before the High Court that the failure of the state to issue a new birth certificate to someone who has undergone gender reassignment (commonly known as a sex change operation) was a breach of Article 8 of the Convention. The High Court ruled that the failure of the state to recognise a sex change by a transgendered person infringed her rights of privacy and family life. This was the first declaration of incompatibility of Irish law under the 2003 Act.

Note: The judgment does not strike down the existing law in Ireland as a decision on unconstitutional legislation would. The matter must now be formally referred to the Oireachtas by the Taoiseach.

> Under s.5(3)(3) The Taoiseach shall cause a copy of any order containing a declaration of incompatibility to be laid before each House of the Oireachtas within the next 21 days on which that House has sat after the making of the order.

6.3 Damages

If a declaration of incompatibility is made, a party to the proceedings can make a written application to the Attorney General for damages for losses sustained.

A procedure is set down in the Act for the assessment of damages. Under the ECtHR victims of breaches of the Convention are entitled to 'just satisfaction' (Article 42 ECHR). The Government may appoint an adviser to advise them on the amount of appropriate compensation and regard must be had to the principles and level of compensation ordered by the European Court of Human Rights.

Summary

The concept of human rights has been developing for centuries. After World War II there was a concerted effort to establish frameworks to prevent human rights abuses. The Council of Europe established the European Convention of Human Rights and Fundamental Freedoms with its own machinery for enforcement.

The Articles and Protocols which have added to the rights are 'framework' rights. They have required interpretation by the European Court of Human Rights.

In Ireland the Convention can now be used to challenge the actions or inactions of the organs of the state. Convention rights can be relied upon in the High Court or Supreme Court. The courts must interpret national law in line with the Convention and judgments of the ECtHR so far as is possible. If there has been a breach of the Convention remedies may be awarded by the national court. The national court may also award damages for breach of the Convention.

QUESTIONS

1. What is the difference between an absolute and qualified human right? Give an example of each type.
2. Consider the situations below and consider whether any provisions of the ECHR may be used to argue against the provision. Can you anticipate any justifications that the state may put forward to try to justify the limitation of the right?
    a) Harpal wishes to join the prison service. He is a Sikh and has been told that he cannot join the service unless he signs an undertaking to wear the uniform and to be clean shaven. He cannot sign the undertaking due to his religious beliefs.
    b) Your client Mike has just had his luxury holiday home in Turkey requisitioned by the authorities. He has been offered no compensation and is told that the new policy is to facilitate welfare policies in the state.
    c) Alexi lives in Moscow. He attends a private academy for gifted piano players. He is accused of theft at school and is whipped ten times as a punishment.
    d) Sean is arrested by the police in the middle of the night. He is badly beaten in the police van and when he requests some insulin for his diabetes he is told to, 'wait for a while and if you co-operate we can sort that'. He is not permitted access to legal advice for the first twelve hours.
3. In which courts in Ireland can the issue of whether a law complies with the ECHR be raised?

REFERENCES

Burns, S. (2007). 'Terms of Law', *National Law Journal*, vol. 157, 736.

European Court of Human Rights (2006). Annual Report.

Ovey, C., and White, R. A. (2002). *European Convention on Human Rights* (3rd edn). Oxford: Oxford University Press.

STUDY SKILLS

At the end of this chapter you should:
- Have an awareness of your own study style.
- Consider possible advantages and disadvantages of other study and learning styles and be aware of the importance of learning effectively.
- Develop strategies of reading with a purpose and taking notes effectively.
- Appreciate some strategies for revision and examination techniques.
- Have an understanding of the types of questions, case studies or research tasks that you may encounter.
- Be able to practise and develop your own interest and knowledge of law and question-answering techniques by using some of the suggested study topics in this chapter.
- Build confidence in being able to adapt your study styles, consider different methods of study and become an 'independent learner'.
- Understand the importance of noting the sources of information you rely on and of including a *References* Section and *Bibliography* at the end of a written project or essay.

1 *Your own Study Style and Attitude to Study*

Question: Do you enjoy studying? Are you indifferent about your studies, or is it a task you actively dislike and that you 'put up with' to achieve a certain result? Does this apply to all or most subjects you study? Which topics do you find the most enjoyable?

Key Points: There is clearly no 'right answer' to this question. If you do not enjoy studying and would rather do anything instead, you need to address this for the sake of your life balance and enjoyment and to enhance your learning achievements. One way of doing this is to consider different ways of learning, taking notes and studying, which you may find more satisfying and which will help you achieve your goals. Trying some changes to the way you work can make study more interesting, effective and rewarding. We can now expect to change our career more than once during our lifetime and to engage in 'lifelong learning'. Awareness of study skills and learning patterns can make this process less stressful and maybe even enjoyable. The skill of 'learning to learn' (a phrase coined by the educational writer Rogers) is an important **transferable skill,** which can be applied both to academic tasks and more pragmatic, work-based tasks.

Questions
Consider these questions and whether you could change *one aspect* of your study pattern to see if it makes study more interesting, rewarding or challenging.
1. Do you have a separate, quiet place to study at home or in a library away from other distractions?
2. Do you study for long periods of time (say in 2–3-hour blocks), shorter time frames such as one hour, or do you snatch time and skim over material in ten minutes, hoping 'this will do'?
3. Do you plan your workload and tasks?
4. Do you actively participate in classes, study group work, internet tasks and consider yourself an 'active learner'?
5. Do you write up a revision timetable and try to stick to it?
6. Do you always dread final assessments and examinations and consider that you will never obtain the grade you think you deserve?

Key Points: Try to change one aspect of your study pattern. For example, let's say you have set aside a Wednesday afternoon from two to five o'clock to study and prepare for an assignment on a topic. This is the only free afternoon you have in the week for this task. Give yourself small 'goals' and set yourself a brief timetable before you start. Give yourself *short* breaks every 45–50 minutes. This may just mean moving away from the computer screen or book to make a cup of tea or making a *short* phone call. You should then return to your task refreshed.

Example: You have been asked to prepare a short ten-minute presentation for the class as part of the Assessed Work element on 'The Court Structure in Ireland'.
1. **Planning.** Spend five to ten minutes planning how you will tackle the task, taking into account the time restraints you have and the information you require (Planning Stage). A suggestion of how a task might be planned is given below.
2. **Research.** Spend thirty minutes looking through notes and reading from a book and/or website(s) and making brief notes (Research

Stage). Remember to note down where you obtained the information.

3. Have a five- to ten-minute break.
4. **Planning and Writing**. Spend ten minutes planning the structure of the presentation. Having done the research you will be aware of the key points. If you are using software for your presentation you need to consider how many chunks of information you will give in electronic format.
   - Introduction — tell the audience what you are going to explain.
   - Subject matter — outline of the different courts.
   - Summary — remind the audience of the key points you have made.
5. Spend thirty-five minutes writing up the key points on the first half of the slides you will use, referring back to the notes you made at Stage 2 and looking up any extra points or clarifications that you need. Congratulate yourself as you are over halfway through your task!
6. Have a ten-minute break. Do not get distracted: return to the final part of your task.
7. Spend thirty minutes writing up the key points for the second five minutes of your presentation, including the summary slide, again doing any extra reading or research that you need to address any point about which you are unclear.
8. **Reviewing/Including References**. Spend five minutes ensuring you have the references for where the material was obtained and looking over to check for any mistakes before printing or submitting the work.
9. The assignment is finished, ahead of schedule, in 135 minutes.

This might seem a long-drawn-out process for one piece of work. It is an example of how planning, and breaking down tasks into their component parts can help your learning and approach to assessment tasks. The task was broken down into manageable chunks, which is the key to approaching tasks which may seem off-putting. Set yourself a realistic target and then stick to it as far as possible. Try to get into the habit of concentrated working in 'pockets' of time, for example forty minutes at a time. If you try to fully concentrate for much longer than this you will become less interested, less effective and more likely to abandon the task until later. You may find that you can only fully concentrate for thirty minutes at a time. If so, work with this. You could try to extend your concentration time, as remember you may be required to focus in an exam setting for two to three hours, so it would be useful to try to get used to slightly longer spells of concentration time.

In the task above, various skills and aspects of learning aspects have been addressed. Research skills, selecting relevant information to address the issue, identifying the core points and summarising skills have all been engaged. By the process of gathering this information you came to understand and assimilate the material by translating it into a format in which you can talk about it and present it to colleagues.

2 Methods of Effective Learning

Effective learning means being able to demonstrate your knowledge in an assessment situation and to apply your knowledge in a practical, work situation. It requires more than remembering concepts and information. It requires understanding and application of knowledge and ideas. For example, we may be able to remember a mathematical formula such as the cosine rule without understanding when it can be used and why it is significant.

To understand concepts and recall them we need to process and work with information and to 'translate' it into a form which makes sense to us. We all have different ways of recording and processing information.

Question: Which of these approaches best describes your style when you attend lectures, seminars or tutorials?
1. You tend to remember most of the content of the lecture or seminar; you don't take any notes but hope that there will be a handout or access to the key points online.
2. You try to write everything down.
3. You try to identify the key points as the lecture progresses.
4. You write some notes and hope they are relevant.
5. You doodle and draw diagrams.

2.1 Taking and making notes

Note-taking comes in different formats and you may have already found your own preferred way of taking notes. The purpose of taking notes is to remind you of key points which the speaker has made, points about which you may be unclear and on which you want to seek clarification or ask the speaker about. They may contain references which you are expected to locate, and research to supplement your notes. You will also make notes from textbooks, cases you read and articles in journals, newspapers and internet resources. In making notes you are 'translating' information into your own format which is meaningful to you. There are different ways of taking notes, and you may find a combination of methods works best for you.

Question: Assuming that you take some notes in a lecture or seminar session, do you write them down lineally, for example:
- tort
- law of negligence
- elements of duty of care
- breach of duty by failing to exercise reasonable care
- causation of loss/damage?

(This is how most books are formatted, with headings and sub-headings.)

Do you draw diagrams? If you studied science, maths or geography diagrams will already be part of your pattern of learning. Diagrams can also be used in the form of charts or 'mind maps' in subjects unrelated to maths or the natural sciences. Drawing diagrams makes you actively engage with the material and you are more likely to think about the content, establish links with other material and ask whether there are other aspects that could be added to the mind map.

Mind-mapping can be used to collect and organise ideas at any time in your studies. It enables you to map your thoughts on a particular topic in a structured way and to use the way remembered ideas lead on to other associated ideas. Some people have memories which can use visual cues very effectively, and mind maps tap into this memory style.

This type of note-taking may not appeal to you, or you may find it more useful for consolidation and revision at the end of the course.

Another point worth considering is using colour in your note-taking, not only to brighten up your notes but as another way of customising and making the material familiar and becoming comfortable with key concepts. This does not mean obscuring all your notes with fluorescent highlighter, but judiciously selecting key parts of the material to enhance your understanding.

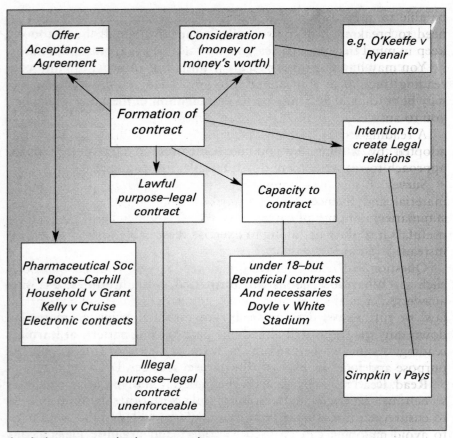

A mind map on topics in contract law

2.2 Effective reading: reading with a purpose

A distinction is often drawn between reading for pleasure (a novel or magazine article) and reading with a purpose (course materials, holiday brochure, report, contractual materials, etc.).

Reading a complex chapter of a book, a detailed report, journal article or legal case may be off-putting, particularly if it is lengthy or deals with a complex area or a subject that you have not yet become interested in or confident about. You will have other demands on your time, too, so you need to adopt an effective reading approach.

There are strategies to help make reading and distilling information more effective. The aim is to become an 'active reader': this helps you sift relevant information, identify relevant points and be able to apply the information to relevant situations. Again, you need to break the task down into manageable 'chunks' and always keep in mind that you are reading with a purpose or aim in mind.

You may have been set particular questions to address from your reading (such as in the Case Studies in this book). Alternatively, you may be reading a text or online resource to find information to enable you to answer a question, compile a report, etc.

A reading strategy which was developed by Williams in 1989 and adopted by a number of educational researchers is the **SQ3R** approach to reading: Survey, Question, Read, Recall, Review.

Survey. Begin by scanning the document and get a feel for the material and its potential usefulness. Look at the title, headings, summaries, date written. Come to a view about whether it may be useful. If it is of no use to you, do not read it: look for another source instead!

Question. To read effectively you need to ask yourself questions such as, 'What do I need from this text?' A broad overview, detailed answers, a critical analysis of the development and current state of the law, or further reading and references mentioned in the text? Jot down any specific issues you need to address or answer from your reading. Asking yourself these questions helps you to read with a purpose and focus on the important parts of the text.

Read. Read through the useful paragraphs in detail. This may take some time, depending on the complexity of the subject matter. Read to ensure you understand the material. Focus on the key points. Try to avoid making notes at this stage, but if you need to clarify your understanding of a complex point you may want to jot down a diagram or key word(s).

Recall. When you have read the relevant parts, run through it again. At this stage you are **testing yourself** on what the text is about. You are 'separating the wheat from the chaff', i.e. identifying the key points. It is at this stage that you can begin **making notes.**

Educational researchers recommend reading and understanding the text **before** making any notes. This ensures that you have an overview of the material first. You understand and process the information into your own words in note-making, to make the concepts and information **personal** to you. You are likely to make fewer, more accurate and relevant notes if you adopt this approach, so it can save you time and result in more effective notes. **Select** relevant information to note and try not to write down too much detail. Make a note of the number of any page or paragraph that is particularly useful. Make sure you space out your notes on the page (allowing for extra details or diagrams later). If you need to take down a direct quote from the material, ensure that you keep a note of the full reference, including author and title of the book or article, etc. (see below for more information on references).

Review. This is the final stage, in which you reinforce any ideas you have gleaned from the material. Scan through the material again to make sure you have not missed any important points. Check your notes to make sure they reflect the aim of the reading task. Summarise to yourself the key points of the material you have just read. You could also make a note of any other authors or material referred to which you could follow up later.

3 Referencing Material

Quoting somebody's work, whether from a textbook, website or thesis, etc., without attribution (i.e. giving it credit or referring to it in your work) can constitute plagiarism.

It is conventional academic practice to refer to research studies, textbooks, etc. on which a writer relies. This is an important requirement for writing essays in any area, including legal essays.

3.1 Referring to case law

Whenever possible you should give the full case name and citation (legal reference) when referring to a case. It is a convention to either underline case names or to place them in italics, e.g. *Scaife v. Falcon Leisure Group (Overseas) Ltd [2007] IESC 57.*

If you are referring to an Act or Regulations, write its title in full: any abbreviation should be explained in brackets. If in doubt, avoid abbreviations.

3.2 The Harvard referencing system

3.2.1 Referencing in your work

This means giving attribution to a source in the body of your work. The Harvard system is accepted academic practice (though there are other accepted forms of referencing). You should check with your academic institution what form of referencing they require. The institution's library will often have information in paper/electronic format that gives guidance on referencing.

In the Harvard system you write the name of the author(s), the year of publication and the relevant page number **in the body of your**

work. In a paragraph relying on the views of an academic writer a short reference to the writer, date of publication and page number is included. For example, 'It could be argued that if a defendant was proved to have an intention to seriously injure or kill a foetus, a murder conviction could be secured (Hanly 2006, p. 209).' Only direct quotations or direct use of phrases or concepts or ideas need to be attributed in this way. You should avoid having too many attributions in your work.

3.2.2 References at the end of your text

At the end of your answer, project, etc. you should include a **List of References**. This is a list of the books, articles, online resources, etc. you have used to research your work. Even if you have not quoted or made direct reference to them, they will have informed your views and writing.

There is a specific format for referencing books, journal articles, etc. The main points to note are:

- The list should be laid out alphabetically by authors' surnames.
- Each item should begin with the author's or authors' surname(s) and initial(s).
- Then the year of publication.
- The title of the book should be set out in italics.
- Include the number of the edition, if relevant.
- The place of publication and the publisher.
- Even if you refer to only one or two books you should list the sources.

A list of references might look like this:

List of References

Clear, D. (2006). *Geographical Constraints on Motorway Construction*. Dublin: Roadway Press.

Flannel, M. (2001). *Horizontal Alignment in Difficult Terrain: An Engineering Guidebook*. London: Practical Press.

Stone, A. (1996). *Rock Anchors and Other Stabilising Influences*. Cork: Foundation Press.

There are different ways of referencing journal articles, chapters in books, articles in compilations, etc.: for further details refer to your library's guidelines.

3.3 Information on the sources you should record

To comply with the Harvard system you need accurate references. Although it may seem time-consuming it is an essential part of the compilation of your work and if you adopt the practice at the start of your studies it will soon become second nature.

It is important to note down the following information when you are making notes.

Author(s), e.g. J. Nestor. If there are a number of authors, write down all their names.
Full Title of the book/article, e.g. *An Introduction to Irish Family Law*.
Date of publication, e.g. 2007.
The number of the edition (this is usually given on the first page of the book, before the Contents page), e.g. 3rd edition.
The page number of the relevant quotation or discussion.
The publisher, e.g. Gill & Macmillan
The website reference, if relevant, and the date accessed. Online resources should include the full http reference and the date accessed. *For example*: The Law Reform Commission Report on Spent Convictions (LRC 84-2007); http://www.lawreform.ie/Spent%20 Convictions%20Report%20Final%20July%202007.pdf (accessed 24 January 2008).

4 Revision

OVERVIEW

• Personal revision style.
• Revision staregies and active revision.
• Revision timetables as an essential tool.
• Sources of information/help.

There are no hard and fast rules about revision. What suits you as an individual? Have your past techniques worked well?

It may be worth considering some new strategies if you want to improve revision and exam performance.

4.1 Previous questions and format of assessment/exam

Make sure that you know what type of assessment you will be faced with and the format of the paper. Issues such as how many questions you have to answer and within what time frame are important for your planning. Use the library at your institution or the internet to look at assessments or exams that have been set in the past (but remember there may have been changes to the syllabus in the material you have covered as well as changes in the type of assessments set). In this way you become familiar with the type of question set and you can practise past questions by first going through your notes and then making a short plan from memory and 'filling in the blanks' by going through your notes again.

A revision timetable makes effective use of limited time. It is part of strategic revision. Split your topics into manageable chunks of material. Note your progress, ticking off areas you have covered and marking areas you need to go over again.

4.2 Key points

4.2.1 Active revision is effective revision

Effective revision is more than simply looking over the course material again and again. It should be more **active** than this because it involves organising material and finding ways of understanding and remembering the information which suit **your** particular learning style. Although the time you set aside for revision is important, the approach and attitude you adopt and the techniques you use to revise are more important.

The thought of having to revise can seem daunting, but do not panic. Revision skills and techniques can be learned and refined.

Active revision means working with the material and topics you are studying, not just re-reading books and notes and other resources. Simply re-reading is known as 'passive revision', which can be tedious and ineffective and make you want to go to sleep rather than give you confidence going into an exam. You have to work with the material, to fully understand its significance and be able to remember and apply key points in the examination.

Different subjects demand different methods, but in general active revision involves using or doing things with the material in a way that helps it to stick in your mind.

4.2.2 Working with the material: stages in revision

1. Reduce the amount of information you have on each topic to a manageable size by condensing the notes down to key words and concepts. (You can do this in a variety of ways.)

2. Summarise your notes on a topic from the various sources you have collected together.
3. Draw the main points from these notes using headings and key points.
4. Try to reduce these notes further to one side of A4 paper using only the main headings and a few associated key words.
   A mind-map can capture all these techniques in an economical way.

Look at past papers to see the types of question that are asked. If you were in the lecturer's position what topics might you select? Try writing some essay plans with and without your notes in thirty-minute blocks.

4.2.3 Making learning wall charts/large diagrams
You may find that rather than reducing notes to A4 sheets you prefer to produce larger diagrams/headings detailing key points on particular topics. Use pattern, colour, diagrams and drawings in your wall charts and display them where you will have an opportunity to look at them for some time and absorb the information. If you have a strong visual memory this method can really help the remembering process.

4.2.4 Making recordings of notes
Recording notes onto CD or other medium may be very effective for students who have a strong auditory memory. Playing the CD when travelling by train or car, for example, can be an effective revision tool. By compiling the recording and selecting the key points you are working with the material.

4.3 A revision timetable
Drawing up a revision timetable may be the best and most effective forty-five minutes you spend in weeks of revision. Revision is a type of project which can be managed, and a timetable helps you to be more effective at revision.

Question: What benefits could you gain from a revision timetable?
Key Points: It is a time-effective way of organising a schedule. It should:
• identify topics that you need to learn

- set out blocks of time in forty-five-minute sessions (as a maximum) for each topic or sub-topic
- give you confidence that you can cover the material and go into the exam feeling reasonably confident.

Monday	Tuesday	Wednesday	Thursday	Friday	Saturday	Sunday

Question: Why do you think the maximum time slot for revision is set at 45 minutes?

Key Point: You can only concentrate effectively and be interested, active and effective in revision if you break it down into manageable topics.

Once you have drawn up your revision timetable be prepared to alter or refine it as you go along. Some general suggestions about working with the timetable are:

- Tick off your subjects as you complete them. Revision is a staged project — recognise that you have completed each stage.
- Set yourself *realistic targets* and stick to the timetable as much as possible.
- Build in time for work and family commitments and free time for sports, etc. into the timetable.
- Mix together the subjects that you feel more comfortable and confident with and those you always put off.

4.4 Other revision ideas

4.4.1 Computers as revision tools

A computer offers the opportunity to organise, reorganise and delete material without having to write everything out every time you make a change. It allows you to make notes as you go along, file them easily and add to or update them in your revision period.

4.4.2 Revising with others: study groups

Working with a small group of other students who are also revising can be an effective process. Other students can make you keep the whole revision process in perspective rather than letting it make you over-anxious. You may find that one of your group is particularly good at planning and can draw up an effective revision timetable. Working together to produce condensed revision notes or to 'brainstorm' answers to questions is particularly useful. Each of you will have different ideas to contribute and may raise issues that others had not considered. You are co-operating rather than competing with other students taking the exam.

4.4.3 Help!

If you are having difficulties with a particular topic or revision generally, try to solve them by talking it over with colleagues and your lecturer. If you find you are becoming unnaturally anxious, do not suffer in silence. See your lecturer or find other sources of help in your institution, such as a student counsellor. Use these resources — they are there to help you.

5 Examinations

5.1 Timing in an exam

Remember to watch the time carefully in the exam and try to complete the required number of questions. It is impossible to do yourself justice if you only have time to attempt eighty per cent of the paper. Do not try to perfect an answer on a favourite area to the detriment of the third and fourth questions. If you do overrun, despite your best efforts, have a go at the fourth question even if you only have fifteen minutes left. You will have to make your essay an 'enlarged' plan and very snappy. Keep to the point and try to reach a conclusion.

Remember, if you have worked through the year, submitted assignments and completed tasks and required reading you will have been assimilating information as you go along. Revision and the exam are the final, albeit most stressful, stages of this process. The exams are designed to allow you to demonstrate your knowledge and understanding of relevant points. They are not designed to trip you up. If you answer the question set, giving reasons and authorities for your answer in a clear and comprehensible manner you should have nothing to fear. Write your answers clearly; a useful technique is to imagine the assessor or examiner is new to the study of law. This can help you to write in a clear, simple style (without being too informal or chatty). Remember to back up your answer or points with legal authorities: examples of cases and Acts, etc.

6 *Some suggested additional study topics*

A Explain the scope of the right to life under Article 2 of the Irish constitution with reference to the recent High Court case of *MR v. TR and Others [2006] IEHC 359.*

B Using the judgments in the case of *MR v. TR and Others [2006] IEHC 359* explain the different functions of the courts and Oireachtas and the extent to which it is permissible for the Courts to review or interpret legislation. (Suggestion: access the case through BAILII and outline the facts (in your own words).) Explain the reasoning of the Court in this judgment.

C CASE STUDY

Using the BAILLI site, access the case of *Antony Clabby v. Global Windows Limited (Defendant)* and *An Post [2003] IEHC 53.*

Consider the following questions on the judgment. You will find it useful to refresh your memory on the elements required for negligence liability outlined in Chapter 4.

1. Which Court gave judgment in this case?
2. What was the nature of the plaintiff's claim against Global Windows (the manufacturer)?
3. Summarise the facts that gave rise to the case in fewer than 150 words.
4. Briefly (under 80 words) outline the elements referred to by the judge that a plaintiff must prove for a successful negligence action.
5. What did the earlier case of *Barclay v. An Post and Another [1998] 2 ILRM 315* (which is referred to in this judgment) decide?
6. Did the judge in the Global Windows case consider that Global Windows had ignored any manufacturing standards relevant to the plaintiff's particular injury? Where is this stated in the judgment?
7. Summarise the court's finding on the absence of a duty of care and lack of causation in this case (in under 120 words).

D *The Occupiers' Liability Act 1995*

Jack is a landowner who owns a large deserted farm with a set of derelict outbuildings, which is near to a newly built housing estate.

Explain to him the scope of the Occupiers' Liability Act 1995 and how it may apply to him. Outline any steps he may take to minimise any potential liability.

E Critically examine whether there is a 'compensation culture' in

Ireland. Suggestion: use the following report to research the area. *Effect of Insurance on Society (in Ireland)* presented to the Society of Actuaries in Ireland by Marian Keane FSAI and Patrick Grealy FSAI, November 2002.

Use other more recent newspaper articles or material from the web. *Remember to*: check the status and authenticity of any website; check when the information was written; and keep a record of the full website reference and the date it was accessed and to include this in the References section of your report.

F   Explore areas of concern within the Irish Prison Service. Read the Prison Chaplains' Report for 2006/2007, which is accessible via a good search engine.
G   Research the concept of recidivism in Ireland and write a brief summary (in under 800 words) covering:
•   the meaning of the concept
•   rates of recidivism in Ireland
•   reasons that may be advanced for recidivism.

Include a list of references at the end of your answer showing where you obtained the information (either in paper/ and or in electronic form).
H Alex is a plasterer and also a keen amateur snowboarder who lives in Scotland. He wishes to go to work in Spain or southern France in order to intensively train with a view to becoming a professional snowboarder. In the short term he plans to stay for four months (for the winter season) and the following year he hopes to buy and renovate two properties in Southern France and set up a business called Le SnoBoard Experience.

Outline the source and extent of his rights as an EU national to live and work as a plasterer on a freelance basis in France or Spain.

I   European Union law
In under 1,500 words draft a report outlining the main provisions of the Reform Treaty signed in Lisbon in December 2007. Make sure you include any sources of information that you use. A good starting point is the CER (Centre for European Reform) Guide to the Reform Treaty by Hugo Brady and Katinka Barysch, which can be accessed at www.cer.org.uk/.

REFERENCES

Buzan, T. and B. (2000) *The Mind Map Book*. BBC Worldwide Ltd

Gibbs G., Morgan A. and Northedge, A. (1999) *Teaching in Higher Education: Theory and Evidence*, Chapter 6, 'How students learn'; Chapter 8, 'How students develop as learners'. The Open University.

Holland, J.A. and Webb, J.S. (1991) *Learning Legal Rules* (3rd edn). Blackstone Press Ltd.

GLOSSARY OF LEGAL TERMS

Actus reus: A Latin phrase meaning the action or omission required for a criminal offence to be committed.

Adversarial system: A legal system in which one party argues their case against another. It relies on advocacy and can be seen as a form of legal 'contest'.

Advocate: Someone who presents a case on behalf of a person.

Agent: A person or organisation that has the authority to enter into contracts on somebody's behalf (the principal).

Alternative dispute resolution (ADR): An umbrella term for different methods of settling disputes out of court. It covers conciliation, mediation and arbitration.

Amendment: A change made to an Act or contractual document.

Amicus curiae: A Latin phrase meaning a friend of the court. Refers to an impartial person with expert legal knowledge who may inform the court. The Human Rights Commission may apply to court for this status in relation to intervening in and informing the court on human rights matters.

Arbitration: A form of alternative dispute resolution that takes place outside the court system. It is governed by the Arbitration Acts 1954–85.

Arrestable offence: An offence which is arrestable without a warrant (defined by s.4 Criminal Law Act 1997).

Assault: A type of tort where a person is put in fear of violence. An assault can also be a criminal offence.

Assign: To transfer property to another.

Attorney General: The government's legal adviser, appointed by the Taoiseach (Article 30 of the Constitution).

Balance of probabilities: The standard of proof required to prove a civil claim.

Barrister: An advocate who represents a party in Court. (Also known as Counsel.)

Bill: A legislative proposal that becomes an Act after being passed by the Oireachtas.

Brehon Law: The original system of law in Ireland which developed until the Anglo-Norman invasion by Strongbow in 1169 and the establishment of English laws in Ireland.

Burden of proof: This concept determines which party in a case must prove their claims. In a criminal case the prosecution bears the burden of proof. In a civil case the plaintiff bears the burden of proof.

By-laws (or bye-laws): Rules made by a body such as a county council for the regulation of a district or property e.g. parking by-laws.

Cartel: A group of undertakings who engage in anti-competitive practices together.

Caveat emptor: A Latin phrase which means 'let the buyer beware'.

Central Criminal Court: The criminal division of the High Court.

Chief Justice: The President of the Supreme Court.

Circuit Court: A court which has limited civil and criminal jurisdiction.

Citation: The method of referring to a case, statute or legal provision generally, e.g. *Kelly v. Hennessy [1995] IESC 8*.

Class action: A civil action brought by a group of people.

Commercial Court: A division of the High Court which can hear commercial disputes of over €1m.

Common Agricultural Policy (CAP): The agricultural policy of the EU.

Common Customs Tariff (CCT): The tariff that applies to the importation of goods across the external borders of the EU.

Common law: Law which has been developed by the courts applying the rules of precedent. Common law legal systems include Ireland, Australia, US, Canada, India, and England and Wales.

Common market: An economic model where the participating states operate a customs union, have a common policy with regard to trade with third countries and liberate the factors of production within the trade area.

Companies Registration Office (CRO): Office responsible for the registration and regulation of companies in Ireland.

Comptroller and Auditor General: An independent officer responsible for auditing and issuing reports on public bodies.

Condition of contract: A condition in a contract is a fundamental term of the contract, breach of which entitles the innocent party to repudiate the contract.

Consideration: An element, meaning 'money or money's worth', necessary for the formation of a binding contract.

Consolidating legislation: Legislation which brings earlier, separate legislation together in one piece of legislation.

Contract: A binding legal agreement.

Contra proferentem: A Latin phrase that describes the approach of the courts towards an exclusion clause. It means it is interpreted strictly, against the person seeking to rely on it.

Cooling-off period: A period of time during which a consumer can withdraw from a contract without suffering adverse consequences.

COREPER: The Permanent Representatives Committee responsible for preparing the work of the Council of the European Union.

Corporation: A legal body which has a separate (corporate) personality distinct from its shareholders or members. A limited company is a corporation.

Council of Europe: The grouping of states which was established after World War II to promote co-operation and the establishment of democratic constitutions in Europe.

Counsel: Another name for a barrister. In Ireland there are junior counsel and Senior Counsel (SC).

Court of Auditors: An institution of the EU that audits the EU's accounts and the EU budget.

Court of Criminal Appeal: The appeal court for criminal law issues.

Court of First Instance (CFI): A court of the European Community. There is a right of appeal to the ECJ.

Court of last resort: The term for a court against whose decision there is no appeal possibility. In Ireland the court of last resort is generally the Supreme Court.

Decree: A court order, e.g. a decree nisi.

Defamation: A tort that consists of publishing a false statement concerning a person (or corporation) to another. The statement must damage the reputation of the person. Defamation can be either libel or slander.

Defendant: A person charged with a criminal offence or a person against whom a plaintiff brings a civil action.

Delegated legislation: Law which is made under the authority of an Act of the Oireachtas. It is also termed secondary legislation or subordinate legislation and is typically made in the form of a statutory instrument.

Derogations: Provisions which allow rights to be restricted in certain circumstances.

Direct Effect: Provisions of EU law which give rise to rights or obligations and which individuals may rely upon before their national courts.

Directive: A type of EU law, addressed to member states, which sets out the goal to be achieved by a set date and which gives each member state a choice of form and methods of implementation. Defined by Article 249 EC.

Directly applicable: Describes a European Union legal provision capable of having legal effect without a national implementing measure (e.g. an Article of the Treaty and EC Regulations).

Director of Public Prosecutions (DPP): An independent legal officer responsible for bringing prosecutions. The DPP enforces the criminal law in the courts on behalf of the people.

Disclaimer: A clause or notice which aims to prevent civil liability arising.

Dissenting judgment: A judgment that differs from the judgment of the majority.

Distinguishing a case: A situation in which a court declines to follow an earlier, binding precedent because the case before it can be distinguished from the precedent on matters of law or fact.

Duress: Force by injury, imprisonment or threat. Duress operates as a defence to some criminal offences. If it is present it may cause obligations under contract to become voidable.

Equity: A form of law originally developed by Courts of Equity to alleviate the harshness of certain principles in the common law system. The Courts of Equity were fused with the common law courts in the 1870s. Equitable principles now form part of the civil court structure.

Estoppel: A principle created by equity. A person who by their conduct or words leads someone to think a state of affairs exists and the other person relies on that statement or conduct to his detriment, is estopped (stopped or prevented) from later claiming that a different set of facts or state of affairs existed.

EURATOM: The European Atomic Energy Community formed under the Treaty of Rome.

European Central Bank (ECB): An institution of the EU. The central bank for the euro (the European single currency).

European Convention of Human Rights and Fundamental Freedoms (ECHR) (1950): The convention set up by the Council of Europe to protect human and political rights within Europe.

European Council: An institution of the EU, comprising the heads of state and the commission president, which meets regularly to formulate the major policies of the EU.

European Court of Human Rights (ECtHR): The court that interprets and applies cases under the European Convention of Human Rights and Fundamental Freedoms. It is based in Strasbourg.

European Court of Justice (ECJ): the court of the European Union; based in Luxembourg.

European Economic Area (EEA): An area where states have entered into an agreement to be bound by EU rules of free trade, even though the states are not part of the EU. Norway, Iceland and Liechtenstein are part of the EEA.

Exclusion Clause: A clause in a contract that attempts to exclude liability for breach of contract or other type of liability. Also referred to as an exemption clause.

Express term: A term that is made part of a contract in writing or orally.

Force majeure: An unforeseeable and unavoidable event.

Grand Chamber: The full court of the European Court of Human Rights in Strasbourg. Comprises 17 judges.

Habeas corpus: A Latin name for a type of court order used in situations where a person alleges they have been unlawfully detained. The order requires the detaining authority to bring the person before the court and justify the continued detention.

Harmonisation: A policy of the EU to bring member states' laws into line with EU policy.

Implied term: A term of a contract implied by an Act or by the court.

In camera: A case heard in private without public access.

Indictable offences: Offences which can be tried on indictment, i.e. by a jury.

Injunction: A remedy ordered by a court to compel or restrain a party from carrying out an act.

Inquisitorial system: A legal system in which a judge or examining magistrate makes inquiries. The trial and evidence is 'managed' by the presiding judge, who can question witnesses, etc. It may be contrasted with the adversarial system of justice.

Inter alia: A Latin phrase frequently used in legal arguments and judgments to mean 'among other things' or 'including'.

Invitation to treat: A phrase in contract law that describes a step inviting a contractual offer. Goods on display in a shop are invitations to treat.

Irish Human Rights Commission: Body established to protect and promote human rights under the Constitution and under international agreements.

Judicial review: An action that challenges the decision of a public body, officer, tribunal or court on the grounds that it has overstepped its powers or acted contrary to its legal duty. An action for judicial review can be also brought to challenge the constitutionality of legislation.

Jurisdiction: The extent of the power or authority of a court or tribunal. For example, the Central Criminal Court has jurisdiction to hear murder cases.

Labour Relations Commission: A body established to conciliate in employment and labour disputes.

Law Reports: Published reports of the courts.

Legal authority: A case, statutory provision which is relied upon in legal argument, or a discussion or essay on the subject.

Legislature: The law-making body of the state. In Ireland the Oireachtas is the legislature.

Limitation period: The time in which an action must be brought before the courts before it is time barred.

Liquidated damages: Damages that can be precisely quantified.

Mareva injunction: An injunction granted to prevent a defendant removing assets from the jurisdiction pending a trial.

Margin of appreciation: A concept used by the European Court of Human Rights to allow contracting states different standards and viewpoints in relation to some issues.

Mens rea: A Latin phrase meaning the mental element (guilty mind) required for the commission of a criminal offence.

Minor: A person under the age of 18 (under the Age of Majority Act 1985).

Mitigation: A contract law principle where a plaintiff has to reasonably reduce or mitigate their losses after a breach of contract. In criminal law a plea of mitigation is made to try to reduce any possible sentence which may be imposed after a finding or plea of guilt.

Mr/Mrs Justice: the mode of address for judges of the Supreme Court.

Mutual recognition principle: A principle of EU law whereby goods, services and qualifications which satisfy national requirements in one member state should be accepted by other member states, unless there are good grounds for non-recognition.

Natural right: A classification of a human right as a basic right that exists because of our humanity. It is not an artificial or legally created right.

Neighbour principle: The principle in the tort of negligence that defines the scope of the duty of care.

Next friend: A term for somebody who brings an action on behalf of a plaintiff who is a minor or unable to sue due to an incapacity.

Novus actus interveniens: A Latin phrase meaning an intervening event that interrupts a chain of causation. It may be used as a defence to a negligence action.

Nuisance: A type of tort protecting the use and enjoyment of land.

Obiter dictum: A Latin phrase meaning the part of a judgment which is not directly binding but contains a statement made 'by the way'. The plural is obiter dicta.

Objective justification: A principle developed by the ECJ which allows a party to argue that steps taken were necessary in the circumstances to achieve a legitimate purpose and the steps go no further than is necessary to achieve the purpose.

Offeree: The party who receives a contractual offer.

Offeror: The party who makes a contractual offer.

Omission: A failure to do something.

Personal Injuries Assessment Board (PIAB): The statutory body established to deal with personal injury claims away from the formal court setting.

Personal representatives: The persons who administer a person's will after death and who are appointed in the will.

Persuasive authority: A case decided in Ireland or elsewhere (Canada, UK, USA being examples) which, although not strictly binding, can be used in support of an argument and which the judges may rely on and refer to in making a judgment.

Plaintiff: The person who initiates a civil action, also known as a claimant.

Preamble: An introduction to legislation which often sets out the purpose of the law.

Precedent: A rule developed by the judges requiring that a relevant principle of law (ratio decidendi) decided by a relevant court should be followed in a later case unless there are good reasons to depart from the judgment.

Preliminary Ruling: A procedure by which a national court can refer an issue of European Union law to the European Court of Justice for a ruling under Article 234 EC.

Prima facie: A Latin phrase often used in legal arguments. It means 'at first sight or appearance'. For example 'the facts reveal a prima facie case'.

Primary legislation: Legislation which is of the highest status. In Ireland, Acts are primary legislation. In EU law, Treaty provisions are primary legislation.

Principal: A person who gives instructions to an agent and who is contractually bound by the actions of an agent.

Private law: The forms of law that primarily regulate the law between private persons (including corporate bodies). Contract, tort, land law and family law are examples of private law subjects.

Private Residential Tenancies Board: A body that uses alternative dispute resolution to resolve tenancy disputes.

Proportionality: A principle used by courts which requires certain measures to be used in order to achieve a legitimate goal and to go no further than in necessary in the circumstances.

Protocol: An international agreement or convention that adds to an existing agreement. For example, the Protocols to the European Convention on Human Rights add further rights.

Public law: The forms of law that primarily regulate the law of the state and the obligations of the citizen towards the state. Criminal law, constitutional law and the law of judicial review are examples of public law subjects. There are overlaps between private and public law.

Qualified majority voting (QMV): The system of weighted voting given to member states which is used in votes in the Council of the European Union.

Ratification: The formal adoption by a state of a Treaty; or the adoption or confirmation of a contract by a principal of a contract originally made by an unauthorised agent.

Ratio decidendi: A Latin phrase meaning the binding part of a judgment which can form a binding precedent for later cases.

Recidivism: The practice of re-offending after having served a sentence.

Repeal: The formal cancellation of a previously enforceable Act. Acts may be repealed in whole or in part by later legislation.

Reserved judgment: A judgment given at a later date than the hearing of evidence, etc. Contrast this with an *ex tempore* judgment, which is given at the time.

Respondent: The person who responds to a claim, e.g. in a Small Claims Court action.

Restorative justice: A model of criminal justice 'resolution' that focuses on the impact of the crime on the victim and aims to restore the victim's position, while encouraging offenders to reform and not to re-offend.

Rules of remoteness: Principles of law developed by the courts to limit the types of damages that can be awarded for breach of contract and tort claims.

Separation of powers: A constitutional principle which aims to divide the functions of the organs of government to ensure that each function can act as a 'brake' or check on excessive power of another.

Single European Act 1986: A treaty of the European Economic Community which accelerated progress towards the internal market by altering voting procedures for harmonisation measures and developed new areas of Community competence.

Single internal market: A geographical area where the factors of production (labour, goods, services and money) can move freely, without being affected by national borders.

Small Claims Court: A user-friendly court, attached to the District Court, which hears consumer disputes concerning goods and services of below €2000 in value.

Specific performance: An order of the court based on equitable principles compelling a party to fulfil a contractual obligation.

Standard of proof: The level of proof required for a party to be successful at a trial. In a civil case the plaintiff must prove their case on the balance of probabilities. In criminal cases the prosecutor must prove the case beyond reasonable doubt.

Statute: Another word for an Act of the Oireachtas.

Statutory Instrument (SI): Secondary legislation made under the authority of a statute.

Statutory interpretation: The approaches used to interpret words in statutory provisions and delegated legislation.

Strict liability: Liability which is imposed without proof of fault.

Subpoena: An order in a civil action requiring the attendance of a witness at a trial to give evidence. It may also compel a witness to bring specified documents to a trial for use as evidence.

Subsidiarity: A principle of EU law which means that action should be taken at the lowest possible level (regional or national level).

Summary offence: An offence which has no right of trial by jury.

Supremacy of EU law: A principle of law established by the ECJ which requires all member states to comply with EU law irrespective of national and constitutional legal provisions.

Tort: A civil wrong.

Tortfeasor: A person who commits a tort.

Treaty: An agreement between countries.

Treaty of Rome (1957): The founding treaty of the European Economic Community

Trespass: A term covering a number of torts of wrongful interference with property, land or the person.

Tribunal: A body established by statute with judicial functions to rule on specific areas, for example the Employment Appeal Tribunal.

Trustee: A person appointed to administer a trust for the benefit of the beneficiaries. A trustee has fiduciary duties.

Unenumerated constitutional rights: Rights that are not specifically mentioned by the Constitution, but have been created by the High Court or Supreme Court, for example the right to bodily integrity under Article 40.

Universal Declaration of Human Rights (UNDHR): The declaration made by the General Assembly of the United Nations in 1948. Specifies the human rights that should be upheld by the UN Charter.

Vicarious liability: Liability imposed on a party for the actions of another. For example, an employer has vicarious liability for torts committed by employees in certain circumstances.

Violenti non fit injuria: A Latin phrase meaning that the defendant consented to a tort. It is a defence to a tort action.

Void: To have no legal effect.

Voidable: A voidable contract is one that one party is entitled to rescind (end). If the party fails to rescind the contract, it continues and has full legal effect.

Waiver: A situation or a formal document where a person expressly or impliedly agrees to give up a legal right under tort or contract.

SOME USEFUL WEBSITES

Amnesty International
www.amnesty.org/
An organisation that campaigns for and researches human rights.

Attorney General
www.attorneygeneral.ie/slru/restatements.html
Office of the Attorney General and Restatements of the law.

British and Irish Legal Information Institute (BAILII)
www.bailii.org
Access to important case law.

Central Statistics Office
www.cso.ie/statistics/CrimeandJustice.htm

Centre for European Reform
www.cer.org.uk/

Citizens' Information Board
www.citizensinformation.ie/categories

Companies Registration Office (CRO)
www.cro.ie/

Council of Europe
www.coe.ie

Courts Service of Ireland
www.courts.ie/

Department of Enterprise, Trade and Employment
www.entemp.ie/
Contains detailed explanations of employment rights and legislation,
aspects of intellectual property, etc.

Department of Justice, Equality and Law Reform
www.justice.ie/

Department of the Taoiseach
www.taoiseach.gov.ie/
Includes a search facility for government documents.

Director of Public Prosecutions
www.dppireland.ie/

Economic and Social Research Institute
www.esri.ie/
Conducts research on social and economic change in Ireland.

Equality Tribunal
www.equalitytribunal.ie/

Eur-Lex
http://eur-lex.europa.eu/
Access to European law.

Europa
www.europa.eu
The European Union internet portal.
http://europa.eu/abc/eurojargon/index_en.htm
A glossary to help decipher Eurojargon.

European Committee for the Prevention of Torture and Inhuman or Degrading Treatment or Punishment
www.cpt.coe.int/en/

European Consumer Centre
www.ecic.ie

European Court of Human Rights
www.echr.coe.int/echr/
www.echr.coe.int/echr/EN/Header/Case-Law/HUDOC/HUDOC+database/ The case law of the European Court of Human Rights.

European Court of Justice
http://curia.europa.eu/

European Parliament
www.europarl.europa.eu/
www.europarl.ie/ —- European Parliament office in Ireland.

Financial Regulator
www.ifsra.ie/

Free Legal Advice Centres
www.flac.ie/

Irish Council for Civil Liberties
www.iccl.ie/

Irish Human Rights Commission
www.ihrc.ie/

Irish Legal Information Initiative
www.ucc.ie/law/irlii/
Recent cases and an archive.
www.ucc.ie/law/newirlii/index.php
Supplies access to recent Irish cases, search facilities and references
to academic writings.

Labour Relations Commission
www.lrc.ie/docs/Welcome/

Legal Periodicals Index
www.legalperiodicals.org/
Run by IRLII at UCC.

National Consumer Agency
www.nca.ie/
www.consumerconnect.ie/
Consumer site of the NCA.

National Crime Council
www.irlgov.ie/crimecouncil/index.html

National Treatment Purchase Fund
www.ntpf.ie/

Oireachtas
www.oireachtas.ie/
Home page of the Oireachtas. Includes details of Bills and Acts.
http://acts.oireachtas.ie/
Acts of the Oireachtas and Delegated Legislation. Recent Acts can
be accessed from this site.

Personal Injuries Assessment Board
www.piab.ie/

Statute Book
www.irishstatutebook.ie/
Includes statutes and statutory instruments up to 2005

United Nations
www.un.org/rights/
The UN and human rights.